REGIONAL COOPERATION AND INTEGRATION
WITHIN INDUSTRY AND TRADE IN SOUTHERN AFRICA

The Making of Modern Africa
Series Editors: Abebe Zegeye and John Higginson

Regional Cooperation and Integration within Industry and Trade in Southern Africa

General approaches, SADCC and the World Bank

JENS HAARLOV

Avebury

Aldershot • Brookfield USA • Hong Kong • Singapore • Sydney

Published by
Avebury
Ashgate Publishing Limited
Gower House
Croft Road
Aldershot
Hants GU11 3HR
England

Ashgate Publishing Company
Old Post Road
Brookfield
Vermont 05036
USA

British Library Cataloguing in Publication Data

Haarlov, Jens
    Regional cooperation and integration within industry and
    trade in Southern Africa : general approaches, SADCC and
    the World Bank. - (The making of modern Africa)
    1.Africa, Southern - Economic integration
    I.Title
    337.1'68

Library of Congress Catalog Card Number: 96-86406

ISBN 1 85972 412 4

Printed in Great Britain by
Antony Rowe Ltd, Chippenham, Wiltshire

Contents

Map and tables

Preface

Regional cooperation and integration has both politically and economically been a key element of Southern African history in the 20th century. The Southern African Customs Union, SACU, was established in 1910 and has roots even further back. The Central African Federation between what are now Malawi, Zambia and Zimbabwe was in the 1950s and early 1960s hotly contested by the African political movements and abandoned in 1963. Tanzania was part of the seemingly promising but in the end not workable East African Community (1967–77). In 1979 South Africa unsuccessfully attempted to weave the Southern African nations into a formal net of cooperation and nonaggression pacts by launching the Constellation of Southern African States, CONSAS. The creation in 1980 of Southern African Development Coordination Conference, SADCC, was the response of the Front-line states to CONSAS. SADCC was made possible by the independence of Zimbabwe in 1979/80. SADCC aimed at uplifting the economic wellbeing of its peoples by reducing external dependence, especially on South Africa. The donor community considered SADCC as a useful vehicle for larger, mostly infrastructural investments, and for manifesting their anti-apartheid stand. SADCC steadily built up its activities in the 1980s, while other attempts to implement regional cooperation and integration in the third world crumbled. This was probably due to SADCC's approach or working method. It was characterized by no infringements on the sovereignty of the member states; it focused on common interests and benefits as well as a pragmatic working method which was step-by-step orientated, and decentralized. These principles carried SADCC far in some sectors, but when it came to industry and trade, problems seemed to emerge and progress was very slow. At the same time the economies of the individual SADCC countries began to change in the second half of the 1980s. The state driven, centralized and inward looking model, which the majority of SADCC member states had ended up with was definitively stuck and unable to solve the problems at hand. Stabilization and structural adjustments policies were introduced with assistance and conditionalities from the international community, not least the International Monetary Fund and the World Bank. However, there was apparently little attention by any of the involved parties as to how these policies affected the possibilities for regional cooperation and integration. And the policies of SADCC and the World Bank on the regional level did not seem to take into consideration the new situation in the individual countries.

I found this interplay of what seemed to be conflicting strategies and practices by different actors on the national and regional level an interesting study object with considerable importance to cooperation and integration in the region. It was, according to my preparatory studies, not thoroughly investigated in available academic research and constituted a lacuna in discussions on the experience of regional cooperation and integration. Moreover, it could be combined with my prior studies of SADCC's industry and trade policies. Thus in 1992, a research outline for the book was made and discussed with my PhD supervisor Barry Munslow, the University of Liverpool, as well as with knowledgeable people in Denmark such as Roger Leys, Knud Erik Svendsen, Finn Tarp and Jens Erik Torp. All were supportive regarding the main issues and gave constructive comments as to the further work. In early 1993 a field trip was arranged. It brought me to Mozambique, South Africa, Botswana and Zambia. In Mozambique the staffs of the Ministry of Industry, and Energy, the Ministry of Commerce and other institutions were extremely open and helpful. Without forgetting anyone a special thanks is extended to Luís Videira, Lúcia Bhatt, Carmélia Chiau, Francisco Carrajola, A. Roque Chiale, Felisberto Ferrão and Madalena Anastácio. From the rest of the trip a warm debt of thanks is due to Emang Maphanyane and Jan Cedergren, Garborone, Rob Davies and Patrick Ncube, Cape Town, Gavin Maasdorp, Durban, and Kwaku Osafo, Lusaka, for inspiring discussions and logistical support. Barry Munslow has provided prompt guidance, suggestions, and ideas, as well as with firmness and forbearance watched the timing of the endeavour. However, none of those mentioned or others can be held responsible for possible errors and omissions in the book for which only I can be blamed. I shall also express my gratitude to family, friends and colleagues in the Ministry of Foreign Affairs, who have all shown impressive patience and understanding during the elaboration of the book. Finally, the book would never have been possible to conclude without the love, inspiration and support from my mother and my three daughters, Ditte, Pernille and Siri.

Abbreviations

ACP	African, Caribbean and Pacific Countries/States
ADB	African Development Bank
ANC	African National Congress
ASEAN	Association of South-East Asian Nations
CACM	Central American Common Market
CARICOM	Caribbean Common Market
CEAO	West African Economic Community (Communauté Economique de l'Afrique de l'Ouest)
CIRE	Inter-Ministerial Commission for Enterprise Restructuring (Comissão Interministerial de Restruturação das Empresas)
COMESA	Common Market for Eastern and Southern Africa
CONSAS	Constellation of Southern African States
EAC	East African Community
EC	European Community
ECU	European Currency Unit
ECA	Economic Commission for Africa
ECOWAS	Economic Community of West African States
EFTA	European Free Trade Area
EPRF	Export Pre-Financing Revolving Fund
EPZ	Export Processing Zones
ESAF	Enhanced Structural Adjustment Facility
EU	European Union
Frelimo	Front for the Liberation of Mozambique (Frente da Libertação de Moçambique)
GATT	General Agreement on Trade and Tariffs
GDP	Gross Domestic Product
GNP	Gross National Product

GREI	Unit for the Restructuring of Industrial Enterprises (Gabinete de Restruturação de Empresas Industriais)
ICD	Industrial Coordinating Division
IOC	Indian Ocean Commission
IMF	International Monetary Fund
ITC	International Trade Centre
LAFTA/LAIA	Latin American Free Trade Association / Latin American Integration Association
MIGA	Multilateral Investment Guarantee Agency
Mts.	Meticais
MRU	Manu River Union
OAU	Organisation of African Unity
ODA	Official Development Assistance
NAFTA	North American Free Trade Agreement
NATO	North Atlantic Treaty Organisation
NGOs	Non-Governmental Organizations
NIEO	New International Economic Order
NTBs	Non-Tariff Barriers
OECD	Organisation for Economic Corporation and Development
PFPs	Policy Framework Papers
PRE	Economic Recovery Programme (Programa de Rehabilitação Economico)
PTA	Preferential Trade Area for Eastern and Southern African States
RECF	Regional Export Credit Facility
Renamo	Mozambique National Resistance (Resistência Nacional Moçambicana)
S.A.	South Africa
SACU	Southern African Customs Union
SADC	Southern African Development Community
SADCC	Southern African Development Coordination Conference
SAPs	Structural Adjustment Programmes
S.A. Rand	South African Rand
SITC	Standard International Trade Classification
SITCD	SADCC Industry and Trade Coordinating Division
SNAAD	System for Non-Administrative Allocation of Foreign Exchange (Sistema Não-Administrativo de Alocação de Divisas)
SRBC	SADCC Regional Business Council

TAZARA/TANZAM	Tanzania – Zambian Railway/Tanzania–Zambian
TNEs	Transnational Enterprises
UDEAC	Central African Customs and Economic Union (Union Douanière et Economique de l'Afrique Centrale)
UK	United Kingdom
UN	United Nations
UNIDO	United Nations Industrial Development Organisation
UTRE	Technical Unit for Enterprise Restructuring (Unidade Técnico de Restruturação das Empresas)
US	United States
USAID	United States Agency for International Development
US$	United States Dollar
VAT	Value Added Tax
ZACPLAN	Zambezi Action Plan

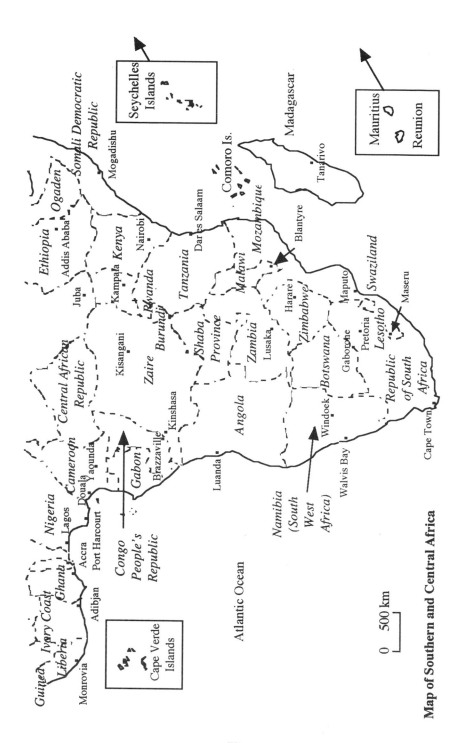

Map of Southern and Central Africa

Seychelles
Islands

Mauritius
Reunion

Somali Democratic
Republic

Ogaden

Ethiopia

Mogadishu

Addis Ababa

Madagascar

Tananrivo

Comoro Is.

Dar es Salaam

Mozambique

Kenya

Nairobi

Kampala

Rwanda

Tanzania

Blantyre

Juba

Malawi

Burundi

Harare I

Zimbabwe

Swaziland

Maseru

Central African
Republic

Kisangani

Zaire

Shaba
Province

Zambia

Lusaka

Maputo

Pretoria

Lesotho

Cameroon

Yaounda

Kinshasa

Brazzaville

Botswana

Gaborone

Republic
of South
Africa

Douala

Gabon

Angola

Windoek

Nigeria

Lagos

Congo
People's
Republic

Luanda

Namibia
(South
West
Africa)

Walvis Bay

Cape Town

Accra

Port Harcourt

Ghana

Ivory Coast

Adibjan

Guinea

Liberia

Monrovia

Cape Verde
Islands

Atlantic Ocean

0   500 km

xv

Meeting the challenge of regional integration into the 21st century: a foreword

Barry Munslow

As the 20th century draws to its close, we should pause a moment to reflect upon the incredible drama of upheaval and change which has swept the continent of Africa over the past four generations. With few exceptions, it was only in the final quarter of this century that independence and majority rule was won for the countries of southern Africa. These struggles have taken a heavy toll, but they have created seeds of hope amongst fields of despair. One of these seeds of hope is a growing commitment towards regional cooperation, haltingly, not without setbacks, often struggling to move beyond the lowest common denominator form of cooperation, but struggling nonetheless to build positive linkages, approaches and attitudes of working together.

It was developments in the final quarter of the 19th century, the discovery and mining of diamonds and gold in South Africa, that created the economic conditions for the emergence of a regional economic sub-system in southern Africa, with South Africa at its hub. One of the great ironies is that the final quarter of the 20th century found South Africa's neighbouring states trying to create a regional organisation for cooperation, the Southern African Development Coordination Conference, SADCC (later Southern African Development Community, SADC), which actually excluded for most of the time the key actor and generator of regional economic integration – South Africa itself. The reasons of course were political rather than economic, the continuation of white minority rule within the Republic of South Africa itself. The SADCC regional cooperation spent much of its existence trying to survive grave acts of destabilisation initiated by the National Party government of South Africa who rightly saw SADCC as a challenge to its political project of continuing minority rule.

A democratically elected government in South Africa from 1994 opened up the prospect of a synthesis of the existing and deep seated forms of actual economic integration becoming harmonised with the institutional political organisation form for regional cooperation – SADCC. South Africa's entry into the organisation offers up a whole new range of prospects. Once again, this is not without problems, not the least of which are the vast disparity that exists between the size of the South African economy compared with its neighbours, the long period of South Africa's isolation from the rest of Africa, possible resentments felt by other states about the threat of being overwhelmed and so forth. Yet now at least, if the blinkered vision of narrow nationalist short term interests can be persuaded of the potential longer term benefits to be reaped by rulers and citizens alike, then further progress can be made.

What other alternatives exist in the face of globalisation imperatives? Individually the countries of Southern Africa are weak and lack a competitive edge. By cooperating together it may be possible to create a more viable economic base. It may prove possible to harness the dynamic of capital accumulation on South Africa to give an added dynamic to economic development throughout the region, harnessing finance, investment, 'know-how' and technology, as well as translating this into mutually beneficial package deals between the countries.

One of the most positive new expressions of this impetus is the Maputo corridor linking Gauteng and Mpumalanga provinces in South Africa with Maputo province in Mozambique. Corridors as a concept offer the opportunity of diminishing the importance of the existing political demarcations and divisions, emphasising instead the mutuality of benefits that can be realised. Their aim is to use the transport spine to facilitate accelerated trade, industry, development, the spread of knowledge and a better cultural understanding. Improving the infrastructure is often central to this process. Clearly such initiatives require care and sensitive handling with respect to the mutuality of benefits, minimising possible negative environmental and social costs. Yet the potential benefits are great. Corridors will play an ever greater role within the globalised economy and can greatly facilitate regional markets.

The Maputo corridor has the advantage of building on what already exists. Its potential benefits include economies of scale, reducing distribution costs and time savings, vertical integration of upstream and downstream production and of primary and secondary sectors, improving access to suppliers, tourism and market access more generally. Above all, the corridor impetus should encourage industry and trade.

Developing trade and industry through regional cooperation is the key focus of this important monograph by Jens Haarlov. Haarlov has produced a highly detailed and up to date study of regional cooperation and integration in industry and trade in southern Africa. Many of the debates discussed in this monograph are closely argued with chapter and verse provided. There is considerable space given to the subtleties of the processes. There are three main themes in the volume. The first outlines the multiple approaches which exist to regional cooperation and integration. The second outlines and explains the limited progress to date within SADCC of industry and trade cooperation. Finally, and importantly, there is an analysis of the role of the World Bank and its policies with regard to regional cooperation and integration.

This study charts the high aspirations initially of SADCC's plans for industry and trade development and goes on to analyse why these were frustrated. Haarlov champions the need to develop trade and industry within the region yet details clearly and analytically how these efforts were stalled, mainly due to the lack of consistency between SADCC's regional initiatives and the simultaneous changes in the macro-economic set-up and development strategy in the individual countries. He identifies a new approach in the making: a structural adjustment adapted market integration approach. Herein lies the innovative nature of the study. The author highlights the inadequacies of the Bretton Woods Institutions in their ability genuinely to incorporate the imperative for regional coordination into their agenda. Their original perspective was one of the individual countries opening themselves up to the global market. A second minority tendency, much less vocal initially within the World Bank, was hesitantly moving towards the argument for regional cooperation. These views were decidedly in conflict and the author provides a country case study of Mozambique to try to illustrate in part how these issues play out. In effect, the national structural adjustment programmes do not take into account the need for regional coordination and undervalue the importance of regional markets.

The case study of Mozambique demonstrates that the existing structural adjustment programmes have been very general in their nature with no specific consideration being given to regional exigencies in relation to tariff reform, foreign exchange allocation and the promotion of exports. Furthermore, the notion of promoting local industry does not appear to be seriously addressed.

It is precisely with a view to finding a way out of the current impasse that I have highlighted the current very active Maputo corridor initiative in this foreword. Let us consider the potential reciprocal benefits. Turning first to Mozambique, there is the opening up of South African markets to Mozambican producers. Existing advantages of cheaper labour costs will need to be complemented by more efficient management, technology and capital investment, above all, perhaps, by a simplification of the myriad bureaucratic impediments of unreformed administrative structures and laws. This is accompanied by an opening up of global markets facilitated by the attendant economies of scale associated with the corridor development.

Of central importance is employment creation within Maputo province, but hopefully spreading in time into Inhambane and Gaza provinces, then further northwards to the centre of the country. There would be both income generation and tax base development following on from increased private sector investment. This in turn would allow the government of Mozambique to reduce its dependence on debt and aid and rely ever more upon the fruits of its own internal development dynamic.

Institutional advantages to Mozambique include sharing the cost and responsibility for the marketing and promotion of corridor projects. There are opportunities for improving the management of the natural resource/ environment base and building cultural and social linkages.

The potential benefits to South Africa, in particular Mpumalanga province but also Gauteng, mirror these advantages. One can add the 'debt boomerang' factor, which is that a destitute Mozambique on the borders of the heartland of the South African economy can only exacerbate social problems in South Africa. The parallel is that between Mexico and California, North Africa and Southern Europe. Development in the south of Mozambique will help to stem the tide of economic migrants seeping into South Africa, swelling the pressures on urban environments and creating further demands on creaking social services, in particular health and education. Such boomerang factors have a two-way effect, however, exacerbating crime networks and social ills such as drugs abuse in Mozambique as South African overspill. Conversely, a successful corridor cooperation between Mozambique and South Africa may prove to be an important point of inspiration for broader initiatives of cooperation and integration in the region. SADC's 1996 signing of protocols on trade and other pertinent issues could signal that a new beginning is underway.

Jens Haarlov provides an indispensable background with this study to understanding the intricacies of the challenge of industry and trade coordination within a regional framework. It is not an easy task. Yet if development is to be made more sustainable, then greater innovation and effort is required to maximise the vast potential scope for regional cooperation.

Finally, it is with great pleasure that I welcome the study by Dr Haarlov as one further fruit of the research initiated from the University of Liverpool in the early 1980s through the European Southern African Research Group. Jens Haarlov was an active collaborator, with a distinguished research record from his base in Denmark. Paul Jourdan of the ANC, who worked with us, has been driving the corridor initiatives forward within the Government of South Africa. There are many others from our research network in the 1980s whom I am sure would like to join me in commending Dr Haarlov's important research contribution in this volume. As the original convener of this international research network and subsequently at the supervisor of Dr Haarlov's thesis, which provided the basis for this study, I can only say how pleased I am to welcome this important specialist publication which can encourage the overall sustainable development effort.

1 Introduction

1.1 Main area of focus, time and place

In the last 50 years the number of nation-states has increased dramatically. At the same time the period has been characterized by an internationalization of the economies of the individual countries, mainly through trade and investment. Functional links between nations in areas such as transport and energy supply have also expanded significantly. Pollution and migration are examples of issues which by their very nature call for action by more than one state. Peace and security between nations demand fora in which the delicate questions can be resolved. The case for international cooperation appears to be as strong as ever. It can take place on a global as well as on a regional level. The two levels can be contradictory as well being complementary. Global free trade in relation to regional trade arrangements is a case in point. The focus of this book is on regional economic cooperation and integration, which the nation-states enter into on a voluntary basis. The geographic area under scrutiny is Southern Africa. The trend towards cooperation and integration between nation-states is found both among industrialized countries and among countries in the third world. Regarding the latter country group *The Courier* (Traoré, 1993) states that:

> The narrowness of these countries' individual markets condemns them to join forces if they are to develop their industries and reap the benefits of economies of scale, attract foreign investors by organising a frontier-free market ... This is a recognized and accepted need.[1]

In Africa an ideological quest for unity and attempts at economic cooperation and integration accompanied the decolonization process in the 1950s and 1960s. In 1980 and in 1991 in The Lagos Plan of Action and The Abuja

Treaty, respectively, the African countries actually committed themselves to strive towards an African Economic Community 'in order to foster the economic, social and cultural integration of our Continent' (Organization of African Unity, 1991, p.4).[2] According to the Abuja Treaty it should be reached through six stages of ever increased cooperation lasting up till 2025.

In 1988 the World Bank's Vice-President for Africa came out with a statement which indicated a growing recognition in the Bank that economic cooperation and integration is necessary in order to tackle Africa's development problems.

> The World Bank is coming round to the view that Africa's economic future may lie in economic integration. Why? The continent is simply too sub-divided – ... Too many trade barriers, too much competition for the same scarce resources human, institutional and financial. And from a business standpoint, markets that are simply too small to sustain industry and investment. ... For the message is clear: only through cooperation will there be convergence between Africa's great resources and its great needs (SADCC, 1988d, p.77ff).

If this need to integrate and cooperate is acknowledged as a point of departure the essential question becomes how to proceed from need to deed? Historic evidence seems to suggest that there have been fluctuating phases of ups and downs for cooperation and integration attempts. Failed and abandoned regional ventures are abundant. They often create bitterness between nations and increase nationalistic sentiments of jealousy and antagonism. The end result can be worse than the starting point. Therefore, countries appear to be well advised to choose with extreme care an approach that is precisely suited for the country group in question, taking full advantage of prior experiences, the possibilities and limitations of the actual situation and future perspectives for the region.

The concentration on regional cooperation and integration among countries is not tantamount to perceiving it as a perfect cure against all development ills. Large countries such as Nigeria or India which history easily might have separated into various independent countries, are living testimonies that for example a huge internal market and common public services are no guarantees for development. However, it is an assumption of the book that for the chosen region, Southern Africa, regional cooperation and integration are among the essential important ingredients, if the region is to prosper and grow, or put in more negative, but perhaps more realistic terms: to avoid marginalization and oblivion in a dynamic world economy.

Southern Africa is pragmatically defined as the member states of the regional organization the Southern African Development Coordination Conference, SADCC. When established in 1980 SADCC consisted of nine countries. In

1990 the newly independent Namibia joined its ranks, and democratic South Africa became the 11th member in 1994.[3] In the latter year the member countries were: Angola; Botswana; Lesotho; Malawi; Mozambique; Namibia; South Africa; Swaziland; Tanzania; Zambia; and Zimbabwe. Key data on the countries in the region are presented in Table 1.1 in which comparative information on Denmark and the United Kingdom (UK) is also included. It might be noted that Southern Africa covers an extremely vast area of land, whereas its population only totals 125 million. This is a bit more than double the population of Britain, but the surface it covers is 28 times the size of the British Isles. The most populous African state, Nigeria, with 100 million inhabitants, covers a territory of less than one-seventh of that of Southern Africa. Income per capita places the majority of countries in the category of low-income economies but with notable exceptions of Namibia, South Africa and Botswana, which are in the middle and upper-middle categories. Economic comparisons reveal that the ten SADCC countries can muster approximately a quarter of the strength of South Africa. South Africa's Gross Domestic Product, GDP, is in turn only four-fifths of the Danish and one-ninth of the British GDP. Moreover, it can be noted how high population growth and external debt as well as dependence on foreign aid are major problems for a large number of the countries. An additional characteristic for Southern Africa is that approximately 90 per cent of the value of exports consists of minerals or agricultural products with little or no value added through processing in the region (African Development Bank, 1993b, p.4).

Among the SADCC countries Tanzania, given its geographic position and economic links, might just as well be said to belong to an Eastern African regional group. Angola could from a geographic point of view be tied up with Central Africa. Economically, Angola has few links to any African country. As a consequence of Angola's high purchasing power this may change after peace is firmly established. The rest of the SADCC region has considerable linkages between the countries which were created over the last century. They are especially strong in the areas of trade, migrant labour and transport. They were shaped before decolonization, and reflected typically the needs of the economic powerhouse of the region, South Africa. At the same time South Africa had to make certain concessions and trade-offs, where the concrete circumstances made this necessary and convenient. For example, the Portuguese state was paid in gold for each migrant worker South Africa recruited in Mozambique; Zimbabwean industry was granted entry to the South African market, and a new rail link was built to Swaziland from Richard's Bay in South Africa. SADCC's original aims were precisely to reduce these links with South Africa. They did this in the name of the international boycott against apartheid South Africa, but equally in order to improve their own development potential. The official view was that the links to South Africa were unequal and a sign of undesired dependence to the

3

benefit of South Africa. In the founding document of SADCC the *Lusaka Declaration* the countries state that '... it is necessary to liberate our economies from their dependence on the Republic of South Africa to overcome the imposed economic fragmentation and to co-ordinate our efforts toward regional and national economic development'.[4] Individually and acting on the basis of short to medium term national interests the majority of SADCC countries sought in parallel to reap the maximum benefits from the unavoidably continuous ties to South Africa. On its part South Africa also performed a double-strategy of both stick and carrot. It offered, for example, attractive rates on transport routes through its territory, but at the same time it waged a covert war and instigated other acts of political and economic destabilization in the region with the aim of maintaining its traditional links.[5] It should be stressed that the book will not beyond these remarks encompass any general introduction to the region. Likewise, it is outside the scope of the book to make a general evaluation of SADCC's success in reducing its economic ties with South Africa.

The period in focus in the book is the mid 1980s to the beginning of the 1990s. Events before and after are only included when they are judged to be of utmost interest for the topic under discussion; they will not be treated separately and/or in their own right. Strategically, the period is extremely interesting. It combines the political breakthrough of the democratization process in South Africa with a turn around in the economies of most of the original SADCC countries. They move from inward orientation as well as a dominance of the state and central controls to more liberal and open economies, both internally and externally, with the private sector in a decisive role. At the same time the ANC both before and after the April 1994 elections renounced drastic economic measures, and stressed the need for maintaining macroeconomic balances and an economy conducive to private sector led growth. This should in turn finance improvements for the majority. In the SADCC countries democratization and higher human rights standards gradually gained ground in the beginning of the 1990s although the process had its backlashes, and it was precarious in several countries. The overall image seems to picture a region with broadly similar economic and political systems by the end of the period in focus. Gone is the South African destabilization of its neighbours, SADCC's attempts to reduce its dependence especially on South Africa, the vicious civil wars in the region, and the impediment to regional cooperation and integration which the conflicting economic and political systems entailed.

The emergence of peace in the region coupled with economic and political liberalization might turn out to be conducive to regional cooperation and integration. The blackboard is wiped clean, some of the previous hindrances on the ground are cleared, and the political interest in preserving peace and improving living standards is very strong. In this context the existing close ties between South Africa and the majority of the SADCC countries are rare assets in a third world setting. However, because of the economic dominance of South Africa they can, if not carefully handled, also be reasons for countries to withdraw from the process. In 1994 at the time of concluding this book the discussion has been very intense in Southern Africa about which model of regional cooperation and integration might best serve the region. This includes the way to deal with varying national interests, and of paramount importance is the avoidance of models of cooperation that contain the seeds of their own dissolution. The book cannot contribute directly to this debate. However, indirectly there might be elements which the involved parties might find useful.

The book aspires to contribute to the accumulated knowledge and lessons learned in Southern Africa by analyzing the general approaches to regional integration and cooperation as possible tools for a deeper insight into chaotic reality. And, not least, to search for explanations as to why SADCC did not succeed in advancing regional cooperation within trade and industry in the 1980s. Moreover, the book tries to place regional cooperation and integration in the context of macroeconomic change among the SADCC countries by the end of the 1980s. It seeks to identify the possible regional policies of the chief proponent behind the quest for a new macroeconomic dispensation – the World Bank. This is done both generally and within the structural adjustment programmes between the Bank and the individual SADCC member states. In this way the book enters into another large field of analysis: the discussion of the virtues and problems of structural adjustment in general and Africa in particular. However, it is important from the outset to stress that the purpose is not to advance any independent judgements on structural adjustment as such. Regional integration and cooperation remains at the centre of the discussion, but the World Bank and structural adjustment inevitably have to enter the analysis, because they significantly influence the possibilities for regional cooperation and integration. It should also be noted that the International Monetary Fund (IMF) only is mentioned when the circumstances make it relevant. There is no attempt to systematically define its specific position or possible divergencies with the World Bank in relation to structural adjustment. Focus is on the latter as the voice of the Bretton Woods institutions in relation to the issues of the book.[6]

The organic inclusion of the structural adjustment policies – natural as it might seem with the wisdom of hindsight – was generally not taking place in academic analysis of regional cooperation and integration[7] or in regional policy making by African states, when the research for the finalization of this book was initiated in 1992. The Abuja Treaty of 1991 for achieving an African Economic Community by the year 2025 was for example celebrated without regard to the influence of structural adjustment on existing plans for regional integration (Organization of African Unity, 1991). In an African context the African Development Bank (ADB) broke the ice in its Development Report

5

for 1993. Its message is that structural adjustment and regional integration should be combined. The report states that 'Structural adjustment programmes are national responses to national economic crises and they are implemented without regard to their regional consequences.' The report also admits that economic integration in Africa has been 'pursued with little or no regard for the conduct of national macroeconomic policies' (African Development Bank/ African Development Fund, 1993a, p.ii). The African Development Bank (ibid.) holds the view that:

> ... irrespective of how bold and courageous structural adjustment programmes are, they are not likely to have a significant impact on the growth and development process, in the absence of more substantial progress with regional integration. The basic premise of this argument is that given the smallness and fragility of individual African economies, their outward-oriented programmes of structural adjustment may be necessary, but not sufficient to achieve self-propelling growth in a world that is increasingly being partitioned into trading blocks, ...

On the academic scene R. Davies of South Africa (1992) initiated a discussion of the World Bank's agenda regarding regional integration in a *Working Paper* from 1992. At the same time economists from the World Bank with A. Mansoor in a prominent role[8] began contributing to the debate on a possible new approach to regional integration in Africa, which took into account and actually advanced the national structural adjustment programmes. This innovative debate has been integrated in the discussion of various approaches to regional cooperation and integration under the heading 'the adjustment adapted market integration approach'.

1.2   Main issues

To sum up from the above: regional cooperation and integration in Southern Africa in the 1980s and beginning of the 1990s is the area of research for the book. It is analysed in relation to three central elements: general approaches, SADCC and the World Bank. The latter is examined under two headings: one is the general policies of the World Bank on regional cooperation and integration, and another is the country specific structural adjustment programmes' consequences for regional cooperation and integration. Moreover, the field of investigation is narrowed down to industry and trade, when analyzing the attempts by SADCC and the contents of World Bank policies. The key questions or issues and their sequencing are sketched below. They can be found in more elaborate terms at the introductions to each of the four main chapters.

Firstly, what tools in the form of general approaches do we possess in order to penetrate and understand the chaotic reality and conflicting tendencies that are present in the period under study? Likewise, ways and means are sought to identify, organize and characterize dangers, limitations and potentials of attempts at regional cooperation and integration, not least SADCC. The ambition is also to answer the question of whether a new approach is in the making, with the point of departure in the World Bank's structural adjustment programmes.

Secondly, what characterizes industry and trade in the region? A knowledge of basic features and interlinkages is deemed necessary for understanding and discussing both World Bank and SADCC's initiatives. On the other hand, what has SADCC tried to implement in the areas of industry and trade? How and why did the initiatives fare so badly?

It is a central hypothesis that the new macroeconomic setting promoted by the World Bank is among the key factors behind the inappropriateness of SADCC's policies. Therefore, the third cluster of questions focuses on which general policies the World Bank seeks to promote in the area of regional cooperation and integration? The question is posed in relation to the Bank's general policy writings, to its interventions at SADCC conferences, and to a specific initiative which the Bank appears to be venturing into on a regional level at the beginning of the 1990s.

However, as World Bank policies at the regional level are assumed to be somewhat inconsistent both generally and between the general and the operational level the book proceeds with a country focus. Here, an attempt is made to assess the impact of national structural adjustment policies on the countries' ability to further regional cooperation and integration. The focus is again on industry and trade, and Mozambique is chosen as a country example. Key questions are the following. Which are the possible direct and indirect regional policies expressed in Policy Framework Papers (PFPs) agreed between the government and the World Bank? How has trade between Mozambique and the region developed under structural adjustment? How do the policies of structural adjustment affect a specific industrial branch, textile and clothing, and its ability to produce for the local and external market?

1.3   Sources, terminology and structure

Both primary sources (government publications, multilateral agency publications, press sources and documents), and secondary sources (books, journals, working papers) have been used in the elaboration of the book. They are included in two separate sections of the select bibliography. The bibliography only contains sources which are referred to in the text or tables. Let me highlight three groups of material. First, the substantial number of documents sourced directly from SADCC, especially on industry and trade policy; second, the documentation of agreements between the World Bank and the Mozambican Government, which are open to the public in Mozambique; and third, the interviews made and primary source material collected by the author during field work in Southern Africa in March–April 1993. The latter included visits to the headquarters of both the SADCC in Gaborone and the Preferential Trade Area for Eastern and Southern Africa, PTA, in Lusaka, as well as to ministries and factories in Mozambique. The field trip also brought the author to South Africa. There material was collected in various institutions, and extremely rewarding discussions were held with excellent scholars of regional cooperation and integration including R. Davies of the University of Western Cape, G. Maasdorp of the University of Natal, C. McCarthy of the University of Stellenbosch, and P. Ncube of the University of Cape Town.

It is appropriate at this point to warn against the possible errors contained in the statistical sources on African development. They are due to the generalized situation of few resources and low institutional capacity in many of the links in the chain that gather, process and present the data. Moreover, there are economic activities and movements of people that per definition escape the official statistics: for example the illegal trade and illegal migrants. However, in the view of the author the possibilities of inaccuracies cannot and should not prevent the use of statistical information to illustrate points of the analysis and to identify overall trends. The important thing is to be aware of the problems, and not to over interpret small statistical differences.

A few remarks on terminology: the organization SADCC changed its name to Southern African Development Community (SADC) in August 1992, when a new Treaty was signed.[9] However, as the main emphasis of the analysis is before that date I shall keep to SADCC, except when references are specifically made to the new aspects of the organization after 1992. I likewise keep the name European Community (EC), throughout the book, except if reference is specifically made to the period after 1 January 1994, where it changed to the European Union (EU) after the adaptation of the Maastricht Treaty for Closer European Union.

The book consists of four main chapters, each with a separate introduction and summary. The following chapter, chapter 2, deals with the general approaches to regional cooperation and integration. In chapter 3 an outline is given of the main characteristics of industry and trade in the region as well as analyses of SADCC's futile attempts in this area. Chapter 4 seeks to identify and scrutinize overall World Bank policy and practice on regional cooperation and integration relevant to Southern Africa. The contents of chapter 5 discuss the regional implications of the World Bank's structural adjustment policies with Mozambique as a country case. Finally, there is an overall summary of the book.

Notes

1   A. Traoré is assistant editor of *The Courier*, which is published by the European Commission and covers areas of interest for cooperation between the African, Caribbean, and Pacific countries, the ACP group, and the European Community under the Lomé Agreement.

2   Reference is also made to Browne and Commings, 1985.

3   South Africa became a member of the reformed SADCC – Southern African Development Community, SADC, at the meeting of the SADC Heads of State and Government in Gaborone, 29 August 1994.

4   The full and correct title of the Lusaka Declaration is: *Southern Africa toward Economic Liberation*, (SADCC, 1984f, p.3).

5   See note 18 in chapter 5 with references on both destabilization in general and on the specific case of Mozambique.

6   See also chapter 5, note 1.

7   An article by J.-C. Boidin (1988) in *The Courier* is a rare example of an awareness of the issue. He poses the question 'whether the ACPs [see note 1 above] can reconcile their stabilisation and adjustment policies – which will remain, basically, national, liberal and geared to the short and medium term – with their economic integration strategies – which have a regional, voluntarist and long-term approach'. Another example has been found concerning regional integration in Latin America and the Caribbean. Structural adjustment programmes were initiated there in the beginning of the 1980s, and not as in Africa mid to late 1980s. The knowledgeable G. Rosenthal, General Secretary of the Economic Commission for Latin America writes (1989, p.13) about the experiences of the 1980s: 'There was also a weakening of the institutions responsible for promoting and monitoring the integration process, while at the same time the gap was widening between the objectives of formal integration commitments and national economic policies, which reacted to urgent short-term imbalances and frequently followed a path of adjustment and trade deregulation incompatible with past integration commitments.'

8   See chapter 2, note 65.

9   The three documents which were approved in August 1992 were: SADCC (1992c); SADCC (1992d); and SADCC (1992e).

2 General approaches to regional cooperation and integration

2.1 Introduction

One has to overcome certain mental barriers before being able to critically discuss the issues of regional cooperation and integration. Frankly, who wants to be seen as advocating uncooperative attitudes in international relations or worse – disintegration. Integration is value loaded like 'progress', or 'welfare', writes C.V. Vaitsos (1978, p.719), and R. Davies (1992, p.3) compares integration to 'motherhood' or 'apple pie' that almost everyone can agree are good things. In Africa one could witness the dichotomy of an ideologically forceful drive for unity and Pan-Africanism running parallel with the fact that the majority of countries obtained their independence with nationalism as a key slogan and mobilizing force in the late 1950s and early 1960s. In no other regional organization in the world is the word 'unity' built-in as in the Organisation of African Unity (OAU) and the United Nations Economic Commission for Africa (ECA) has had the promotion of regional cooperation and integration as a key area of action since it was set up in 1958.[1] My own experience from working in Africa[2] is that one finds a peculiar coexistence within African political elites of a profound sympathy for African unity and at the same time a deep distrust and feelings of superiority and inferiority between neighbours. Do these two tendencies neutralize each other and make regional integration efforts tantamount to jumping up and down on the same spot – like a Masai-dance – fascinating and comforting but not solving the key problems of society? Further, are discussions of integration and cooperation worth the effort, as flows of for example trade and labour seem to take place totally independently of national boundaries, integration schemes and theories? Illegal border trade is thriving in the whole of Africa; South African goods penetrated nearly all African markets even at the height of sanctions,[3] and if one hears French spoken in the centre of Johannesburg it is merely a token of the massive labour inflow to South Africa in the 1990s both from neighbouring countries and far beyond in spite of illegality and the nonexistence of agreements on free circulation of labour. At the same time experience with formal schemes for regional integration has generally been disappointing in Africa, as in the Third World in general. Eastern and Southern Africa can display the most evident example of this in the form of the East African Community, which was dissolved in 1977 after ten years of existence.[4]

However, the kaleidoscopic and often contradictory tendencies in the real world are to me simply justifications for attempting to organize and systematize perceptions and knowledge, and to introduce possible linkages, relationships and models. The models, general approaches or 'ideal types' are not found in their pure form in reality. They are most often mixed and intermingled with other models and developments in different areas, but often one type tends to dominate in a given period: that general approach can then be called the paradigm. This must not obscure that the merit of any of the models is one of a simple tool. It may enable a better understanding of reality, and be helpful to the identification of reasons, trends and possible future developments. In this case it shall assist in opening the can of regional integration and cooperation in Southern Africa, and give clues as to whether what we find is hot air, worms, a nutrient for sustainable development or a mixture of the three. The interpretation of reality that the general approaches allow for, will facilitate intervention and action which in turn will influence future developments and new analysis.

The purpose of this chapter is more specifically, through the presentation and discussion of the general approaches, to be able to locate and identify potentials and possible limitations of the existing attempts to forge regional cooperation and integration in Southern Africa. Especial attention is attached to enabling an understanding of SADCC. However, the ambition is to get around the major clusters of approaches. An innovative aspect may be the inclusion of the embryonic theorizing around regional integration under structural adjustment.[5] The built-in normative guide to these efforts is to attempt to identify a path and a structure that might be able to exploit the seemingly rich possible benefits from regional cooperation and integration, without at the same time sowing the seeds of the scheme's own self-destruction. This goes hand in hand with an eclectic attitude, so that one is not bound to one specific theoretical complex, but is free to utilize the best of various approaches, in order to maximize their usefulness for the analysis in question.

I shall start out with a basic distinction between cooperation and integration. This is followed by a section on regional cooperation. Thereafter the focus shifts to regional integration, which will be analysed under four different headings:

- market integration approach;
- development integration approach;
- adjustment adopted market integration approach;
- neo-functionalist approach.

The chapter will conclude with a summary, perspectives and a brief attempt to place SADCC within the general approaches to regional cooperation and integration.

2.2 Defining regional cooperation and integration

No universally accepted definitions exist of the two concepts regional cooperation and regional integration. Indeed, one could chose, as do I.C. Orantes and G. Rosenthal,[6] to interpret cooperation as a 'style' within a broader defined regional integration concept. The 'grand old man' of regional integration theory, P. Robson (1990, p.3), also prefers an all embracing definition. To him 'international economic integration' is 'a state or a process that derives its importance from its potential for enabling its participants to achieve a variety of common goals more effectively by joint or integrated action than by unilateral measures'.[7] However, I will argue that first there are sufficient differences in substance to justify two distinct categories; and secondly, that the dichotomy cooperation/integration seems to be increasingly used in discussions, concerning type of regional interaction that is desirable in Southern Africa, which makes it convenient to apply for the purpose of this book.

Regional economic integration was originally confined to the theory of customs unions, elaborated by J. Viner in 1950. According to Viner (1950, p.5) a customs union is defined by: '1. The complete elimination of tariffs as between the member territories. 2. The establishment of a uniform tariff on imports from outside the union. 3. Apportionment of customs revenue between the members in accordance with an agreed formula.' The more analytical definition within the same school of thought was delivered by R.G. Lipsey. He defined the theory of customs unions as: '... that branch of tariff theory which deals with the effect of geographically discriminatory changes in trade barriers' (Lipsey, 1960, p.496). However, in order to achieve increased applicability and usefulness for real life analysis the definition has to be expanded in economic terms and include the political level, too. As I see it, it must contain both the issue of sharing markets and common institutions, including decision making.

B. Balassa (1961, p.4) approaches the issue '... as a process and as a state of affairs. Regarded as a process, it encompasses various measures abolishing discrimination between economic units belonging to different national states. Viewed as a state of affairs, it can be represented by the absence of various forms of discrimination between national economies.' This is supplemented by H. Kitamura (1966, p.45) who focuses on the institutional aspect: 'Economic integration is, thus, a process in which an attempt is made to create a desirable institutional framework for the optimization of economic policy as a whole'. J. Tinbergen (1965, pp.76–82) combines the two definitions through the useful distinction between 'negative and positive integration'. The former denominates the abolition of barriers between countries, for example the 'reduction of import duties or the expansion of quotas'. The latter implies the building up of institutions with the task of avoiding market distortions, to redistribute income between countries, regulate unstable markets, and prepare economic policies. This is then put into an interstate political setting by E.B. Haas (1971, p.6) in his definition of integration:

> The study of regional integration is concerned with explaining how and why states cease to be wholly sovereign, how and why they voluntarily mingle, merge, and mix with their neighbours, so as to lose the factual attributes of sovereignty while acquiring new techniques for resolving conflict between themselves.[8]

Balassa (1961, p.4) and Kitamura (1966, p.43) are also helpful regarding contributions to defining the concept of regional cooperation as distinct from integration. For Kitamura 'cooperation between independent nation-states may include a wide range of actions relating to technically well-defined fields, such as patent laws or communication.' To Balassa 'cooperation includes various measures designed to harmonize economic policies and to lessen discrimination ...'. However, it seems that Balassa's diminishing of discrimination is next to impossible to distinguish from the process of integration. Nye's (1971, p.230) discussion, within a neo-functionalist framework, of 'partial integration schemes' is parallel to the concept of cooperation we try to establish. He defines them 'as limited sector integration ..., agreed specialization and allocation of market shares, joint services, and jointly owned public corporations'. World Bank economist F. Foroutan (1992, p.27ff.) joins in and adds joint infrastructure projects when he defines cooperation 'as broadly as possible to include everything from joint projects, such as the Beira Project in SADCC, to tax harmonization, harmonization of public administrative rules, national statistics, health and education standards, transportation policy or the like.'[9] From the four contributions I distil five clues suggesting that a definition of cooperation at least should be able to encompass: 1) the technical sector coordination; 2) harmonization of policies; 3) common promotion of production; 4) common running of some public services; 5) execution of joint projects. We will now turn to E.B. Haas. His definition of cooperation is brief and open-ended: 'Regional cooperation is a vague term covering any interstate activity with less than universal participation designed to meet commonly experienced need' (1971, p.7). However, the common perception of a need could be misleading, as agreement on action regarding a certain project might stem from a variety of reasons among the cooperating nations of what the problem and benefits really are. Orantes and Rosenthal's integration style that corresponds to the cooperation concept is called 'integration at micro level' or 'project integration'. It has a useful emphasis on the advantage of the cooperation for all participants and stresses that cooperation is not necessarily a stage in a fixed line of evolution. Their definition is as follows: '[Cooperation] aims at promoting interdependence through specific activities which involve an intrinsic benefit for the participating countries, but which are not necessarily conceived as stages leading to the emergence of a larger unit' (Orantes and Rosenthal, 1977, p.22).

True to my eclectic point of departure, I shall now contribute with my own definitions which combine what I see as the best and most useful in the above, and add elements that I judge are lacking. Thus, regional integration is defined as 'a process through which a group of nation states voluntarily in various degrees share each other's markets and establish mechanisms and techniques that minimize conflicts and maximize internal and external economic, political, social and cultural benefits of their interaction'. I shall define regional cooperation as 'a process whereby nation states in common solve tasks and create improved conditions in order to maximise internal and external economic, political, social and cultural benefits for each participating country'. Thus, in contrast to cooperation the definition of integration includes the issue of general access to each other's markets and building up mechanisms for operating the scheme, but without demanding any specific institutional arrangement. The definition of cooperation underlines that the point of departure and objective are buried in the individual nation states. They act together in specific areas where they judge that they together stand a better chance of enhancing development opportunities than when acting individually. Common institutions are not excluded but administering activities may span from a semi ad hoc basis to more formalised fora. This leads us to the next section on regional cooperation.

2.3   Regional cooperation

Regional cooperation has often been treated as an appendix or sub-sub-category of regional integration. The reason for this is partly that some of the elements of regional cooperation are derived from the development integration approach, partly probably because the cooperation approach is much more diverse and academically difficult to analyse schematically than, for example, market integration and development integration. However, the many problems attached to implementing the latter, and on the other hand the necessity for individual nation states to cooperate to enhance development opportunities have brought renewed attention politically and academically to regional cooperation.

Regional cooperation was defined in the above as a process whereby nation states in common solve tasks and create improved conditions in order to maximize economic, political, social and cultural benefits for each participating country. In an evaluation of existing arrangements it is important to note that the cooperative efforts can take place on a continuum stretching from a systematic framework, aiming at continuously increasing the level of cooperation; to an episodic style, where cooperation is limited to scattered projects created more by coincidence than intent. We can now return to the fields of action that regional cooperation may contain. The elements are not specified in the definition as they are not necessarily all present in each regional cooperation attempt. Moreover, although the list probably represents the major relevant forms for regional cooperation presently, it is non-exhaustive, because other examples exist and new ones can be added. In relation to the items mentioned in 2.2, the list below has been rearranged and supplemented by the administration of shared natural resources and common ground in confronting and cooperating with extra-regional countries and institutions:

1   execution of joint projects, technical sector cooperation, common running of services and policy harmonization;
2   joint development of common natural resources;
3   joint stand towards the rest of the world;
4   joint promotion of production.

I shall elaborate on these points one by one. (1) Joint projects can be executed in all areas of cooperation, but will typically concentrate upon infrastructure in a broad sense. Roads, railways, bridges, telecommunication links, energy transmission lines etc. can often be singled out for profitable common investment. The implementation of some transport projects will link landlocked countries to the sea and give both the landlocked and the country with the seaport an interest in the construction of, and mutual benefit in, the use of the facility. The establishment of improved transport facilities between cooperating countries can also be part of a conscious attempt to overcome hindrances to trade between countries. Foroutan (1992, p.28) writes: '... the pay-off to cooperation in realizing joint projects is likely to be considerable. The experience of SADCC, often mentioned as the only example of successful integration in South-Saharan Africa, is a good example'. However, only the coming years will tell whether the rate of return on SADCC's many infrastructure projects lives up to expectations.

Technical sector cooperation also typically concerns areas such as transport, communication and energy. The aims would be to make the links between the participating states as efficient as possible and to reduce costs thanks to a more optimal use of facilities. The cooperation in for example transport may be limited to synchronizing airline timetables, but can also lead to the creation of joint public or private companies for the running of railways, airlines, harbours and maritime services. This was for instance the case in the East African Community where public common services were responsible for these areas. At the 1992 Annual Conference of SADCC the World Bank representative called for the creation of jointly owned regional operating authorities to cater for infrastructure activities and public utilities (World Bank, 1992e, p.3). However, a whole range of more 'soft' public services might be identified as potentially benefiting from regional cooperation. Let me stick to one of the most obvious: education, training and research. With the small size of most African economies and the limitations to public expenditures there is a strong case for pooling resources as regards specialized training institutes. Agricultural and medical research and the combat of various pests and diseases are obvious candidates for prearranging fields of specialization at universities in each country or for creating common institutions.

Policy harmonization can cover such areas as industry standards and commercial law, but can, at least in principle, also reach the level of macroeconomic policies; but in practice, results in economically sensitive areas have typically not gone beyond statements of intent. Policies towards environmental issues have a character that calls for regional policy harmonization. In a group of cooperating countries the localizations of common services and/or institutions can often be an area of tension and controversy. However, it can also be used, consciously, to create a better balance between the member states by, for example, favouring the lesser developed countries in the allocation process. I will argue that it is within this line of thought that the SADCC Secretariat was located in one of the smaller (albeit prosperous) member states and the Sector Secretariats were placed in the various member countries. The EAC experienced both conflicts and attempts to dampen contention in relation to the distribution of the common services.[10] The distribution of leadership posts in common organizations contains the same dichotomy of conflict and appeasement. In SADCC there seems to be a consensus that the Head of the Secretariat shall be from a larger member country, while the Deputy post created in the beginning of the 1990s must come from one of the smaller states.[11]

(2) Natural resources have a tendency not to respect national boundaries, and will often be shared between two or more countries. Therefore, there is frequently a point in analyzing whether cooperation in this field is desirable and feasible seen from both an administrative, technical and economic point of view. Areas that are prone to this kind of cooperation are for example

desertification, wild life, marine resources and river basin development.[12] Several river development organizations exist in Africa, mostly in West Africa. The World Bank found in 1979 that the tasks of these organizations were vital, but results were mixed. They were diagnosed as having 'overly ambitious objectives, inadequate finances, and the lack of qualified staff', and there was a lack of consistency between the plans of the river organizations and the national development plans (World Bank, 1989, p.158). River development is often linked to energy production which in itself, as noted above, also has a cooperative potential. In Southern Africa we have the Zambezi river with the Kariba dam and electricity generation both on the Zambian and Zimbabwean bank of the river and downstream at Cahora Bassa in Mozambique. SADCC has, since the late 1980s, tried to start up a programme for an integrated development of the Zambezi river basin in its totality.[13] The preservation of wild life is a cooperating sector of SADCC, but not one that can boast of many results. Mozambique and a democratic South Africa will probably cooperate on the development of game parks in southern Mozambique in conjunction with the giant Kruger National Park along South Africa's border to Mozambique, and will possibly link up to a national park in the south east corner of Zimbabwe.

(3) The joint stand towards the rest of the world has several aspects. Let me distinguish between the following:

(A) joint seeking of funds for regional projects;
(B) joint stand in international organizations (e.g. OAU, United Nations (UN), World Bank, African, Caribbean and Pacific (ACP) countries);
(C) joint marketing of regional products or services, e.g. tourism, transport services and key export products;
(D) joint seeking of favourable relations with other regional blocks or individual countries;
(E) joint position towards a common enemy;
(F) joint rules for foreign investment in the region.

(A) is what SADCC, with apparent success, has been able to perform since its inception in 1980. In 1991 SADCC reported that 89 per cent of project funding was expected to come from foreign sources out of a total budget of US$ 7.5 billion (SADCC, 1991b, p.32).[14] Regarding (B), the six SADCC countries constituting the 'front line states' (Angola, Botswana, Mozambique, Tanzania, Zambia, Zimbabwe) have been able to reach common policies, especially concerning the liberation of Namibia and the struggle against apartheid. These policies have to some extent been taken over and promoted by SADCC, but in this context the remaining SADCC countries Malawi, Lesotho and Swaziland have mostly had the role of sleeping partners. (C) has been attempted by SADCC in the area of transport routes from the sea to the hinterland – the Dar es Salaam and Beira Corridors, and region-wide tourism promotion is in preparation.[15] Cooperation in marketing of certain commodities and processed goods is an obvious possibility for Southern Africa, including a democratic South Africa. Ironically enough, private enterprise and the free market have created the world's most efficient primary product selling cartel: diamonds from De Beers of South Africa. Producer nations have unsuccessfully tried to challenge this cartel, and Botswana has taken the next logical step of simply buying a share in De Beers. Point (D) is what for example the Caribbean Common Market (CARICOM) has tried, in relation to the United States and the North American Free Trade Agreement (NAFTA). The Central American countries have a regular dialogue with the EC,[16] and the Association of South-East Asian Nations (ASEAN) – with the combined weight of their growing economic importance – have held successful consultations with the EC countries on political and economic issues. The Nordic–SADCC Initiative from 1986 is an innovative concept of North-South region to region cooperation on more effective aid, production, trade, financing and culture. However, in the beginning of the 1990s one tends to conclude that very little beyond the scope of better aid delivery has been achieved.[17] (E) is naturally of special importance for military pacts, but it can certainly also be relevant for economic cooperation. SADCC is an example of this in its relation to apartheid South Africa.[18] The cohesion of the ASEAN countries, especially after the American withdrawal from Vietnam and Vietnam's invasion in Cambodia in the 1970s, was based on common fear of communist expansion. The West African Economic Community (CEAO) owes much of its ability to survive in difficult waters to the member countries' fears of being dominated by Nigeria and the rest of English speaking West Africa. (F) The common rules for foreign investments in a region may be seen as an attempt to avoid countries engaging in self-destructive competition by offering the most favourable conditions possible to the foreign investor. Instead of neutralizing each other's offers in this way, the regional partners could agree on a joint level of incentives on the basis of the productive environment in the region in comparison with other parts of the world. However, this area is one of the most disputed and difficult to approach from a regional point of view, as each country wants to be in a vantage position to attract investments and interests are simply not the same in countries with different levels of industrialization. Political orientation and not least stability is also of paramount importance, not least for the investors evaluation of a given incentive structure. In the beginning of the 1990s one can witness separate discussions in each SADCC country of how to imitate and adapt Mauritius' success with Export Processing Zones.

(4) Joint promotion of production within the cooperation approach is sometimes difficult to distinguish from industrial planning and development in the development integration approach. The simplest way out of this is, in

19

my view, to establish that the latter is implemented as a countervailing measure to alleviate negative distributive effects of the across-the-board market integration approach, whereas joint promotion of production within the cooperation approach exists in its own right. The overall economic objective of the latter is to benefit from the possibilities of specialization and the economies of scale permitted by access to markets in more than one country. This will ideally increase the level of industrialization and create employment opportunities. This may require, as Orantes and Rosenthal (1977, p.22) note, 'adoption of complementary measures – free trade in the articles to be manufactured'. Green (1980, p.A46) tends to see this more as a question of creating an 'imaginative linking of production planning with trade' that ensure 'balanced production and export opportunities' and 'reduces demands on hard currency', 'possibly under an agreement specifying targets and prices and providing for annual clearing'. Ravenhill (1985, p.210) sticks to already established industries in his discussion of realistic alternatives to hitherto failed regionalism in Africa and proposes that 'emphasis would be on utilising existing regional production in an effort to match regional surpluses and deficits.' The obligations of market access for members are reduced to 'quantities agreed in interstate negotiations, and ideally payments ... would be made in local currencies.' P. Ndegwa (1984, p.33) writes on the same lines:

> Roughly balanced trade (including energy, transport, communications and other 'invisibles') or agreed target levels of imbalance seem more likely to promote preferential import liberalisation and its counterpart of increased export opportunities than free or preferential trade.

In his systematization of experiences in the area, Robson (1990, p.197) distinguishes between on the one hand 'the "complementarity agreements" [that] involves trade liberalization for certain existing industries or project groups in the context of a deliberate planned rationalization of production'; and on the other hand, an approach which is also limited to specified products or industries, but 'takes the form of measures to promote and regulate investment in new regionally based industries that enjoy economies of scale, so as more economically to meet the combined demand of member countries'. The above measures have been attempted to varying degrees in different regional groups. One can mention the intention of the Latin American Free Trade Association (LAFTA) to create a network of complementarity agreements;[19] ASEAN Industrial Projects, seeking to establish new large scale regional industries and the ASEAN Industrial Complementation program, aiming at promoting greater complementarity among existing industries,[20] and the Central American Common Market (CACM) program for integration industries that should cover the whole market in Central America.[21] The

Andean Pact had a strong element of regional industrial sector planning with a view to locating new regional industries and rationalizing production of existing plants.[22] Attempts were also made in the East African Community (ECA) to distribute industrial investments in some specific branches in certain countries.[23]

However, none of the mentioned programmes progressed in accordance with initial high expectations. Rather, they have stagnated, collapsed and/or been abandoned. Leaving more specific circumstances aside, this has its background in various crosscutting conflicts. One is between the state intervention and planning contained in industrialization programmes and on the other hand the free market, private initiative approach. The balance of political power in the participating states have typically been in favour of the latter.[24] The second contradiction is between relatively developed countries and countries in the initial phase of building up an industry. Add to this the conflicting impulses of external forces, both international organizations, governments and transnational enterprises,[25] the ever present force of opportunistic nationalism[26] in politics in the participating countries, as well as the relatively weak bureaucracy and planning capacity.[27] This has lead to very time consuming and unproductive bureaucratic battles over location of industries, over market access, over sharing of costs etc. However, one must bear in mind that in most of the cited examples the promotion of production has been part of across-the-board development integration efforts. Robson (1990, pp.202 and 214) concludes: 'Narrower arrangements limited to particular sectors or industries may well be more suitable'. He also prefers 'fiscal and other incentives which is expected to work broadly in the desired directions'. The latter was generally not possible with the large market distortions in most developing countries in the 1970s and 1980s, but this might have changed with the market oriented policies of the late 1980s and 1990s. Regarding the 'narrower arrangements' the argument is difficult to comprehend as the failed schemes did focus on specific industries and sectors. However, in an earlier writing Robson (1985, p.619ff.) shed some light on this, as he refers to 'smaller groups of countries – two or three even, if necessary overlapping, and possibly resting on joint financial participation in capital, profits, tax revenues, and even manning.' They must be backed by 'community guidelines' and 'adequate incentives'. A relevant question here is whether this kind of flexible cooperation might stand a better chance of success when it is part of a loose cooperation arrangement, than when it is a component of overall integration schemes? My hypothesis on current levels of knowledge is that the problems of equity can be more easily overcome in the looser arrangement, but on the other hand the drive to actually reach an agreement as such will be weaker than if it were part of an integration scheme. The focus of the following chapter on SADCC's experiences with industry and trade cooperation in the 1980s will hopefully shed some light over this.

21

To wind up this discussion of regional cooperation, two additional concepts must be presented. One is 'incremental': we will later see its specific role in the neo-functional approach, but all the same it may be applied here as an important characteristic of cooperation. I shall broadly define it as a step-by-step approach, starting out with the most simple and noncontroversial areas and from there venturing – if the ice can bear it – further cooperative initiatives. Ravenhill (1985, p.213) does not offer any definition, but writes: 'An incremental approach to regionalism in Africa based on the identification and implementation of limited functional projects ... appears to avoid many of the problems that have beset the more grandiose schemes based on an integration of markets'. This quote contains the other catch word – 'functional'. Again it can be, and is, used both independently and as a part of a neo-functional (and functional) analysis.[28] Preferring the former in this context, the meaning of the word in discussing the cooperation approach is that the cooperation must focus on areas and tasks that the involved countries see as important in order to sustain their existence, and at the same time to which they have an obvious interstate interest. Vaitsos (1978, p.736) writes for example: 'Instead [of all embracing schemes], it needs to concentrate sectorally or inter-sectorally on the functional fulfilment of specific goals and tasks.' Orantes and Rosenthal (1977, p.23) expand this to the organizational set-up, stating that 'institutions must be created as a function of the needs which are to be jointly satisfied, and that the emphasis must be placed on transactions, not on legal instruments'. This calls, according to the authors, for task-specific, decentralized agencies, which do not 'necessitate regional institutions with supra-national characteristics' (ibid., p.24). Ravenhill (1985, p.212) supplements this important dimension of the cooperation approach in the following way: 'Flexible, functionally-specific organizations have the advantage of impinging little on the sovereignty of participating states: decision-making power remains concentrated at the national level'. Thus, in the cooperation approach, regional interaction is a supplement to national development efforts and can not substitute these.

Cooperation has both a raison d'etre of its own and can also be seen as a result of the frustrating experiences with general integration attempts. However, in the beginning of the 1990s influential circles within the neo-liberal economic school are advocating regional cooperation in Africa from a different perspective, as the following quote indicates. It originates from the World Bank economists de Melo and Panagariya's (1992a, p.20) conclusions from a 1992 conference on the 'New Regionalism in Trade Policy':

> African markets remain small, and efforts at regional integration will only divert attention from efforts to integrate Sub-Saharan Africa with the World economy. The role of regionalism in Africa should therefore be limited to cooperation on matters that have an obvious regional dimension.

The authors mention such areas as transport, education, information and the environment. Elements discussed above, such as promotion of production and common rules for foreign investors, do not belong in the cooperation universe of the neo-liberal interpreters. This is an aspect which could give rise to conflicts in the future. Moreover, African countries might not agree that regional integration in one form or the other is excluded on the agenda of future development options. Views in the World Bank also appear divided on the issue, as section 2.6 and a later chapter will reveal. We will now turn to the first of four approaches to regional integration.

2.4 Market integration approach

Mentioned above was J. Viner and his book *The Customs Union Issue* from 1950. It became a point of departure for discussions of regional integration in the second half of this century. Viner has been seen as the father and inspirer of an approach[29] that analysed the costs and benefits of customs unions solely within the sphere of movements in the market place and their implications on welfare in the participating nations and in the wider world. However, customs unions had existed long before Viner, and ironically, Viner was generally opposed to their creation. Before the unification of Germany in 1870, the leading province-state, Prussia, signed a host of customs union agreements with other German enclaves from the 1820s onwards[30] – known collectively as the German Zollverein. The building up of infant industries behind protective customs walls was discussed already in 1885 by the German economist F. List (1885).[31] For the student of Southern African affairs it is of special interest to note that more than 40 customs arrangements, protocols and conventions were celebrated in the period 1889 till 1942 between South Africa or before 1910 the four states that comprised South Africa, and Basutoland (Lesotho), Bechuanaland (Botswana), Swaziland, Southern Rhodesia (Zimbabwe) and Northern Rhodesia (Zambia) (Viner, 1950, pp.157–60). Before Viner's study, according to Lipsey (1960, p.497), it had been generally accepted that customs unions were beneficial and would increase world welfare. The argument ran along the following lines: 'Free trade maximises world welfare; a customs union reduces tariffs and is therefore a movement towards free trade; a customs union will, therefore, *increase*, world welfare even if it does not lead to a world-welfare *maximum*.' Viner's terms of reference for the study that led to his book were – on the basis of the strong American support to regional economic cooperation in Europe – to analyse the possibilities and limitations of customs unions.[32] What Viner from his neoclassical economic theory and free trade position showed was, however, that no predetermined answer could be given as to whether a given customs union is beneficial or not. It all depends on how much trade is created, in relation to how much trade is diverted by the establishment of the customs union.[33] Trade creation represents the substitution of high cost domestic production with a cheaper source placed in another country inside the customs union. Trade diversion is the substitution of a low cost product from outside the union with a higher cost source from inside the union. That Viner (1950, p.44) wants to emphasize the possible negative effects of a customs union is evident from this quotation:

> It will be noted that for the free-trader the benefit from a customs union to the customs union area as a whole derives from that portion of the new trade between the member countries which is wholly new trade, whereas each particular portion of the new trade between the member countries which is a substitute for trade with third countries he must regard as a consequence of the customs union which is injurious for the importing country, for the external world, and for the world as a whole, and is beneficial only to the supplying member country.

Viner (ibid., p.51ff.) identified a range of different situations and conditions that theoretically might lead to a situation where trade creation was larger than trade diversion. I shall not go into these technicalities, but quote a more simple presentation by him: 'Customs unions ... are unlikely to yield more economic benefit than harm, unless they are between sizable countries which practice substantial protection of substantially similar industries' (ibid., p.135). Thus, for Viner competition between industries in different countries of the customs union was important, because this would lead to a situation where production would be rationalized and the most efficient producer would capture the market. If production solely is complementary there is no drive for improvement of production methods and even a very high cost producer can dominate the whole customs union market. This argument has been discussed intensely within the market integration tradition,[34] and according to R.F. Miksell (1963, p.211) and G. Maasdorp (1992b, p.139) the conclusion is that welfare will be maximized if the economies both are competitive and *potentially* complementary, which undeniably from a common sense point of view also seems most logical and constructive. Further, the benefits from a customs union are claimed to increase if foreign trade constitutes a relatively small part of GDP. Thus, apart from potential complementarity the developing countries do not seem to fit well into the traditional theory's requirements. Trade is generally low between regional partners, foreign trade constitutes a relatively large part of GDP, and only a small part of the produced goods are competitive on the regional markets, mostly within light manufacturing industry. The bulk of primary exports do not have markets in the region.

Before going further into the discussion of the approach, the standard types of market integration will be presented.[35] This is important as the customs union is only one of the forms that market integration can take. It may rather be seen as a stage in a process of ever diminishing discrimination between the national units. First, we have the free trade area. It is characterized by the abolition of tariffs between the members, but each one keeps its own tariffs towards the rest of the world. The next step is the customs union which has the added trait of a common external tariff. Thereafter follows a common market. It supplements the customs union with the free flow of factors of production – labour and capital – among the member states. Economic union is next on the ladder. Apart from the accumulated elements of the stages hitherto it features prominently some degree of coordination and harmonization of macroeconomic policies. The ultimate level, according to Balassa (1962, p.2), is the total economic integration that 'presupposes the unification of monetary, fiscal, social, and countercyclical policies and requires the setting-up of a supra-national authority whose decisions are binding for the member states'. However, I would assume that the last stage on the basis of the characteristics more appropriately might be called 'political union'. The various stages can be illustrated by the following table.

Table 2.1
Stages in the market integration approach

Characteristic/ integration form	No internal tariffs	Common external tariffs	Free flow of labour and capital	Harmonized macro- econ.	Supra- national ins.
Free Trade Area	*	–	–	–	–
Customs Union	*	*	–	–	–
Common Market	*	*	*	–	–
Economic Union	*	*	*	*	–
Political Union	*	*	*	*	*

* = implemented
– = not implemented

Adapted from Balassa, 1962, p.2 and Nye, 1968, p.860

Obviously, the schematic form cannot do justice to the wide variety of regional organizations that are found. Moreover, some organizations do not follow the indicated sequence and others have added elements that do not form part of the market integration model, but for example belong to development integration. Nevertheless, in order to illuminate the merits of the model I shall give some illustrations of how the categories of the table can be applied. An example of a free trade area is the European Free Trade Area (EFTA). On a level below this and outside the table, the Preferential

Trade Area for Eastern and Southern Africa (PTA) has since its establishment in 1982 tried to implement its preferential treatment in the shape of gradual tariff reductions on specific goods from companies that satisfy certain conditions. However, in the beginning of the 1990s PTA seems to be aiming at creating a free trade area soonest and a common market before the year 2000.[36] Southern African Customs Union (SACU) is a prototype customs union and can be traced back to 1889/90.[37] SADCC in its original shape does not fit into the market integration approach, but the essential characteristics embedded in its new treaty of 1992 for the creation of SADC are the free flow of goods, labour and capital and harmonization of macroeconomic policies,[38] which are parallel to what here is called an economic union. That stage is what the EC is struggling to implement and expand with the Maastricht Treaty of closer European union in the beginning of the 1990s. The United States (US) can be seen as an example of political union with common institutions, but still leaving a wide range of issues to the discretion of the participating states.

Back to the costs, benefits, gains and critique of the market integration approach. The gains of market integration, according to Lipsey (1960, p.496), are a consequence of:

1   specialization based on comparative advantage;
2   economies of scale. Unit costs decrease as production increases;
3   changes in the terms of trade, as a result of tariffs and increased bargaining power;
4   forced changes in efficiency due to increased foreign competition;
5   a change in the rate of economic growth.

Traditional customs theory normally only dealt with (1), but recognized also some importance of (2) and (3). Four and five were left out completely. Thus, the issue of development is difficult to grasp within the theory. Added to this, are the restrictive assumptions and the static character of the theory. Among the assumptions are:[39]

–   perfect competition in transparent markets;
–   free flow of labour and capital inside but not between countries;
–   no transport costs;
–   tariffs as the only trade restrictions and balanced trade between countries;
–   prices reflecting the opportunity costs of production;
–   resources, e.g. labour, fully employed.

Deviations from these requirements in real life – not least in developing countries – limit the applicability of the theory. High unemployment, prohibitive transport costs and distorted markets have been more apt descriptions in most of the Third World during the last 30 years. The static character of the theory makes it inappropriate to contemplate, for example, changes in the comparative advantages of a given country. It is a frozen image of the existing distribution of the elements which constitutes the background for productive activities. That these may thaw and shift over time, e.g. due to deliberate intervention such as improved infrastructure or education, the theory cannot convincingly reflect. In R.F. Miksell's (1963, p.205) words:

> However, the effects of the creation of regional markets on the more fundamental problems of developing countries such as increasing opportunities for profitable foreign and domestic investment, broadening the export base, achieving balance of payments equilibrium, mobilizing unemployed resources and avoiding economic dualism, have been largely neglected.

Miksell (ibid., p.206) would like to see a more dynamic analysis of market integration directed towards: 'their impact on the direction of investment in the developing countries for future output rather than limited to analysis of the welfare implications of shifting existing trade patterns.' It is argued that trade diversion – at least in a period – could be necessary in order to create the conditions for sustained growth. For example, industrialization through import substitution could be reached with fewer costs and larger benefits within a region than in each individual country.[40] Axline (1977, p.84ff.) writes:

> Thus, trade diversion is the main means of expanding production, as firms attempt to supply other countries' markets, even though this may reduce each economy's national income ... the development gains in the form of savings of scarce foreign exchange and expansion of production (although inefficient in world terms) outweigh the costs in the form of national income foregone by protectionism ...

He is supplemented by Balassa (1965, p.83), who concludes that:

> The choice is therefore not so much between free trade and import substitution in an integrated area, as between import substitution within national frontiers or in the framework of a free trade area (customs union).

This discussion is marked by the dominance of the import substitution industrialization in most developing countries in the 1960s and 1970s, and by two assumptions. One is that the export of primary products could not act as the engine of development, and the other is that a jump directly from the internal market to the world market in industrial products would be the exception among developing countries.[41] This is of key interest for discussions

27

around 1990, for although the many limitations in implementation of the import industrialization policy have been revealed, the two assumptions still seem to apply, at least to the area in focus in this book.

Defending regional protected markets among developing countries against attacks from the adherents of a universal free trade system, Miksell (1963, p.229) emphasizes one more argument which has also gained prominence in recent years, viz. the learning process which regional integration offers to national business before full exposure to world market competition. He puts it this way: 'I believe, trade and competition in industrial products among developing countries will provide the experience and discipline for them to sell their industrial products on world markets, thereby broadening the export base of the entire region'.

Thus, relevant and constructive critique of assumptions, the static character and the restricted analysis of gains and costs were raised against Viner's initial analysis that per se seemed to rule out any real benefits from developing countries engaging in market sharing arrangements. Together with the next point concerning the distributional aspects of the market integration approach, this critique constitutes the background for the formulation of an alternative form of the development integration approach.

Inside a regional market with free flow of goods, labour and capital the invisible hand or spontaneous force of the market will, in principle, allocate production to where competitive advantages make production costs low, other conditions favourable and profits high. This is the essence of the effective allocation of resources. However, the same forces tend to lead to a pattern where the areas that are already relatively developed will attract the major part of the new investments, employment opportunities, technological innovations and other characteristics of modern development. The lesser developed areas will tend to stagnate or 'roll back' in terms of development. They become poles of stagnation, whereas the former become poles of growth. This process has been named 'polarization' or 'backwash'.[42] The latter was used by Myrdal (1957, p.26) in his pioneering 1957 analysis of the phenomenon. He showed how both economic and non-economic factors contributed to a 'cumulative process' of upturns in some and downturns in other areas:

> If things were left to market forces unhampered by any policy interferences, industrial production and ... almost all those economic activities which in a developing economy tend to give a bigger than average return – and, in addition, science, art, literature, education ... – would cluster in certain localities and regions, leaving the rest of the country more or less in a backwater.

Labour and capital flows to the most developed areas are vehicles in the process of disfavouring the lesser developed areas, according to Myrdal.[43]

They are reinforced by the lesser developed area's low level of education and health, a deficient transport system and general poverty. Both economic and non-economic factors are 'interlocking each other in circular causation' (1957, p.30). Counteracting the backwash effect or polarization is the 'spread effect', working through the demand that the developed area places on raw materials from the lesser developed areas. It may in turn create new developed agglomerations there. There is, according to Myrdal (ibid., p.34), a tendency for the spread effect to be most effective the more developed a country is, mostly because of better infrastructure and markets. In contrast:

> ... part of the curse of a low average level of development in an under-developed country is the fact that the spread effects there are weak. This means that as a rule the free play of the market forces in a poor country will work more powerfully to create regional inequalities and to widen those which already exist ... poverty becomes its own cause.

The spread effect will be even weaker if it has to cross national boundaries between developing countries than when it operates inside one country. This gloomy picture is not basically changed by an added possibility of creating a spread effect: it can happen because of dis-economies emerging in the relatively developed area (ibid., p.35).[44] They may consist in over-congestion resulting in prohibitive prices of land and housing, high costs of labour, pollution etc., and have the potential of making the industrialist decide to locate outside the developed centre. However, I would argue that it is not likely that this would be sufficient motivation to move to another developing country. There is normally excess labour and land available in other parts of the original country of location, and fear of the unknown and a wish for close proximity to the centre will reinforce a choice to stay within the known boundaries. However, special efforts made by the state can influence this process.

The backwash or polarization process (I shall use the latter concept henceforth) is a key to understanding the way in which regional integration has proceeded in the Third World. Polarization has simply been seen at work all too often, and developed into being the main political stumbling block for an expansion of regional integration or reason for its dissolution. An example of the latter is the EAC, where Kenya seemed to get the lion's share of benefits.[45] The Central African Federation was biased towards Zimbabwe, where industry clustered especially in Harare or Salisbury, as it was then called.[46] As an non-intended side effect the Southern African region thereby got its own expression for the polarization effect – its called 'bambazonke', which means that everything goes to Harare.[47] The CACM has been plagued by conflict between the less developed countries such as Honduras and the better off ones such as El Salvador.[48] The development integration approach

29

can to a large extent be seen as an attempt of finding ways and means of reducing the negative effects of the polarization process.

2.5   Development integration approach

The development integration approach is born out of the problems and dysfunction of the pure market integration approach. The previous section has outlined the critique of the market approach's static character, its sole focus on how trade creation and trade diversion will influence welfare, and its tendency to widen economic differences between lesser and more developed areas, when market forces are left to function on their own. The development integration approach's answer to this is to change the agenda in three areas: 1) the objective of the integration process; 2) the timing and level of interstate binding commitments; 3) the distribution of cost and benefits of the cooperation.

No commonly accepted stringently defined new objective can be identified, but the following should give a good idea of how the static welfare maximum is substituted by a dynamic development oriented goal. M.I. Blejer (1984, p.9) states that the emphasis is on: 'attaining dynamic transformations in the economic structure'. Orantes and Rosenthal (1977, p.26) write: 'The integrated development style has as its explicit objective the acceleration of the economic and social development of the countries' members ... and is oriented towards the optimization of economic policy as a whole'. Thus, with the redefinition of objective the use of protected markets becomes perfectly logical, according to the adherents of the development integration approach. Blejer (op. cit.) writes:

> Tariff protection and interference with free trade are considered justified when the social welfare function is redefined to include future as well as current consumption and other non-economic objectives and when there are imperfections, externalities, and distortions in commodity and factor markets.

To round off the discussion of objectives it should be added that the achievement of some degree of industrialization is often an implicit or explicit extra purpose of the development integration approach. C.A. Cooper and B.F. Massel (1965a, p.462) write in an article where they try to locate a theoretical basis for dynamic development through customs union membership: '... we accept industrialization as a legitimate policy goal and consider how membership in a customs union may enable a less developed country to achieve more economically the ends served by protection.'

Turning to the second major difference, Balassa (1961, p.10) agrees that a larger dose of state intervention in the economy is necessary in developing country groupings than in integration arrangements among developed countries:

> It has been widely accepted that a higher degree of government intervention is likely to be necessary in Latin-American integration projects. This reflects the proposition that present-day underdeveloped countries need more state interference in economic affairs than do advanced economies, since, in the former, market incentives are often not conducive to development.

Exactly how far an integration group will go in its intervention in the market mechanisms follows no fixed rules, but depends on how, under the given circumstances, the states perceive that their objectives are best served.

Regarding the level of common decision making it might have been noted that the binding commitments between the member states of an integration group, and indeed the creation of supra-national institutions, came in at a rather late stage in the market integration approach. Naturally, common rules and regulations must be implemented that underpin market development, but they are mainly seen as technical and not – as in the development integration approach – the backbone for furthering the integration among the countries. Orantes and Rosenthal (1977, pp.25 and 27) write that in the development integration approach 'co-ordination of policies becomes a simultaneous – or even prior – requisite for trade liberalization ... to prevent, among other problems, unequal inter-country distribution of the benefits deriving from the process.' Therefore, 'the transfer of faculties [to common institutions] will have to begin at a very early stage in the process.' Axline (1977, p.103) asserts that 'the logic of integration among underdeveloped countries foresees little likelihood of success if integration is undertaken at relatively low levels, and a greater possibility of success only if a relatively high level of political integration is undertaken at the outset.'[49] If this was not achieved Axline reckoned that the 'disintegrative dynamic' of the market forces would stall the integration.

The third key element to unlock the development integration approach is the treatment of the distribution of costs and benefits stemming from regional integration. The main question is how the negative consequences of the above discussed polarization process can be avoided through a more equitable distribution of the proceeds from integration. However, opponents of the approach will claim that the interventions very easily eliminate economic gains which the integration has brought about for the group as a whole. And if they do so, the process of integration should not have been initiated in the first place. Robson (1990, p.202) is aware of this dilemma and captures well the dichotomy between the ideal economic demands and the requirements of political cohesion of a regional group in his assertion that there may be 'trade offs between considerations of efficiency and those of equity'; and 'the objective is to bring about profitable specialization subject to the requirements of balanced development'.

The methods applied to bring about a more equitable distribution of costs and benefits in a regional integration group can be organized and presented in various ways. I have in earlier writings settled on defining two major groups: 1) compensatory mechanisms; 2) corrective mechanisms (Haarlov, 1988, p.22). By doing so, I followed Axline, but for example Robson has a similar, though more descriptive distinction between 'income transfers' on the one hand, and 'instruments to effect a change in the emergent pattern of resource allocation' on the other hand.[50] According to Robson, the corrective mechanisms can further be subdivided in two groups: 2a) initiatives that seek to achieve their aims through incentives and other manipulations of the market mechanism; 2b) interventions that through administrative measures and planning strive to change the pattern of development. However, this distinction could be spelled out from the outset, and I miss a distinction between changing general conditions for investments and establishing specific incentives. Also, the compensatory mechanism is too vaguely phrased in Robson's definition in order to capture what the groups are engaged in. Therefore, I prefer the following division into four broad groups:

(1) pure fiscal compensation;
(2) improve conditions for development;
(3) incentives for a changed pattern of production;
(4) planning of new industries and agreements on distribution of production.

At the same time as this gives a better overview, it illustrates a continuum from less to increasingly more state intervention in the economy in order to bring about the desired equity. (1) The pure fiscal compensation is a statal transfer of money from the countries that gain from a larger market to the member states that bear the costs of this process. This poses immediately the relevant question of how to estimate benefits and costs between countries.[51] One can try to estimate lost customs revenues or put a price on trade diversion, i.e. the extra price that a country must pay by importing certain goods from a regional partner instead of getting them more cheaply from the world market. Following this line of thought, there should also be a price on the costs of an industry closing down – the negative side of trade creation, and conversely a value assessment of the gains from industry expansion – the positive side of trade creation. These calculations are extremely complex and probably impossible to conduct with any accuracy, especially as the number of members of a group increase and the type of goods exchanged become more and more diverse. Also, there can in one country very well be examples of areas that benefit and others that stagnate. Therefore, fiscal compensation between countries must be more a question of estimates and a result of negotiations and trade offs, where the pure compensation is but one of the issues that together form a package solution. In CEAO fiscal compensation has been paid from the two most developed members to the five lesser developed countries through the Community Development fund. However, the flows appear to have been relatively small and unstable (Robson, 1983, pp.56ff. and 64ff.). Pure and well-functioning fiscal compensation is in Africa, to my knowledge, only found in SACU. Income from the customs union made up between one and two thirds of public revenue in the lesser developed members in the mid 1980s (Hanlon, 1985, table 1.B). In SACU the common revenue pool is shared in a way that favours Botswana, Lesotho, Namibia and Swaziland in relation to South Africa. I shall not go into the details of the revenue sharing formula, but the essential features are to secure the less developed countries at least an equivalent of 17 and a maximum of 23 per cent import duty on all goods, compared to an average real external tariff of 9 per cent, and on top of this an extra 42 per cent. It can be argued as Maasdorp and McCarthy do[52] that the revenue sharing formula takes into account both the trade diversion and the polarization effects; moreover, it entails a compensation for lost fiscal discretion and has a built in income stabilization factor. However, whereas the minimum 17 per cent import duty have a counterpart in other countries' excise levels, the origin of the 42 per cent is lost in obscurity. It has no economic basis but is rather a negotiated political price for securing the cohesion of the customs union. However the SACU agreement also has elements which are problematic for the less developed countries:[53] especially the exclusive administration of the arrangement by South African institutions and the fact that payments to the member states in a given year are based on the movement of goods two years back. Moreover, the pure fiscal compensation as such has the basic weakness of not targeting and taking action in order to influence the creation of jobs, the establishment of industry etc. in the less developed areas.[54]

(2) Action has been taken, but only indirectly, in the second arena for counteracting the negative distributional consequences of free trade. Typical examples are the improvement of basic infrastructure such as roads, railways, telecommunications, energy transmission and education, especially technical training so important for investment in human capital, which can be put into productive use in future industrial development. Both improved infrastructure and better education will reduce the costs for investors when localizing production in the area in question, and ideally give the poor areas a competitive edge they have lacked. In the beginning of the 1990s in Africa the only mechanism in a regional integration group, that among other things invests in improved conditions for productive investment, is the solidarity fund of the CEAO (Mansoor, 1992, p.433).[55] A similar Fund for Cooperation Compensation and Development exists in the Economic Community of West

African States (ECOWAS), but it has not become operational up to the time of finalizing this book. However, in the EC this kind of intervention totally dominates assistance to disfavoured regions. It is known as the structural policies and is principally implemented through three structural funds.[56] The structural policy is officially justified because 'the existence of wide disparities might jeopardize the successful implementation of the internal market programme ...' (Commission of the European Communities, 1992a, p.2). Thus, allocations from the structural policy have been used to achieve political acceptance for steady progress in market integration from the poorest and most reluctant members, often in the form of package deals. The overall aim of reducing regional disparities is split into five operational objectives that target different types of affected areas and social groups: for example, regions lagging behind, regions with industrial decline, long term and youth unemployment, adjustment of regions dominated by agriculture and fisheries. It was only after 1987/88 that the regional policy got off the ground with a five year budget of around 60 billion European Currency Units (ECU). Two-thirds were earmarked for regions lagging behind. The distributed amounts correspond to less than 0.5 per cent of total EC GDP, but the support received represents 3.5, 2.9, and 2.3 per cent of GDP in Portugal, Greece and Ireland respectively, and an even larger part of their investments – eight per cent for Portugal, 11 per cent for Greece, and seven per cent for Ireland. The structural policies are therefore assumed to have a real positive impact on growth possibilities in these countries,[57] although they cannot guarantee the creation of production and employment.

(3) The third type of intervention seeks through various forms of market incentives, to motivate the economic agents to locate economic activities in lesser developed areas and countries within an integration group. This may for example be done through:

a)   development banks;
b)   favourable investment incentives;
c)   slower rhythm of general tariff reduction than in the rest of the countries;
d)   maintenance of certain internal tariffs.

a) Development banks attached to an integration scheme can have a special arrangement – a soft window – allowing for loans with exceptionally favourable conditions to, for example, projects that enhance the productive capacity of the lesser developed regions or members. Loans for complementary industrial development were part of the agenda for the EAC Development Bank, but according to Hazlewood it never really had any impact due to restricted funds and lack of clear objectives.[58] The Central American Bank for Economic Integration has among its objectives 'long term investment projects in industries of a regional nature or of interest to the Central American

34

market ...' and has played a small but positive role in the economic development in the region in spite of the generalized crisis in Central America and CACM in the 1980s, according to an independent survey from 1989 (SIDA, 1989).[59]

b) The favourable incentives to attract intra- and extra-regional investments in the lesser developed areas are preceded – at least according to the idealised requirements – by a harmonization of investment codes among the participating states. After that is achieved, the less developed countries will receive special permission to offer conditions e.g. tax rebates that are more favourable for the investor than the general rules. Intentions to establish such an arrangement are found in both ECOWAS and CEAO (Robson, 1990, p.204), but as the common regulation of foreign investments, as discussed above, has had no success till the time this book is written, neither has there been any specific favouring of investments in lesser developed countries. An incentive to invest in a lesser developed country may also be a temporary protection of products from newly started industries on the home market from competition from other member states. In the SACU agreement article six provides for infant industry protection for a maximum period of eight years in Botswana, Lesotho, Nambia and Swaziland. However, the impact has been very limited due to the smallness of the markets and the use of escape clauses and other kinds of opposition from South Africa.[60] The incentives to localize investment in specific areas and create a better balance than the existing one and that emerging in a regional group, can be done both with and without an overall agreement and plan for the distribution of industry. A general problem for the use of market incentives to influence allocation of productive activity has been the market distortions regarding prices, exchange rates etc. that have generally characterized developing countries in the 1970s and 1980s.

c) Less developed countries in a regional group can be granted permission to reduce tariffs towards the regional partners in a slower pace than the rest of the group. This device should in principle give the economically weaker countries the necessary time to adjust policies, and the temporary and gradually reduced protection is a strong market incentive for industry to rationalize, strengthen its technological, managerial and financial situation and take other initiatives to increase competitiveness. Thus, the less developed members should ideally stand a better chance of avoiding an overkill of industries that with proper preparations would survive on the larger market. The EC has had these kinds of gradual tariff reductions, when admitting new members, for example Greece, Portugal and Spain, and such a system is intended but has not been implemented in ECOWAS.

d) A system of fixed intra-regional tariffs that favour industry in the lesser developed countries is found in CEAO and the Central African Customs and Economic Union (UDEAC). The internal rates are, according to Foroutan:

35

'... separately determined for each enterprise, product, country of origin and country of destination.' The purpose is '... to reduce the competitive disadvantage of the least developed members by applying a lower rate of duty on products originating in these countries than similar products produced elsewhere within the group'. Simultaneously, the least developed countries apply higher tariffs than what is the norm in the rest of the group, against imports from more developed regional partners (Foroutan, 1992, p.23).[61] These measures will probably make industry profitable in countries which would have had difficulties in attracting and maintaining industry under free market conditions. On the other hand, the system tends to minimize incentives to improve conditions for effective production in a less developed country, and reduce the advantages of regional markets in terms of specialization and scale economies. The system in itself can end up by maintaining a wholly inefficient and costly pattern of production.[62]

(4) Concerning the fourth form of development integration, agreeing on alleviating regional differences by the establishment of new industries that can deliver to the whole region, distribution of markets for existing industries, so they can specialize and benefit from scale economies, the matching of over capacity by import needs and other forms of administratively planned and controlled integration, I shall refer the reader to the section above on regional cooperation (2.2). As stated, the experiences from attempts to implement these kind of policies in regional groups that are based on liberal economics and market sharing, have for a variety of reasons not been successful – to put it mildly. Nye (1971, p.231) refers to how: 'The countries have not been willing to harmonize even indicative development plans.' Ravenhill (1985, p.209) summarizes the point with the following blunt comment:

> [R]ather, the problem of ensuring an equitable distribution of regional productive activities can be solved only through sectoral planning, and the allocation of industries by agreement among the participating states. Yet this solution is unpalatable for most African countries in that it necessitates a surrender of some critical policy-making autonomy.

Finally, I shall present the concept 'core state'. It is, according to P.C. Schmitter (1972, p.75), 'a sub-region or member-state with a clear economic and political preeminence'.[63] Such a dominant state could be Zimbabwe in SADCC; South Africa in SACU, or Kenya and Zimbabwe in the PTA. The 'core state' has an obvious interest in maintaining access to the whole regional market for its developed industry, but this will undoubtedly create serious imbalances in trade flows with lesser developed member states, at least in the short run. To prevent these from becoming political issues which might induce protection and block integration, the core state may be willing to cede substantial public financial resources for securing the coherence of the group. However, it could be suggested that in developing countries the support from the core state to the less developed member countries would face especially stiff internal resistance, because so many obvious development needs exist in the core state itself. This argument seems highly relevant when discussing the possibilities for a democratic South African being the 'locomotive' for development in the whole of Southern Africa, or South Africa repaying the region for the sacrifices and losses inflicted by its destabilization policy. However, this process will also be affected by other strong forces that tend to discourage attempts to follow the development integration approach as such. One of them (see below) is the adjustment adapted market integration approach to regional integration that in the beginning of the 1990s becomes increasingly important for evaluating the possibilities for future regional integration in Southern Africa.

2.6   Adjustment adapted market integration approach

Around 1990 a new approach to regional development in the Third World surfaced. It represented a break with the attempts to use regional integration as a means for import substitution industrialization behind relatively high customs walls. It strove instead to align regional integration with the basic principles of the structural adjustment programmes being implemented in an ever increasing number of developing countries, under the auspices of the International Monetary Fund (IMF) and the World Bank. Hence, the descriptive title chosen for it: *The Adjustment Adapted Market Integration Approach*. It amounts to an attempt to synchronize regional integration in the areas of trade and industry with the neo-classically inspired liberal, market and outward oriented development policies beginning to prevail in most developing countries, including the SADCC region, in the beginning of the 1990s.

This new approach does not amount to a fully fledged theoretical construction, but this is characteristic of the area of regional integration as such.[64] Neither has it, at the time of writing this book, been presented and published in book form. The following is based on articles, papers and reports from World Bank staff and consultants. Prominent among the authors is the World Bank economist Ali Mansoor. However, the new approach cannot automatically be equated with official World Bank policy. In section 2.3 World Bank economists were quoted as only wanting to allow 'cooperation' in Africa, and the World Bank's attitude towards regional integration will be further scrutinized in later chapters. The work of Ali Mansoor and the other proponents has specifically focused on regional integration in the area of trade and industry in Africa.[65] I find it justified to compare this new trend with the emergence of a new – although somewhat embryonic – paradigm for regional integration theory.[66] This is, however, not a surprising evolution, as it simply belatedly reflects the overall change in Third World development strategies in the 1980s: from a certain dominance of state-led, mostly inward looking strategies, often including import substitution industrialization policies, to market and private sector driven, outward oriented policies with emphasis on liberalization of imports and priority to exports to the world market.[67]

The point of departure for the new approach is the structural adjustment programmes with the objectives of eliminating economic distortions and integrating the participating countries in the world trade system.[68] The main measures to achieve these aims are:

- greater reliance on resource distribution through market prices, for example regarding foreign exchange;
- rationalization and reduction of effective protection towards the world market;
- increasing the role of the private sector in the economy.

The regional integration of the new approach shall in no way be seen as an alternative to the above, but rather as a complementary initiative that will facilitate the way to an open economy in a given country.

This is to be done, in short, through a regional expansion of the markets for goods, services, capital and labour, while at the same time lowering the external protection of the countries. This is meant to ensure greater competitiveness of the economies and therefore improved possibilities to survive and succeed in world market conditions. More concretely the policy entails an introduction of the following measures:[69]

- total abolition of non-tariff barriers (NTBs) towards regional partners on a reciprocal basis;
- reduction of tariffs towards regional partners on a reciprocal basis;
- no discrimination among regional partners of goods or services on the basis of product type or ownership of producing company;
- reduction of tariffs towards the world market;
- free flow of capital between regional partners;
- allowance for firms from regional partners to operate on the same conditions as local firms;
- free flow of labour between regional partners and a free transfer of remittances to home country of the migrants.
- free trade in national currencies against each other, preferably to reach currency convertibility;
- harmonization of macroeconomic policies

The elimination of intra-regional NTBs is given high priority as an immediate, short term measure able to start off the process and at the same time have a relatively large impact, due to the dominance of NTBs in the pre-structural adjustment programme management of external trade (Mansoor and Inotai, 1990, p.23ff).

A certain ambiguity must be noted regarding the reduction of tariffs between regional partners to a level that obviously, to make sense, must be below their external tariffs. On the one hand, this should be avoided, according to the adjustment adapted approach, as it is tantamount to discrimination towards third parties (ibid., p.28). On the other hand, lower internal tariffs are accepted as part of a realistic regional integration effort, but:

> ... regional trade preferences should not be excessive [more than 20 per cent], and should be reduced after a clearly specified adaptation period (say 5–10 years) to prevent significant diversion of efficient trade and to avoid inefficient investment (ibid., p.24).

The external tariffs will never be totally abolished for fiscal reasons, but they shall aim at a level that is lower than if the country had implemented a structural adjustment programme as a bilateral venture with the World Bank. This is possible, because of the efficiency gains the firms will obtain, as a result of the larger regional market. Consequently, the proponents of the adjustment adapted approach disapprove strongly with the possible establishment of new or revived customs unions with high external protective tariffs. Furthermore, it is interesting to observe that the policy of nondiscrimination on the basis of types of goods or ownership for the PTA will imply an abolition of the 'common list' of goods eligible for tariff reduction as well as an elimination of the clauses requiring a majority of local equity capital or management in order for a given company to benefit from PTA tariff cuts.[70]

As will become evident below, the free flow of factors of production is rather important for the consistency and possible success of the adjustment adapted approach. While capital flows might be facilitated by the trend towards currency convertibility, the labour issue is so much more contested and complex. This was seen in the 1980s when Nigeria reversed ECOWAS' progress in this area by expelling approximately one million aliens from other West African states. The high unemployment rates and inability of the African economies to provide jobs for the rapidly increasing population constitute a difficult background for progress. In Southern Africa the African National Congress (ANC) that has a dominant position in democratic South Africa, openly cautions neighbouring countries that a post- apartheid government intends to modify the migrant labour system, which will imply significantly reduced future intake of labourers from the neighbouring states.[71]

Institutionally, the approach wants to emphasize flexibility and selectivity. However, in spite of a perceived dominant non-performance of existing regional organizations it is deemed necessary to work with and through them. The framework of cooperation with regional organizations shall ensure that efforts towards a common market 'will be consistent with and reinforce national adjustment programs instead of pulling in the opposite direction as now occurs' (Mansoor, 1992, p.446). This frank statement is also an interesting contribution to an understanding of World Bank attitudes towards existing attempts at regional integration.

The new approach envisages that the first step in renewed regional integration efforts would be to implement what has already been agreed upon in existing organizations. But from there, flexibility and selectivity emerge in the sense that the countries on a bi- or trilateral basis or in other subsets may advance as far with regional integration measures as they wish. Countries which prefer a slower pace are perfectly free to stick to that, but they have no right to veto the faster ones. In this way the advance will not be determined by the lowest common denominator. This methodology will respect the vast difference in material interest that different countries have in regional integration. However, it is proposed that the most advanced countries be rewarded by additional support from donors, and indirectly the reluctant countries will face substantial pressure not to lag too far behind.

The process towards integration should be incremental and be characterized by bottom-up initiatives, opposed to previous all embracing command and regulation from the state. The private sector should play a major and increasing role in the economy and as a political pressure group. There will be an openness to African countries which are not members of a given regional organization, but which have substantial trade with members. In order not to divert that trade, similar arrangements to those in existence inside the organization could be entered into between a nonmember and interested members. An example of this in Southern Africa would be Botswana outside and Zimbabwe inside the PTA.

The question of distribution of the benefits of regional integration is also discussed in the new approach. The question being asked is, whether or not a form of compensation should flow from the economically more stronger to the more weaker members of a regional group.[72] An analytical distinction between various types of measures is not present in the adjustment adapted approach. The basic argument is that the 'natural' laws of economy will lead to an absolute, overall, increase in income for an effective regional integration scheme, but the relative distribution of rising welfare is by no means given. Based on experience – e.g. from the US and EC – it is more than likely that higher growth, income per capita and level of industrialization will be concentrated in certain geographical poles. This should be seen as the natural order of the day that must be accepted before joining a regional integration scheme.

The natural way of offsetting this, according to the new approach, is to allow the free flow of capital and labour. Remittances from migrant labourers working in the more developed countries to their less developed home countries will reduce the chronic trade deficits of the latter. Myrdal's argument (see 2.4) that labour migration is part of the cumulative deterioration of conditions in the less developed areas is not taken into consideration. Capital will flow from the industrialized poles to profitable investments in the lesser developed areas. This amounts to what in section 2.4 was called the spread effect, which contrasted with the polarization effect. If the spread effect is not deemed sufficient the most beneficial way of compensating, according to the adjustment adapted approach, is to reinforce private sector agents in the weaker areas. Nevertheless the new approach admits that:

> ..., political sensitivity will have to be taken into account in addition to purely economic arguments. Thus, there will have to be workable means of transferring compensation between governments (Mansoor, 1992, p.448).

In devising such a mechanism care must be taken not to eliminate the benefits of the private sector in the advanced areas, and the implementation of 'regional projects' in weaker countries must be avoided. They are likely to be politically motivated and consequently not to be economically viable, and if they were economically sound projects, other sources of financing could be found. The new approach does not specify what projects it especially has in mind, but the very negative attitude is likely to be focused on productive investment, particularly anything that resembles planned regional industrialization.

Examples of schemes that are more attractive to the new approach are the arrangement in SACU implying budgetary transfers of common tariff revenue according to a formula that overcompensates the weaker members, and the Solidarity Fund of CEAO mainly financed by the relatively more developed countries Cote d'Ivoire and Senegal, as they represent the highest trade volumes. In the beginning of the 1990s CEAO is studying the possibility of letting an import tax enter directly into a common account.[73] This would avoid the problems of the core states having to pull out money once it has entered the national treasury. That this is a real problem can be witnessed by the debate in South Africa in 1992 as to whether the country can afford the fiscal drain of transfers to the other members of SACU.[74] In the light of this approach the EC model of sharing part of Value Added Tax (VAT) receipts has the advantage of not being linked to tariffs that are ideally, gradually being reduced.

At this stage an interesting question to the adjustment adapted approach is why it wants to bother to pass via regional integration in order to reach the ultimate objective of universal free trade, and thereby deviate from the traditional logic of the IMF and the World Bank that prescribes a unilateral opening of a country's economy towards the world market, as the ideal remedy. The proponents of the adjustment adapted approach admit that the latter cure '... leads to rapid and extensive restructuring driven by the competition from imports that would channel factors of production to newly profitable activity' (Mansoor and Inotai, 1990, p.28). But here, the advocates of the adjustment adapted approach insert the following:

> Where possible, African governments should adopt such an approach [of unilateral opening]. In practice, however, we are far from a first best situation and a wide gap persists between the objectives and achievements of [World] Bank supported trade liberalization efforts in Sub-Saharan Africa (ibid., p.29).

and further:

> After a decade of structural adjustment efforts in Sub-Saharan Africa, progress with liberalization has been slow and accompanied with reversals. ... A regional approach may offer a new dimension to supplement the unilateral and uncoordinated national efforts of the sort currently being engaged in with World Bank and IMF support. Regional liberalization may be more politically acceptable than unilateral concessions ... (ibid., p.17).

The political aspect is a key to the understanding of the rationale of the adjustment adapted approach. One may argue that if politics[75] did not enter the equation, the new approach was not needed, as the ideal solution of total one-shot liberalization could then be implemented. Lets have a closer look at how a regional solution affects the politics that tend to block liberalization. Firstly, it is asserted that liberalizations will be accepted more readily on a regional basis, because governments can draw upon the positive connotation and sentiments of Pan-Africanism and the OAU and ECA sponsored schemes of working towards a united Africa: to be obtained through integration inside and between regional groups, of which PTA is one.[76] These aspirations are expressed in the Lagos Declaration and Final Act of 1980 and were renewed with the Abuja Treaty of 1991 aiming at African unification in the year 2025. These plans and sentiments are real, but as witnessed by their foot-dragging pace of implementation, they are, in the view of the author, neither self-propelling nor can they provide the engine for other similar schemes.

Secondly, the regional approach is potentially more politically acceptable because – in contrast to unilateral liberalization – it implies trade offs with other countries. There is a clear element of mutual concession involved.[77] This argument certainly holds some truth, but one should not disregard the counteracting tendency of extreme suspicion between unequal neighbours and the difficulty of approving a trade deficit with a more industrialized regional partner, whereas an even worse balance is accepted without qualms towards leading industrialized countries.

The third argument centres around the internal vested interests that are against liberalization – be they state or private agents – that survive and profit from an existing ineffective set up. They will have more difficulties in toppling a binding multilateral agreement with regional partners, than if it was a unilateral opening decided by the local government. They will also gradually be opposed by groups that benefit from the liberalizations. Moreover, donors are expected to transfer resources to the countries engaged in adjustment adapted regional integration in order 'to overcome political obstacles that would not otherwise be removed and which hinder economic progress' (Mansoor, 1992, p.448).

The fourth and probably most important point is that adjustment adapted regional integration will reduce the costs of adjustment,[78] i.e. make the social hardship of transforming the economy, politically acceptable to government. An all out liberalization will imply in an African context, heavy losses in production and employment opportunities, which, according to the new approach, are not possible to offset by growth in expanding sectors. This is due to the narrow industrial base, the extreme market distortions of the past, high costs and inefficient production, under-utilization of capacity, import dependence, a small market, and the lack of investment capital. Even if a country on its own implements wide ranging liberalizations it cannot in isolation reap the benefits of cross border investments, horizontal and vertical integration of firms etc.[79] In contrast to this scenario, the new approach:

> … may diminish the cost of adjustment by forcing competition first with firms that are of comparable level of (in)efficiency. This would allow a reduction of costs, through mergers, acquisitions and takeovers, that may be significant enough to facilitate survival in the world market (Mansoor, 1992, p.442).

To conclude the discussion of the adjustment adapted approach, its proponents – who are up against the conventional wisdom of unilateralism – state with admitted pragmatism and evident cynicism: 'that regional liberalization may yield more lasting and worthwhile results in some cases where extensive unilateral liberalization is resisted' (Mansoor and Inotai, 1990, p.29).

However, this obviously raises the question of whether the adjustment adapted regional integration approach is irrelevant in cases where African governments give in to demands or conditionalities of across-the-board trade liberalization, because they are politically too weak to withstand or because they accept or disregard common people's sufferings, and lack an understanding of how an embryonic industrial base is seriously threatened in the course of an all out liberalization?

2.7   Neo-functionalist approach

The neo-functionalist approach introduced here does not pretend to do justice to the totality of the many interesting corners, innovative aspects and internal developments of the analytical model. The author must be selective in order to establish the essentials of the approach in the brief space available. However, this is difficult as neo-functionalist analysis is indeed, a many-faceted subject. Its founder is the American political scientist and Berkeley professor, E.B. Haas, and among his many followers I shall emphasize J.S. Nye and P.C. Schmitter, who to some extent revised and systematized the approach, and tried to apply it to Third World reality.[80] They delivered their principal contributions between the late 1950s and the mid 1970s. Their primary source of inspiration and analytical challenge is the EC created in 1957. But with the establishment in the 1960s of a number of regional integration attempts in the Third World their focus is tentatively enlarged also to cover regional integration among lesser developed nations. The theoretical inspiration of the neo-functionalists comes from the functional theory of international cooperation that again is a reaction to a federalist approach. This will be elaborated below. The aspiration of the neo-functionalists is to inject social and political science with a capital 'S' into the functional analysis and thereby make it relevant for explanatory and prognostic purposes. Around 1970 Haas even proposed a program for 'computer simulation' analysis that by attributing values to all variables of the approach would be able – through a calculation – to foresee how regional integration groups would develop.[81] This ambition of borrowing the robes of natural science's laws and regularities of behaviour was, however, given up by Haas in 1975. He doubted whether it was worth the 'time and ingenuity', as international behaviour of states with the search for a new international economic order became more 'turbulent' and less rational than before (Haas, 1975, p.17ff. and p.86ff.).[82] The author of the present book holds the view that it anyway would have been a blind alley to try to reduce and summarize real life developments to numbers, instead of pointing at trends, casual linkages, comparable developments, specific factors etc. within a geographic and macroeconomic framework that sets some limits, but at the same time is affected by political and social action. I shall try to give below a general characteristic of the approach and highlight some of the empirical generalizations or hypotheses that are thought especially relevant. But first let's turn to its source of inspiration.

The neo-functional approach is indebted to the functionalist theory of international politics. The latter was developed by D. Mitrany.[83] In his main contribution – *A Working Peace System* – from 1943 he attempted in the midst of war to outline an international system that could preserve and fortify peace, and in this sense the approach is certainly normative. He had three points of departure for formulating his proposition. The first being that nationalism is a very real force that will live on and influence politics for a long time (Mitrany, 1966, p.29). The message that deep rooted national feelings are still highly politically relevant is forcefully brought home by the split-up of the former Soviet Union along national lines, by the war in ex-Yugoslavia and by the growth of Euro-scepticism in many member countries of the EC in the 1990s. The second trait that draws in the opposite direction is that the world 'in its material life ... has moved far towards a common unity'. Mitrany (ibid., p.26ff; see also p.70ff.) explains:

> The economic self-sufficiency of the individual and of the local group was broken up by the development of communications, of new sources of power, of new materials, the opening up of new lands and the rise of mass production, all factors which have bound peoples increasingly together.

It is on the basis of this ever increasing international interaction and 'social interdependence' (ibid., p.97) that improvements in welfare are bound take place, but without ignoring the power of nationalism. The search is on, according to Mitrany (ibid., p.28), for a 'line of action that might overcome the deep-seated division between the needs of material unity and stubborn national loyalties.' This leads us to the third point of departure. Mitrany argues that there is no hope that the use of force or formalism in the shape of conquest, federalism or constitutionalism will solve the problem. Nazi Germany and Imperial Japan had unsuccessfully tried by war to create larger territorial units. Federal arrangements might well be inflexible, torn by national contradictions and hampered by limitations in scope. The constitutionalists had a misplaced belief that formal arrangements, 'blueprints' and 'grandiose juridical gestures' would lead to a world government (ibid., p.31ff.).

Mitrany's answer is to focus on functions. According to him 'sovereignty cannot in fact be transferred effectively through formula, only through a function' (ibid., p.31). He pinpoints ordinary, everyday functions that because of the internationalization of life have become more efficient to administer internationally than nationally. Obvious areas for Mitrany are railways, shipping, communication, aviation and broadcasting, but cooperation could also take place regarding production, trade, distribution, and the negative functions such as police, drug-traffic, security and courts (ibid., p.70ff). In these fields international authorities might be built up. Their territorial coverage and way of operating will entirely depend on how the function is most effectively administered. This tends gradually to reduce the monopoly of the nation state on authoritative action. Mitrany writes (ibid., p.27): 'The functional approach, which by linking authority to a specific activity, seeks to break away from the traditional link between authority and a definite territory'; and further, 'By entrusting an authority with a certain task, carrying with it command over the requisite powers and means, a slice of sovereignty is transferred from the old authority to the new; and the accumulation of such partial transfers in time brings about a translation of the true seat of authority' (ibid., p.31). The network of functional international organizations that is created will little by little take over most of the former key elements of the nation states that in this way are 'sharing', not surrendering, their sovereignty.[84] Functionalism has no fixed end-position which it strives to reach. The process will decide how the actual format will be, but the political dispensation will be a kind of 'World Community' (ibid., p.32). Therefore, the functional approach does not agree with regionalism: 'closed regional unions would mean no more than the extension to regional dimensions of the ideas and ways of the old nationalism ...' (Mitrany, 1963, p.44). Conversely, the universal process of working together and solving practical problems will, according to the approach, avoid crisis, create peace and convince citizens and the states to continue on the functional road, and therefore 'quite naturally pool their sovereign authority so far as the good performance of the task demands it' (Mitrany, 1966, pp.32 and 98).

This latest quotation also points at a key weakness of the functionalist approach. That is the transformation of the material basis to decisions that initiate and further the functional process. Where are the interest groups, political parties and other mechanisms? They seem to be kept out in the cold by the 'good spirit' of functionalism. Haas (1964, p.30) writes convincingly in this connection:

> Functionalists leave themselves open to the charge that their concept of interest and interest politics is either hopelessly utopian or rigorously mechanical. ... Yet without the link provided by a theory of interest politics, functionalists cannot hope to explain why experts ... are going to introduce us to the blessed state of world community.

In contrast, the neo-functional approach 'takes self-interest for granted' and 'banish from our construct the notion that individual actors, groups, or elites regularly and predictably engage in political pursuits for unselfish reasons. All political action is purposively linked with individual or group perception of interest' (Haas, 1971, p.23 and 1964, p.34). I shall not go deeper into this or other possible criticisms of the functionalist approach,[85] but let the neo-functionalist take over. From the functionalist approach they uphold the concept of functions and the rejection of formalistic or legalistic solutions to regional integration. Their aim for the study of regional integration is also normative; Haas (1971, p.4) admits this bluntly and continues:

> The units and action studied provide a living laboratory for observing the peaceful creation of possible new types of human communities at a very high level of organization and of the processes which may lead to such conditions.

However, in contrast to the functionalists, the neo-functionalists do not adhere to the vision of a network of international organizations, ultimately combining into a world political authority or community. The neo-functionalists are more modest and aim at understanding the processes that are conducive to increased regional integration that ultimately will result in a political community or union among the involved nations.[86] They will use the understanding of the process for analytical and prognostic purposes, and hope the insight provided may promote the process. I shall present some of the key tools and hypotheses developed by the neo-functionalists about regional integration.

Central and new in the neo-functionalist's understanding of the integration process are the concepts of functional linkages, spillover, incrementalism, including different negotiating styles, and the role of interest groups and integrationist technocrats. Functional linkages are inherited, or deliberately created connections between tasks or functional areas within a regional group. The standpoint of the neo-functionalists is that there will be a tendency to expand the area of operation from one such task or function to the other. This then constitutes a spillover process. Haas gives here a general characteristic of what type of function has the linkages conducive to a spillover. 'The task, in short, must be both specific and economically important in the sense of containing the potential for spilling over from one vital area of welfare policy into others' (Haas, 1963, p.12). In the context of creating a common market, he directly mentions areas such as unifying railway rates, removing restrictive practices in certain branches of industry, removing import quotas ... and the like (ibid.). A classical case of spillover, but highly actual in Europe in the 1990s, is the establishment of a common monetary policy, because of built up pressure from the functioning of a common market. The reaching of common goals within certain areas will create imbalances in other sectors that then are prone to be included in the integration effort.[87] Schmitter (1969, p.162) summarizes spillover in the following manner and introduces at the same time the useful qualifications 'scope' and 'level':

> Spillover refers, then, to the process whereby members of an integration scheme – agreed on some collective goals for a variety of motives but unequally satisfied with their attainment of these goals – attempt to resolve

47

their dissatisfaction either by resorting to collaboration in another, related sector (expanding the scope of the mutual commitment) or by intensifying their commitment to the original sector (increasing the level of mutual commitment) or both.

The agreement by the involved countries to increase the scope or level of integration will typically happen through an incremental process as opposed to sweeping, constitutional changes. Haas (1971, p.23) explains:

> ... most political actors are incapable of long-range purposive behaviour because they stumble from one set of decisions into the next as a result of not having been able to foresee many of the implications and consequences of the earlier decisions. Ever more controversial (and thus system-transforming) policies emerge, starting from a common initial concern over substantively narrow but highly salient issues. A new central authority might emerge as an unintended consequence of incremental earlier steps.

A politicization of originally noncontroversial issues and of the integration as such is likely to accompany the process. In some early neo-functionalist writings it is asserted that under certain conditions it automatically happens.[88] More intense political debate seems only natural as wider constituencies are covered by the agreements and the costs become more visible. The politicization may lead to the reformulation of common goals.[89] The member states may also feel compelled by the higher level of integration to establish common positions toward third parties.[90] The Lomé Convention or common foreign investment guidelines are cases in point. To the neo-functionalists this is an externalization of the integration.

The styles of negotiation in which the discussions on regional integration are conducted contribute markedly to the end result, according to the neo-functionalists. They identify three main styles.[91] One is the 'minimum common denominator' style. In that case the group only moves as far and fast as the most reluctant member is prepared to go. This is by the neo-functionalists seen as a brake on integration. They hold this view in common with the adjustment adapted approach discussed above. SADCC's consensus seeking way of operating is in principle based on the minimum common denominator style, and has both been seen as a limitation and as a factor of stability and cohesion.[92] The second type of negotiation is 'splitting the difference' style. This indirectly indicates that the countries are involved in a zero-sum game, where the improvement of one country's position always will be to the loss of another member. Thus, negotiations may easily be stalled, and compromises will depend on the parties succeeding in satisfying themselves that roughly equal concessions are exchanged. The third negotiation style is characterized by 'upgrading of common interests' and will typically include package deals.

It will be a variable sum game, where everyone may gain without any losing out. The original conflict will be redefined and a solution worked out on a higher level of integration that includes expansion in level and scope of integration. In this way the spillover process is maximized.

In the attempt to upgrade common interest and develop package deals the integrationist technocrat obviously has an important role to play by identifying and proposing solutions that satisfy all members and at the same time bring the integration forward by containing functional areas which are likely to have a high spillover potential.[93] However, the powerful technocrats do not function in a vacuum. The neo-functionalists found in Europe an indispensable interplay between them and interest groups, whose constituencies were affected by integration, and non-ideological political parties which were favourable towards integration. Thus, the background of a modern industrial pluralistic society became included in the neo-functionalists' conducive conditions for integration.[94]

What triggers off an integration process in the first place? Is it only the converging interests of interest groups and political parties that can be identified as background variables? No, says Haas. Neo-functionalists believe that the opening of the ball may be preceded by 'a dramatic act motivated by passionate ideological commitment'. In Europe the committed 'Europeans' and in Latin America the proponents of the 'anti-dependencia school of thought' managed to present their convictions in a sufficiently convincing way, according to Haas.[95] In Africa the ideological appeal of 'Pan-Africanism' and the concept of 'collective self-reliance' may be said to have had the same function.

In their eagerness to impose pseudo natural laws on social reality, and impressed by the steady growth in integration in the first years of the EC, the neo-functionalists tended to see the spillovers and moves towards higher levels of integration as an automatic process. They have rightly been criticized for that, and made self-criticism of the original version of the approach.[96] The same applies to the overemphasis on the facilitating role interest groups. Indeed, in early writings Haas discouraged the use of the approach in non-pluralistic societies,[97] and one can find sweeping statements about the doubts as to whether regional integration is at all relevant in Africa because of 'the imperatives of state- and nation-building' (Haas, 1975, p.17). This may perhaps explain why the neo-functionalists are so little in focus in the analysis of African integration and why some scholars have little faith in their input.[98] I will, however, argue that it would be a shame to stop here. At least some neo-functionalists have left the dogmas behind, and have broadened their analytical framework, so that it becomes more relevant also for a Third World setting. The conclusion of the neo-functionalists might still be that integration in, for example Africa, is immensely difficult, but such a result is not equivalent to the irrelevance of the approach.[99]

Instead of the quasi-automatic spillover the neo-functionalists have introduced other situations such as spill-back, self-encapsulation and spill-around. Spill-back describes how the integration process may deteriorate. Self-encapsulation depicts how the regional group stick to the original tasks and the countries seal 'themselves off from the perturbing external forces' (Schmitter, 1970, p.39).[100] Spill-around characterizes how members of the integration group agree to increase the scope but not the level of cooperation. They take in new areas, but remain scratching on the surface, and do not dig deep into these or existing common fields.[101]

Nye has tried to systematize the elements of a revised neo-functional analytical model.[102] It contains basically three elements:

A   integrative potential;
B   process mechanisms
C   consequences of integration.

These can be combined with analysis of internal processes in the member states, taking into account that there are also groups opposed to and neutral in relation to integration, and different modes of regional economic integration, for example the five types in table 2.1. All this makes the model more complex, but should also make it more applicable. The key elements of the model A–C have the following subdivisions. In relation to Nye's discussion they have been somewhat simplified by the present writer for reasons of clarity and space.

A Integrative potential	B Process mechanisms	C Consequences
1 Symmetry of units and perceived equity of distribution of benefits	1 Functional and deliberate linkages of tasks	1 Politization
2 Capacity of member states to adapt and respond	2 Rising transactions	2 Redistribution
3 Elite identity and pluralism	3 Socialization of elites and formation of regional groups	3 Reduction of alternatives
4 Shared perception of external situation	4 Ideological-identity appeal	4 Externalization
5 Low or exportable visible costs	5 Involvement of external factors	

Several of the elements included have been discussed above. However, I shall briefly go through the various points in order to present the analyses in a systematic way.[103] A1 refers to the discussion of the significance for a

50

successful integration of economic size among members, whether measured in absolute terms, as GDP per capita, or for example through the level of industrialization. The neo-functionalists do not have a fixed answer. On the one hand, they introduce the innovative concept of the more developed 'core state' that can perceive a self-interest in making sacrifices to further integration (see also 2.5). This is contrasted with two counter tendencies. One is that countries with relatively greater economic power in a group will have a tendency to disregard integration efforts, because they will dominate the region in any case. To this shall be added the negative consequences on integration of the polarization effect (see 2.4), when the partners are of unequal size. Their tentative conclusion, especially relevant for the book, is that particularly in lesser developed countries with fewer resources, differences in size and power may prove to be a disintegrative factor, because the little that exists for distribution will be strongly contested. This might be reinforced by the partners' perception of the situation as a zero-sum game infested with national status and symbolism. Thus, even in a case where conditions are improved for everybody, serious conflicts may emerge over the relative distribution of the spoils. The EAC is a case in point.

A2 highlights that internal instability and lack of cohesion in a country can weaken its ability to respond adequately to regional integration. The neo-functionalists' hypotheses is that the weaker the ability of key economic decision makers to respond and adapt, the more likely it is that the signals from the integration process receive a negative response from the country, and will result in a spill-back. In the 1990s in Southern Africa this would lead to a close watch of, in particular, political developments in South Africa, as the country is decisive for establishing a post-apartheid regional arrangement.

A3 illuminates first how the integration process will be facilitated by shared values among the elites in the member states that control economic policy decisions. Second, pluralism is, as above, a euphemism for the importance of interest groups and political parties. However, here it is correctly placed among other key conditions. Nye writes with special reference to developing countries about their significance: 'The relative absence or weakness of such groups in many less developed countries has been shown to make integration more difficult (though not impossible) by depriving regional bureaucrats of potential allies and by depriving governments of channels of information useful in the formation of realistic economic policy'. I agree with this statement, indicating that the integration process is not automatically doomed when pluralism is weak, but that rather it is a question of degree, and interplay with other elements. The identity in outlook among leaders of member countries is a special but important case. In developing countries, because of low development of interest groups and lack of social cohesion, the leaders' actions can often be characterized by insecurity and ideology, including nationalism. This is a background that may easily end up in conflicts and personal schisms with other leaders. On the other hand, the opposite may also be the case – that the leaders get along very well – and they then often may go further with integration than expected. However, formal agreements can be difficult to implement, as the power of leaders to commit relevant parts of society to the joint objectives is often limited, precisely because of the lack of cohesion in society.[104]

A4 illustrates how a common understanding of the countries' external situation among the regional partners can be conducive to integration: in relation to (1) the global system; (2) a single state and (3) other regional organizations. Regarding (1), the dependence on export of few primary commodities and the perception of being locked in that position by the global economic system have been important motivating factors behind many integration efforts in Latin America and Africa. However, the international dependence may also be so pervasive that it becomes a disincentive to integration. This could explain the weak economic integration in ASEAN up until the 1990s. Concerning (2), integration can be furthered as a result of a sense of 'external threat from a giant neighbour'. The front line states' perception of South Africa could be an example. However, the hegemonic regional state can also directly and indirectly show hostility towards attempts at regional integration and thereby discourage such efforts. Other regional organizations (3) may, by their sheer existence, have a demonstrative effect which is an incentive to copy the initiative. This can also imply practical and material benefits because the countries will obtain a stronger bargaining position when dealing with the other groups. In Europe the creation of EFTA could be seen as a wish to have a common stand towards the EC. The rivalries in West Africa between CEAO and ECOWAS have been mentioned above. They might have furthered integration in CEAO but have certainly weakened ECOWAS. When SADCC was formed in 1980 it was partly a response to South Africa's attempt to promote a counter-union, Constellation of Southern African States (CONSAS).

A5: when the countries involved perceive that a possible regional integration venture is a low cost endeavour their willingness to enter into binding agreements both within and between countries increases. These might in turn spark off the process of creating spillover effects. To use this low cost perception in the initial phases might prove decisive, as it might take time before more stable socioeconomic interests and constituencies favourable to integration have been built up.

Integration among countries with more or less the same level of industrialization tend to lower perceived costs, because less polarization can be expected. Protection of regional industries is a way of letting the outside world pay for internal development, as discussed above in connection with trade diversion. Concerning developing countries international development aid has a definitive influence. Nye (1971, p.216) writes: 'Similarly among less developed countries if the solution to an integration problem can be met largely through the provision of external aid, the costs of the solution are exportable and it may be more likely to be adapted'. In the case of SADCC, the countries' knowledge in 1979/80 that a concerted aid package would be forthcoming if they joined together is a case in point.[105]

We can now turn to the process mechanisms. B1 covers the inherent and deliberate linkages between functional tasks. They will by their economic-technical nature or through package deals etc. further the spillover process and thus the deepening of integration. This has been discussed above. In devising a package it is important, especially in developing countries, to nurture supportive coalition partners for further integration, but at the same time avoid regional integration becoming dependent upon specific political parties. Note the parallel argument about the build up of supportive constituencies in the adjustment adapted market integration approach (see 2.6).

B2 deals with the raising transactions that may underpin the integration process. Transactions may for example be trade, capital movements or communications. It is significant that the level of internal trade in a group is not part of the above integrative potential, but only figures as a process mechanism. This illustrates that the neo-functionalists agree that focus should be on the potential for increased economic interaction in a group, and not, as in the market integration approach (2.4), on a demand for high levels of intra-regional trade before the integration starts. However, increased transactions do not automatically bring the integration forward. They may also – because of for example the polarization effect – lead to spill-back as in ECA or spill-around as in CACM.

B3: the socialization of bureaucratic elites to the aspirations of regional integration is an important process mechanism; if this does not happen the national bureaucrats will be the first to try to stop or slow down the process, as tasks are moved from them to the regional level. Socialization will take place through increased interaction between the national administrations and postings in the regional organization. Socialization of elites may also take place among NGO leaders, as a result of interest groups establishing contacts and forming regional organizations. Thereby their loyalty can shift towards the region. However, according to Nye, this is only a weak tendency. In spite of decades of inter-European NGO cooperation the main focus and activities, e.g. for the trade unions, is still on the national level. In Southern Africa both the SADCC Regional Business Council (SRBC) and the PTA Federation of Chambers of Commerce and Industry are extremely weak in the beginning of the 1990s and still totally dependent on the back up of their respective regional organization, and on donors in the case of SRBC (see also 3.4).

B4: the neo-functionalist hypotheses in this area is that the greater the ideological identity is with the regional integration group, the less is the chance that any opposition will try a frontal attack, and the greater is the willingness to sustain short term losses and for businessmen to invest in the common market. Reference can be made to the adjustment-adapted approach's conscious utilization of the ideological appeal of Pan-Africanism.

B5: external actors may as illustrated above constitute an integrative potential. But at the same time their involvement in the integration process represents a process mechanism. The external actors can be single countries, regional groups or international organizations. For SADCC South Africa's destabilization policy in the 1980s comes easily to mind, as one affected single country's attempt to hinder integration. At the same time South Africa's destructive action strengthened SADCC's internal cohesion and increased its foreign backing. The key role of France in monetary cooperation in West and Central Africa also illuminates the importance of individual external actors on Africa's regional integration groups. Regarding regional groups the Nordic/SADCC Initiative and the regional framework support from the EC to SADCC illustrate the point. Then, there is the IMF and World Bank; their role in relation to SADCC is up for discussion in later chapters. Suffice it to say here that they seem to have discouraged traditional integration, but not substantially supported alternative cooperation attempts (such as SADCC) in the 1980s. In the 1990s they appear to promote their own adjustment adapted model, but the signals are not quite clear or convincing in word or deed. The ECA have played a key role in the creation of PTA, and PTA's dominant foreign cooperation partners seem to be UN agencies. The neo-functionalists hold that a positive involvement may also have negative effects, if the external actor in reality gets a veto-power, and weakens the identity appeal of the regional organization. Some would argue that the massive donor involvement in SADCC has resulted in such a situation.[106] Transnational Enterprises (TNEs) are not among the external actors that the neo-functionalists include in the analysis, in spite of their influence and inclusion in the neo-functionalists' concrete analyses of integration in Latin America.[107]

Finally, the neo-functionalists have deducted four consequences or conditions that on the basis of experiences from integration attempts are likely to occur over time, and in turn influence future development. First there is (C1) the politization of integration. This has already been mentioned above as a natural consequence when wider areas and hitherto exclusive domains of national groups are covered, and as the costs of the process become more evident. Whether politization is 'bad' – i.e. in the neo-functionalists view becomes a hindrance to integration – is difficult to answer. It depends on the political constellations in the member countries. However, what the neo-functionalists, also obviously normatively, call a 'premature politization' is likely to influence the process negatively, as it indicates that integration has not functioned for a sufficiently long period in order for groups benefiting from the process to organize and manifest themselves in support of the venture.

The premature politization should be a typical outcome in developing countries' integration attempts. Reference can be made to the similar line of thought in the above discussion of the adjustment adapted approach in 2.6.

C2: redistribution is – without the neo-functionalists directly saying it – in its essence the effective allocation and organization of production within a regional market. In that process there are also interest groups, political parties, bureaucrats etc., which will benefit more than others. These developments are the effects of the hidden hand of the market, or of the negative integration. Positive integration is, for the neo-functionalists, the upgrading of common institutions and agreements on, for example, location of industry, so that 'the most severe effects of redistribution may be controlled' (Nye, 1971, p.221). Note the parallel to Tinbergen's concepts positive and negative integration, introduced in section 2.2. There will be a tendency for governments to let the indirect or negative integration run its course, while refraining from the more difficult interventions and national sacrifices embodied in the direct or positive integration, according to Nye. Thereby redistribution may develop into a hindrance for integration.

C3: the reduction of alternatives is the consequence of being interwoven in the network of regional agreements and therefore having few other possibilities than to continue on the integration road. However, illustrating the point that it is impossible to calculate politics by formula, there might be dramatic political actors who, because they are more willing to take chances, exploit the members' internal dependence to insist on special benefits. They don't hesitate to create a crisis in the group to reach their goal. Depending on the strength of common interests a crisis may in fact serve as a spark for igniting one more move forward in the integration process.

C4: the process of externalization was also referred to above. It covers the necessity of finding common positions in certain foreign policy areas towards both supportive external quarters, potential members and hostile foreign forces once a number of internal policies have been agreed upon. The neo-functionalist hypothesis is that there is a tendency for foreign policy formulation to run ahead of other internal areas of integration. They hold that such a situation may slow down the integration process, because it can involve highly emotional areas that are difficult to reconcile, and thus create unnecessary conflicts that make package deals more difficult to accomplish.

The discussion of potentials, process mechanisms and consequences can, in principle, be applied to all kind of integration attempts between countries, but its finer details are particularly suited for the analysis of integration attempts somewhere on the five-rung ladder presented in 2.4, and the neo-functionalists are especially keen on the virtues of common markets. Haas (1971, p.12) puts it this way ' Of all issues and policy areas the commitment to create a common market is the most conducive to rapid regional integration and the maximization of a spillover.' However, in 2.2, I showed how they also contemplated regional cooperation, which is equivalent to what Nye (1971, p.230) calls 'partial integration schemes'. He has some interesting observations about their qualities which we will go deeper into now, because the basic elements and terminology of the approach are established. On the positive side, cooperation arrangements exploit the integrative potential that exists in certain sectors, but which might be nonexistent in others and not capable of supporting a fully-fledged integration. On the negative side, they only have a modest effect on the process forces. This is so because transactions do not necessarily rise, the linkages with the rest of the economy are limited and the number of groups involved are restricted. Nevertheless, two process forces are released. They are the building up of a regional identity and the socialization of elites. The relevance of this for an understanding of SADCC's first 12 years seems striking. In SADCC's key theme document for its 1992 annual conference the organization states: 'But more than anything else, the greatest success has been in forging a regional identity and a sense of common destiny among the ten member states' (SADCC, 1992b, p.3). However, there is one more major process mechanism which the neo-functionalists assert is being invoked in partial integration schemes or cooperation: viz. the involvement of external actors – typically bilateral and international donors. Their input to schemes and regional development banks can be essential for the implementation of common endeavours. Moreover, as discussed above, donor involvement may function as an integrative potential, as it makes the countries more willing to go into joint action, because the perceived costs are low. Again SADCC stands out with its 89 per cent external funding of projects, as mentioned above. Obviously, the neo-functionalists are not very satisfied with regional cooperation as it holds few chances of developing into higher forms of integration, and will as Haas notes 'have great difficulty of influencing the policies of their members' (Haas, 1971, p.12). A situation that the next chapter will illustrate is certainly not unknown to SADCC. However, let us conclude on a (relatively) positive note with Nye (1971, p.230): 'a limited scheme is likely to have more effect (even though a slight one) than a grandiose scheme that fails'.

Winding up this section, criticism has been raised regarding the functionalist ideological superstructure and lack of linkage to the political processes, and concerning for example the early neo-functionalists' blind belief in a more or less automatically running integration process, and their failure to include the TNEs among their external actors. However, as this book is not targeted towards final answers to each approach's general quality in itself, but is consciously eclectic, I find it reasonable to conclude that the analysis of regional integration and cooperation has been brought forward through the introduction of the concept of functions that can be more effectively catered for internationally than nationally, and by the work of the neo-functionalists who tried to combine the functional point of departure with innovative concepts and hypotheses, trying to explain how the integration process actually works.

2.8   Summary and SADCC

This chapter has presented and discussed a host of approaches to regional cooperation and integration. This might on the face of it appear confusing, but my postulate is that they are all relevant for understanding the existing organizations, the attempts to break new ground and the discussions on a future regional dispensation in Southern Africa. They may constitute a framework for discussion and analysis, a point of inspiration or raise the alarm about what should preferably be avoided, when closer interaction between nations is the aim. It is my hope that this has been facilitated by drawing in examples from Southern Africa and elsewhere. Let me briefly go through the essentials of the chapter.

The main issue at stake is how to exploit the apparently high potential gains from regional cooperation and integration without at the same time sowing the seeds of dissolution, resulting in a worse end situation than the initial position. In order to avoid semantic uncertainty a distinction is introduced between cooperation and integration. The former is defined as 'a process whereby nation states in common solve tasks and create improved conditions in order to maximize internal and external economic, political, social and cultural benefits for each participating country'. Thus, emphasis is on nation states voluntarily agreeing on joint action in certain areas, where they reckon that each country may achieve an outcome that is more favourable than if it had acted on its own. Integration is defined as 'a process through which a group of nation states voluntarily in various degrees share each other's markets, and establish mechanisms and techniques that minimize conflicts and maximize internal and external economic, political, social and cultural benefits of their interaction'. Here, the emphasis is on trade and creation of organizational structures that can optimize results. A distinction between negative and positive integration is introduced. Negative integration is the simple reduction of barriers between countries, whereas positive integration covers the more delicate agreements on common policies which intervene in the markets and the creation of relevant institutions.

I start out with coordination as an approach, because it deserves a platform of its own and should not be treated only out of frustration with the other approaches, or promoted because of a belief that regional integration will divert Africa from the road to world market integration. The section on cooperation tries to organize the rather heterogeneous subject under different headings. They are basically systematizations of what has been found in different cooperation attempts around the world. The categories are: execution of joint projects, typically infrastructure, technical sector cooperation, running of services and policy harmonization; joint development of natural resources; joint international stand, and joint promotion of production. The categories are not necessarily interlinked or -dependent. Each category may operate in its own right, and the cooperation may be as limited or comprehensive as the involved countries wish. Catchwords are concentration on functional needs, an incremental – step by step – attitude, flexibility, decentralization, no supra-nationality, focus on national needs, consensus decision making style, making sure that the cooperation only goes as far as everybody wants, and that all partners perceive that they receive a reasonable share of the benefits. Main problems are that although the scope of cooperation can be wide, the level is typically not deep: cooperation does not intensify and accomplish changes in key issues. Policy coordination and harmonization are often victims of this. The coordination of positions and action towards the rest of the world can – depending on the existing circumstances – reach significant levels, whereas the promotion of production have had limited success, and met numerous and mostly prohibitive problems. However, it raises the question, whether narrower, flexible arrangements might hold more promise.

In the section on market integration the five-rung ladder model of various types of market integration and their respective characteristics is introduced. Further, we identify the rather ironic situation that what is normally regarded as the theoretical basis and justification for pure market led integration, in fact tends to discourage this. Viner insists that only an analysis based on the concepts of trade creation and trade diversion can indicate whether a given market integration venture will be beneficial or not. A positive answer is likely when the economies of the partners are competitive but potentially complementary and have a low level of foreign trade. Thus, developing countries with a high level of exports of primary products to the rest of the world coupled with imports of industrial goods from outside the region, seem to be poor candidates for integration. This leads us to a criticism of the static principle and restrictive assumptions of the approach. For developing countries one might argue that it would be more constructive to apply a dynamic view, giving priority to creation of investment opportunities and productive use of the labour force, although this might imply costs in the form of trade diversion. Lastly, the section focuses on the backwash, polarization, or as it is also called in Southern Africa, the bambazonke effect of market integration. It covers the situation where industry and development in general cluster in the already relatively advanced countries or areas within a regional group. Thereby some areas become poles of growth – others poles of stagnation – and both the up- and downturn have a self-propelling dynamic. Economic forces that counteract polarization – the spread effect – are normally relatively weak, at least in the short run, and especially in and among developing countries. In contrast, the bambazonke is rapid, forceful and disruptive.

The development integration approach is based on market integration, but tries to take precautions against some of its limiting or self-destructive aspects. It changes the objectives, gives priority to positive integration and ventures to reduce or eliminate the polarization effect by introducing measures aimed at ensuring that the costs and benefits of cooperation are more equally shared. The objective of integration is lifted out of its neoclassical cradle and given a dynamic and development oriented content. Positive integration implies that close political cooperation and binding agreements, and commitments between nations, become part of integration at a relatively early stage of the process. This is not least to secure an equitable part of the spoils of integration for all members, but it gives inevitably the approach a top-down tendency. Four basic methods to achieve or rather approximate this goal are identified. Pure fiscal compensation; improving conditions for development; creating incentives for a changed pattern of production; planning new industries and agreements on distribution of production. They also indicate raising levels of public intervention in the economy. Fiscal compensation is impossible to calculate with any precision and will depend on estimates, interests and negotiations. SACU is a case in point. Improving conditions of production is found in the EC's structural policy. It has a substantial impact in the affected areas and has politically lubricated the integration process. It entails, however, no guarantees that jobs and production will come to the disadvantaged areas. Direct economic incentives to allocate production in less developed areas may be brought about through development banks, various investment incentives, slower rhythm of tariff reductions, or maintenance of certain tariffs. Each has its technicalities, pros and cons, but the general problems are that economic incentives cannot function well where markets are distorted, and a system of incentives require a prior broad agreement on strategy and goals in order to tune the various mechanisms correctly. Development banks, for one, need clear objectives and sufficient resources. Fiscal and other incentives demand harmonization of the base line situation both for intra-regional and for foreign investment; especially the latter has proved difficult to obtain. If the countries maintain some kind of intra-regional tariff arrangements they run the risk of nullifying the basic gains of a larger market, i.e. more effective production for the whole region. Planning new industries and distribution have, as recounted under 'cooperation', not been crowned with success. It has proved difficult to agree on a joint industrial strategy and possible action impinges too much on sovereignty, so that the issue easily falls prey to nationalism, and different material interests depending on the level of industrialization. The whole issue of redistribution within a regional group is to a large degree contingent on the existence of one or more core states that can see external and long term internal benefits in supporting the poorer areas. However, this is not a perspective that will emerge easily in the Third World, because of the generalized lack of resources.

The adjustment adopted market integration approach is an attempt to utilize regional integration to achieve world market integration for a developing country more quickly, and in better order than would be possible if the country implemented on its own a bilateral structural adjustment programme with the IMF and the World Bank. It implies a flexible and reciprocal opening up of free flows of goods, labour and capital between the regional partners. The harmonization of tariffs against the rest of the world as in a customs union is not foreseen, and tariffs shall be kept low and diminishing. Actually, the adjustment adapted approach argues that the reorganization of production and improvement in efficiency thanks to a regional market will enable world market tariffs to be lower than they would be if the country had stood alone. Minimal compensation arrangements to counteract polarization are reluctantly foreseen due to political considerations. The free flow of labour and capital is seen as a key in securing balance in the regional economic development. Industrial complementarity and industrial planning are banned, and the private sector is the all dominant force in developing society. The process will be incremental and bottom-up, as distinct from the development integration's more top-down methodology. The approach will work through existing regional organizations, because they are there, and have to be brought into line. The reason for the need to use regional integration in Africa eventually to secure world market integration is political. The proponents of the approach refer to the strong ideological support for integration in Africa. They emphasize how international agreements in comparison to national schemes on e.g. tariff reductions are more difficult to topple for pro-protection groups, and they claim that the regional bargaining is a better psychological background for liberalizing the economy than a unilateral opening towards the world market. Lastly, but not least, they are painstakingly aware that a unilateral opening towards the world market will have very high costs in the form of eliminating industry and creating social despair. They find that the regional detour is worthwhile, because costs are reduced to a level which it is hoped might be accepted by the politicians. The latter argument could, however, be turned into a question mark: would the approach then accept the stated negative consequences of an unilateral opening, if they were swallowed by the political establishment in a given African country?

The neo-functionalists are next in line. Their hallmark is the understanding of the process of integration and to a lesser degree cooperation. They place more emphasis than the other approaches on the social and political conflicts and configurations which accompany and decide the pace and outcome, and devote less attention to the economic side of it. At the same time the development of the material basis – the economy and technological level – is of utmost importance to the approach, because it is the basis for the constant increase in functions that can be most effectively catered for internationally. The neo-functionalist owe this point to the functionalist theory of international politics, but they do not elaborate the issue as such. The neo-functionalists focus on how there can be a spillover from the joint administration of one function to the other. They introduce the innovative concept of functional linkage that, typically, through an incremental decision making process, gradually increases the scope and level of integration. Influenced by the steady initial progress in the EC the early neo-functionalists writings have a tendency to define the expansion of integration as a law of nature, and interest groups and integration technocrats as the main movers of the process. This made the approach less relevant for developing countries with non-pluralistic systems and weak interest groups. However, in later revisions of the theory interest groups have been placed in a more constructive context as one of several factors to be taken into consideration. Also, the neo-functionalist become less deterministic in their belief in constant progress in regional integration, and develop more refined analytical tools. According to the neo-functionalists, any integration attempt can be analysed systematically through the application of the three headings: integrative potential, process forces and consequences of integration.

I have in the chapter tried to make references to SADCC where relevant, but how can SADCC in its totality up till 1992 be characterized? I shall not go into a dispute over how others over the years have defined the organization. SADCC itself has in recent publications called its mode of interaction 'regional project coordination' and 'functional cooperation'.[108] Within the framework of different approaches discussed above SADCC can be firmly placed under the cooperation approach. This can negatively be deduced from the fact that SADCC does not contain any kind of general market access between the countries. The latter is part of the definition of regional integration. Moreover, SADCC concentrates on functional areas where mutual benefits can be maximized, for example transport, communication and energy, and has been avoiding formalism and elaborate treaties.[109] Its way of operating is incremental, consensus seeking and decentralized, both in the administration of regional areas of cooperation, and in the execution of projects. SADCC adhere to the minimum common denominator negotiation style. National interest will always prevail over regional programmes. Some of the salient points are illustrated in the following quote from one of the driving forces behind the creation of SADCC, the late President of Botswana, Sir Seretse Khama: 'The basis of our cooperation, built on concrete projects and specific programmes rather than on grandiose schemes and massive bureaucratic institutions, must be the assured mutual advantage of the participating States.'[110]

In the absence of strong political parties and interest groups the identity in outlook of especially the heads of state and governments of the front line states constituted, in a neo-functional terminology, an important integrative potential for SADCC. However, this goes hand in hand with their difficulties

61

in committing larger parts of their societies to the implementation of regional objectives, for example within industry and trade. The fragility of the 'Presidents' club' also becomes apparent when newcomers, such as F. Chiluba of Zambia who enters the scene in 1991, are not readily accepted. In the 1990s it will be interesting to watch the relationship between the relatively strong South African interest groups and their embryonic SADCC counterparts. If this interaction and the democratic reforms create an upswing in interest articulation, it might place regional cooperation and integration on firmer ground than has hitherto been the case. Among the various types of regional cooperation, SADCC has concentrated on: (i) the execution of joint projects; (ii) the coordination of technical sectors; and (iii) joint stand towards the outside world. SADCC's impressive list of joint projects mostly within infrastructure bears witness to the first. The second covers much of the work done in SADCC's sector secretariats. The third has two main aspects; one towards apartheid South Africa, the other in relation to the donor community. One may point at a high integrative potential for SADCC as a result of the existence of a common enemy in the shape of apartheid South Africa, and because perceived costs of entering into the cooperation were low, as donors were expected to cover the major part of the bill. South Africa's destabilization policy in the 1980s was a negative process mechanism, whereas the ability continuously to mobilize donor funds for projects must be counted on the positive side. The interaction between state officials, management and technicians in public utilities has undoubtedly lead to higher levels of elite socialization and regional identity, also in wider circles of the population. However, one cannot speak of any broad support for SADCC based in various interest groups. That there is a special difficulty of bending the countries towards policy harmonization has been experienced by SADCC. One of its senior officials states:

> Unfortunately, in essence, the main national planners have remained totally parochial in approach, and have not provided the necessary information to influence the political trade-offs that are necessary in regional integration. The planners have only seen themselves as instruments of [national] political will, when they should influence it towards greater economic efficiency through regional cooperation (Maphanyane, 1990, p.8).

SADCC has within the sphere of a cooperation approach attempted to take up the delicate issues of enhancement of trade, production and investment. How this fared in the 1980s is in focus in the next chapter. In the final chapter I shall briefly return to SADCC's transformation into Southern African Development Community (SADC), according to its new Treaty from 1992. In its articles it appears to reflect a relatively pure market integration approach, but accompanying declarations and analytical papers state that SADC will follow a development integration approach. SADC's intentions are up against Africa's oldest functioning customs union, SACU, and PTA's ambition of creating a common market in year 2000. Chapters 4 and 5 will illustrate that these developments take place within the framework of structural adjustment policies in the individual countries and of initiatives from the World Bank to influence the path of regional cooperation and integration.

Notes

1 See for example Hansen, 1987.
2 The author worked in Africa in two periods, both in Mozambique: 1982–85 in the Ministry of Industry and Energy, and 1989–92 at the Danish Embassy in Maputo. Moreover, working as a consultant for SADCC 1985–86 and employment at the Danish Ministry of Foreign Affairs 1987–89 also involved numerous working visits to Africa.
3 See for example *Finansies and Tagniek*, 1991. According to the South African publication 49 African countries traded with South Africa in 1990.
4 See for example Hazlewood, 1985.
5 The structural adjustment inspired approach (section 2.6) is a useful reference in for example the discussions in chapter 4.
6 Their definition of 'economic integration' is: '... any set of joint activities, promoted by common institutions, which raises the level of economic interdependence among a group of countries' (Orantes and Rosenthal, 1977, p.22).
7 The definition presented has the disadvantage of using the word that it sets out to define in the definition.
8 This definition is a conscious change in relation to earlier definitions that placed more emphasis on shift of loyalties of social groups from the nation state to the new regional level. Thus, for example, the definition in Haas (1963, p.7): '... integration [is] the process whereby political actors in several distinct national settings are persuaded to shift their loyalties, expectations and political activities toward a new and larger centre, whose institutions possess or demand jurisdiction over the preexisting national states.' This definition contains three indicators: 1) political activities; 2) political loyalties; 3) institutions. Nye (1968, p.858) criticizes the definition, because the elements can vary more or less independently, and Haas (1971, p.6, note 5) agrees to this.
9 Besides the useful highlighting of 'joint projects', the quotation reveals the often found inconsistency in use of the concepts integration and cooperation. Tax harmonization would for example normally be

considered beyond the cooperation concept and well into an integration mode, equalizing conditions for the economic actors within an integrated regional market.

10 See for example Ojo, 1985, p.157ff.

11 The choice in 1993 of a Lesotho national for the post as new Deputy for the SADCC Secretariat in Gaborone seemed to prove this general rule, whereas the selection of a Namibian as successor for the Zimbabwean Head of the Secretariat was somewhat of a digression. It might be seen as a wish to draw Namibia closer to the organization, but could also be interpreted at a downgrading of the larger SADCC countries' interest in SADCC; however, most probably, Dr Kaire Mbuende, Namibia's deputy minister of agriculture, turned out to be the best qualified compromise candidate at hand.

12 See for example World Bank, 1989, p.157ff. or Green, 1980, p.A45.

13 Reference is made to the ZACPLAN (Zambezi Action Plan) for the Zambezi river basin development.

14 The report indicates that funding is secured for 41 per cent of total project budget.

15 SADCC has a tourist sector cooperation administered by Lesotho, but at the same time the Southern African Regional Tourist Council with South African participation has existed in parallel. This calls for problems if some kind of merger or division of tasks between the two is not achieved.

16 The so-called 'San José' meetings.

17 See for example Haarlov, 1988, chapter 5; Groes et al., 1989; K. Kiljunen (ed.), 1990, or Oestergaard, 1989b. Reference is also made to the discussion of the Norsad fund in section 3.4 of this book.

18 See the discussion in for example Zehender, 1983.

19 See for example Saigal, 1985.

20 See for example Wong, 1985, p.90.

21 See for example (in Danish) Aalborg, 1986, chapter 4, or Schmitter, 1972.

22 See for example Saigal, 1985.

23 See for example Ojo, 1985, p.158.

24 See for example Wionczek, 1978, p.782.

25 See for example the discussion of the influence of foreign governments and transnational enterprises (TNEs) in Vaitsos, 1978, pp.719–69. He makes e.g. the interesting point that: 'In the case of industrial planning quite distinct attitudes and actions are shown among different TNEs according to their degree of presence prior to integration' (p.735). Thus, TNEs outside that want to get in tend to have a favourable attitude, whereas the existing TNEs benefiting from protection in each national market typically are against regional industrial cooperation. Robson, 1990, p.209ff. also discusses TNEs, especially in West and Central Africa.

His basic conclusion that I tend to agree with, is that they merely 'like any profit-maximising enterprise [operate] by reference to distorted market signals' and the 'basic remedy must be sought mainly in the adoption of a regional industrial strategy and a related fiscal incentive policy for all enterprises, and partly in the adoption of more rational pricing systems throughout the regions so that commercial self-interest and community objectives are better harmonized'. However, he does admit that: 'the market power of the TNEs does enable them to exercise influence and pressure on the member states and the group; they do not merely respond to exogenous provisions.'

26 Clearly, in contemporary Central America, no attainable combination of material pay-offs or affective satisfactions at the regional level can compete with the mobilizational capacity of nationalism'. '... opportunistic nationalist leaders will mobilize their captive clienteles from above in the interests of self-perpetuation in power and in the process, leave behind both a residue of antagonism which will make future regional consolidation much more difficult and a legacy of public policy which will increase rather than decrease their country's dependence on external powers'. These were part of the conclusions of an analysis by the neo-functionalist Schmitter (1972, p.76) of the Central American experiences of regional integration.

27 The scarce administrative skills is one of the reasons for Robson, 1990, p.214, to conclude that across-the board-planned regional integration is not in general practicable.

28 Thus, I disagree with Ostergaard, 1993. He seems to believe (p.44) that the concept functionalist is monopolized once and for all by Mitrany's functionalist international political theory, which is discussed in 2.7, and asserts that others therefore cannot meaningfully use the concept without bringing along the old baggage from the international political theory. This would not be very conducive to the development of theory. The neo-functionalist for example use the concept of functions, but in a different context than Mitrany.

29 See for example Blejer, 1984, p.6ff. or Orantes and Rosenthal, 1977, p.24.

30 In an appendix Viner (1950, pp.141–53) lists more than 100 customs agreements on German soil between 1820 and 1870.

31 Here referred to from Robson, 1990, p.5.

32 See Viner, 1950, pp.3 and 130–2.

33 See Viner, ibid., pp.42–4. See also for discussion of the two concepts for example Lipsey, 1960, p.6ff. and Balassa, 1962, p.25ff.

34 See for example Lipsey, ibid., p.498ff. An interesting discussion of competition and complementarity in regional integration arrangements is also found in Maasdorp, 1992b, pp.137–9.

35 The presentation follows Balassa, 1962, p.2.
36 Concerning the Common Market objective, reference is made to the document PTA, 1992b; and regarding the scrapping of the system of preferential treatment of specific goods and factories I refer to the abolition of the common list and 'study on streamlining the rules of origin', according to PTA, 1993a, p.10ff. See also note 70.
37 See for example references indicated in note 52.
38 Reference is made to SADCC, 1992c adopted by the SADCC Heads of State and Government in Windhoek in August 1992. However, the Treaty is only operational when ratified by two thirds of the member states. See especially article 5, (2) a+d and article 41. The identified aspects of a market integration approach are supplemented by elements of the development integration approach such as a development and growth objective (article 5,(1)a) and principles of equity, balance and mutual benefit (article 4 d). However, their operational significance depends on the protocols that will be elaborated for each sector of cooperation.
39 See for example Robson, 1990, p.14.
40 Miksell, 1963, p.212ff. See also Cooper and Massel, 1965a; Cooper and Massel, 1965b, p.11ff., who links the issue to infant industry protection.
41 See for example Balassa, 1965, pp.73–84 and Miksell, ibid., p.229.
42 According to Robson, 1990, p.170, 'polarization' was first used by Hirschman, 1958. Balassa uses it without this reference in Balassa, 1965, p.122. Myrdal introduces and elaborates on his backwash concept in his book Myrdal, 1957.
43 Note that this is contrary to the position of the adjustment adapted market integration approach. See section 2.6.
44 See also Ndegwa, 1984, p.28 and Robson, 1990, p.170.
45 See for example Hazlewood, 1985 or Ojo, 1985.
46 See for example Barber, 1961; Creighton, 1960; Leys and Pratt, 1960; Palmer and Parson, 1977.
47 See for example Jourdan, 1991, p.26.
48 See for example Aalborg, 1986; Axline, 1977; Orantes and Rosenthal, 1977 and Schmitter, 1972.
49 However, Axline is rather pessimistic regarding the possibilities of reaching such an early political consensus.
50 See Axline, 1977, p.87 and Robson, 1990, p.202. Ojo, 1985, p.161ff. also uses the distinction between compensatory and corrective measures. Ravenhill, 1985, p.209 prefers to distinguish between fiscal compensation plus the work of development banks on the one side and sectoral planning and the allocation of industry on the other side.
51 See for example Foroutan, 1992, p.22 or Robson, 1990, p.203.
52 See Maasdorp, 1982, p.95ff. and McCarthy, 1992, p.12ff. For a discussion

of the pros and cons of SACU see also Henderson, 1985; Hoohlo, 1990; Kumar, 1992; Maasdorp, 1992a; Maasdorp and Whiteside, 1993.

53 See for references previous note.

54 See e.g. Ravenhill, 1985, p.209.

55 See also Robson, 1983, p.59ff.

56 The European Fund for Regional Development. The European Social Fund. The European Development and Guarantee Fund for Agriculture. It must be noted that the EC structural policies are only additional to the efforts that nationally are carried out to support weaker regions, and the allocation of EC funds depend on an active interplay and cooperation with local, regional and national authorities. See also Robson, 1990, p.181ff. and Winters, 1992, p.29ff.

57 The factual information can for example be found through the reference Commission of the European Communities, 1992a and in Commission of the European Communities, 1993a.

58 See Hazlewood, 1985, p.176ff.

59 See also Robson, 1990, p.204.

60 See for example Kumar, 1992, p.7ff.; Maasdorp, 1982, p.90ff.; McCarthy, 1992, p.15ff.

61 For a recent and critical review of the UDEAC tariff and indirect tax regime see World Bank, 1992d.

62 The lack of country specialization within manufacturing industry in West and Central Africa (CEAO and UDEAC) was indeed one of the conclusions in Robson, 1983, pp.53ff. and 167. See also Robson, 1990, p.211ff.

63 Schmitter uses in this context the 'core state' to show how a dominant state can be willing to accept intra regional pay offs, for example generous support to weaker members, in order to be able to use the region to follow and achieve extra regional goals.

64 The lack of explanatory power of theory in relation to a possible regionalization of the world is e.g. taken up in Melo and Panagariya, 1992c.

65 Reference is made to Mansoor, 1992, Mansoor and Inotai, 1990 and World Bank, 1991b.

66 The possibility of a new paradigm in the making is briefly discussed in Davis, 1992, p.8ff.

67 This is, admittedly, a crude generalization of an overall trend and due respect must be paid to the much more diversified empirical evidence, not least regarding the exact composition of strategies and the sequence of their alteration.

68 See Mansoor and Inotai, 1990, p.24.

69 Reference is made to the texts in note 65 from which the points have been summarized.

70 Reference is made to PTA, 1982, article 3, (4), a, (ii) and the special Protocol, Annex III (article 15) on the Rules of Origin – rule two. See also note 36, and the discussion of certain aspects of the PTA in section 3.4 of this book.

71 See e.g. two publications by Davies: 1990 and 1991.

72 See e.g. Mansoor and Inotai, 1990, p.26ff. or Mansoor, 1992, p.448ff.

73 See Mansoor, 1992, pp.433 and 449.

74 See e.g. Maasdorp and Whiteside, 1993, p.42ff.

75 In this connection politics can be translated to the interplay of interests and the balance of forces that makes any government keen to keep social unrest low and the opposition at bay, and which provide a government with incentives to securing as reasonable and advantageous deal as possible in the country's external economic relations, and to promote its own ideological positions.

76 See e.g. Mansoor, 1992, p.446ff.

77 See e.g. Mansoor and Inotai, 1990, p.17.

78 See ibid., p.18 and Mansoor, 1992, p.442ff.

79 Mauritius in the 1980s might be cited as an example of a situation like that, and the country's attempts to make the 'Indian Ocean Commission' function and reach investment agreements with especially Madagascar could be seen in this light.

80 Let me highlight the following contributions from the three authors:
   a Haas, 1958, 1964, 1971 and 1975;.
   b Nye, 1968 and 1971;
   c Schmitter, 1969, 1970 and 1972;
   d Haas and Schmitter, 1965.

81 See Haas, 1971, p.40ff.

82 Haas identifies the concept of international interdependence, or reliance on extra-regional forces and governments – as the culprit of distorting the assumptions of regular regional integration, and emphasizes how this negatively affects the decision-making process in regional organizations:

   The chain of causation, as it becomes longer and more complex, gives rise to attempted package deals which involve more uncertainty in the minds of the actors. The chance of failure is much greater than in the incrementalist situation. No action ensues when the deliberate linkage contrived by the leadership encounters the hesitations of the member governments. Hence policies designed, by deliberate issue linkage, to force the Community into expanding its scope in order to trigger an irreversible process toward political union are likely to fail.

My comment to this is that interdependence has always been there, especially in the Third World. In Europe the heavy dependence on the outside world just becomes more manifest in the 1970s, e.g. with the two oil crises. It is, however, beneficial if it makes the neo-functionalist conscious of how regional integration is subsumed international interdependence, and if it discourages them from embarking on programs for futile computer simulation analyses.

83 The background for the discussion here is the two publications Mitrany, 1966 and 1963.

84 This has a parallel in the way SADCC in its key document from the 1992 Consultative Conference in Maputo, describes the transfer of sovereignty, as a 'change in the locus of exercising sovereignty, rather than a loss of sovereignty' (SADCC, 1992b, para. 12.4, p.33).

85 See for further discussion for example Haas, 1964.

86 See Haas, 1963, p.7 where he refers to a 'political community'. Nye, 1971, p.225 even talks of a federation or political union as the end result. This was later diluted by Haas, 1971, p.31, where he distinguishes between three possible end situations: 1) a regional state; 2) a regional commune; 3) a more complex arrangement of 'asymmetrical overlapping'. The main point and problem is that on the one hand it is necessary with some specification of the end situation in order to be able to evaluate whether progress is made in the integration process, but on the other hand the approach does not contain any fixed, readily defined final way of organizing the community. On the contrary, it aspires to be relevant for analysis of a wide range of different types of integration.

87 The neo-functionalists also refer to this as the process of engrenage. See e.g. Schmitter, 1972, p.8 or Nye, 1971, p.195.

88 Whether the politization process automatically will occur, or which conditions must be fulfilled for it to happen, has been a matter of controversy within the neo-functional approach. See for example Nye, 1971, p.193ff.; Haas and Schmitter, 1965, p.2; Schmitter, 1969, p.164ff.

89 See for example Schmitter, 1969, p.165ff.

90 Ibid. and for example Haas, 1975, p.9ff.

91 See for example Haas, 1963, p.8ff.

92 See for example Anglin, 1983, p.691ff.

93 Deliberately created or overstated linkages between problems or functional areas are in the neo-functionalist terminology called 'cultivated spillover' (Nye, 1971, p.200).

94 See for example Haas and Schmitter, 1965, pp.3 and 60; Haas, 1963, p.15ff.; or Haas, 1971, p.24.

95 See Haas, 1975, p.13.

96 See for example Nye, 1971, p.193ff.

97 See for example Haas, 1963, pp.16 and 31.

98 The conclusion of Oestergaard, 1993, p.41ff., is for example that the neo-functional approach is not helpful for the analysis of regional integration and cooperation in Southern Africa, because of the absence of strong interest groups in the area.

99 See for example Haas, 1971, p.37ff. and Nye, 1971, p.226.

100 Haas, 1971, p.14 sees the Nordic cooperation as an example of self-encapsulation.

101 According to Schmitter, 1970 it is spill-around that best characterized the CACM in the 1960s.

102 See Nye, 1971, p.199ff.

103 This is mainly based on Nye, 1971, pp.199–231 and Haas, 1971, pp.10–18.

104 A reference could here be made to what Hyden has described as the 'soft state' and a dominant peasant based 'economy of affection' that does not place exact demands on, or enters into any interplay with the state. The state exists over and above society, floating like a hot air balloon. See for example Hyden, 1983.

105 It was probably at the Arusha Conference in July 1979 (also known as SADCC–1) among the front line states and between the front line states and donors that the involved African countries were assured that substantial aid would be forthcoming, if they formed an organization such as SADCC. The perspectives of this aid might in turn have assisted in convincing Lesotho, Malawi and Swaziland to join SADCC. The expectations were confirmed at the first Annual Conference in Maputo in November 1980 (SADCC–2). See for example Anglin, 1983; Green, 1981, p.A35ff.; Christiansen, 1992, p.31ff.

106 See for example Oestergaard, 1989b, p.173.

107 See for example Schmitter, 1972.

108 See SADCC, 1992b, p.23 and SADCC, 1993b, p.5.

109 Reference is made to the analysis of the legal and procedural framework of SADCC in Simba and Wells, 1984.

110 Speech held at the Lusaka Conference, where the basic objectives and strategy of SADCC were defined in the so-called Lusaka Declaration with the title: Southern Africa: Toward Economic Liberation. The quote is from SADCC, 1984f, p.3. The Lusaka Declaration is also reprinted in for example Simba and Wells, 1984.

3 Industry and trade and SADCC's initiatives

3.1 Introduction

The intention of this chapter is, firstly, to introduce some basic features and magnitudes regarding industry and trade in the SADCC region. This empirical overview serves as a background both for the presentation in the next chapter of World Bank policies and practice towards regional cooperation and integration in Southern Africa, and for the second focus in this chapter: SADCC's industry and trade programmes and how they fared. The contents and fate of SADCC's industry and trade programmes may highlight some of the theoretical points from the previous chapter, for example how it is comparatively much more easy to expand the scope than to deepen the level of cooperation, and how it is difficult for state leaders to commit both state and private owned industries to put regional plans and agreements into practice. Moreover, the problems of implementing SADCC's industry and trade programme, which will become evident later in the chapter, constitute part of the reason why it is relevant to include a focus on World Bank policies towards regional cooperation and integration.

However, it might be beneficial, as a prelude to the above, to take a quick glance at the arguments for singling out industrial development and trade of manufactured products as the main areas of interest, and thereby leave aside other important sectors such as agriculture and transport. As to the overall relevance and theoretical background I shall limit myself to a few references. The first originates from the excellent connoisseur of industrial development in Africa, R.C. Riddell. He, however, shifts the burden of proof to H. Chenery who in his book *Industrialization and Growth* from 1986 writes (Riddell et al., 1990, p.ix):

Development is now conceived as the successful transformation of the structure of an economy. In his historical studies of modern economic growth, Kuznets (1966) identified the shift of resources from agriculture to industry as the central feature of this transformation ... Historically, the rise in the share of manufacturing in output and employment as per capita income increases and the corresponding decline in agriculture, are among the best documented generalizations about development.[1]

Another scholar with intimate knowledge of industrialization in Southern Africa, C. Stoneman (1989, p.28), puts it this way: 'Industrialisation is the only way that nations develop and for their people it is the only escape route from poverty.' He admits that reforms in the agricultural sector might be important and necessary prerequisites for successful industrialization, but maintains that: 'self-sustaining productivity increases without foreseeable limit come only from industry' (ibid.). I tend to agree with the above, especially when one adds a long term perspective and allows for temporary exceptions such as some of the oil-producing countries.

However, one thing is theory and arguments that, admittedly, are close to postulates in the way they are presented here. But from a much more pragmatic angle, in Southern Africa the imperative of industrialization and achieving world market competitiveness in selected branches become evident. The basic argument is that the present export dominance of mineral and agricultural products in the region must be broken.[2] Why? The main reason is that prospects are extremely gloomy for achieving prices on the world market from which the SADCC countries can thrive and grow. According to the World Bank, the non-fuel commodity price index almost halved from the early 1980s to 1992, and in the same year it reached its lowest level since its inception in 1948. The same source foresees a halt in the downward trend and a slight increase in non-fuel primary commodities from 1994 to the year 2000. This covers, however, a stagnation in mineral prices that constitute 40 per cent of SADCC's export value,[3] and a key assumption is that the period will witness a sustained economic upturn in the industrial countries (World Bank, 1993b, p.58ff), which is not very likely to be the case.

Moreover, long term technological changes militate against the traditional mineral and agricultural export products of Southern Africa. The research into new uses of known and abundant materials, substituting metals with cheap ceramics or copper wire with transmission by light in optic cables, threatens the viability of much mineral production. Biotechnology has many potentialities, some of which might be very positive for Africa, but it is also likely to reduce the demand for traditional crops such as sugar and cocoa because cheap genetically engineered substitutes may be grown elsewhere. This will probably further weaken the sporadic and generally unsuccessful attempts to form sales cartels among primary commodity producer countries.[4]

To aggravate this, the countries emanating from the former Soviet Union, producing a range of minerals similar to the main export earners of Southern Africa, will probably in the next decade desperately seek world market access and position through *inter alia* a relatively low pricing policy. A substantial increase in demand for raw materials from expanding Asian countries is in the author's view probably the only element which may mitigate the negative perspectives for traditional exports from Southern Africa.[5]

How does the regional angle and especially regional trade in manufactured goods come into this? The point of departure is that the 1960s and 1970s industrialization strategy, based on import-substitution in the protected national market of the individual African countries generally failed to create a sustainable manufacturing industry under the given conditions of the world market. This is illuminated by the stagnation and decline in manufactured production in the majority of the SADCC countries in the 1980s, as shown in the next section. At the same time the experience of successful industrialization in developing South-East Asia seemed to underline the necessity for African countries to increase their manufactured exports and ultimately become competitive at least in selected niches of the world market in order to transform their economies and cater for their growing populations.[6] But an abrupt across the board entry into the world market would destroy much industry and institutional capabilities, and pull the carpet from under the livelihood of many workers and as well from under much vested interest in industry and state bureaucracy. Thus, it would probably be economically unwise and politically extremely difficult endeavour for any government – not least in countries where a pluralistic society is in the making, since there, the democratic institutions are not sufficiently developed to absorb and canalize protest, and people will tend to react by violence as this was the only way possible under earlier regimes.[7] However, between the poles of a protected national market and fierce world market competition lies trade between neighbours and in a regional context. A key assumption of this book is that the development of a regional market may avoid the sudden disruption of the political and social fabric of society, because the environment of the regional market has the potential to gradually improve industrial efficiency, raise productivity, increase capacity utilization, give export experience etc. The regional market may identify positions of strength to be built upon and may be a stepping stone towards world market competitiveness. But it would also exist in its own right – as one among several pillars of manufacturing industrial development. As G. Maasdorp (1992c, p.215) puts it: 'The manufacturing sector in Southern Africa needs to grow on all fronts'. They include exports to the world market, import substitution, regional exports as well as informal trade. The realization of the inadequacy of remaining in the old trenches of inward oriented, import substitution industrialization with state intervention versus outward looking industrialization with only the free play of the market forces, was internationally starting to gain ground in the end of the 1980s.[8] The challenge for governments would be to have policies in place that made the different areas of industry mutually supportive and strive to increase efficiency and productivity in all of them, taking into consideration the intimate linkages to investment in human resources, technology development and the availability of physical and financial infrastructure.

In chapter 1 it was emphasized how one must be aware of the fragile basis of much statistical information from Africa, and be very careful not to misuse or over interpret statistical data. These words of caution are most relevant to this chapter. The sources of inaccuracies are innumerable, and call for humility towards the data, not least concerning comparisons between countries and regions of the world. Note must likewise be taken that neither the ever increasing informal sector nor the illegal cross-border trade is reflected in the statistics.

It should also be clear that focus is on manufacturing industry and not industry as such. The latter is the broader term and embraces – apart from manufacturing – also construction, water, energy, electricity and extractive mining, including oil processing facilities. According to United Nations classification manufacturing is defined as: 'The mechanical or chemical transformation of inorganic or organic substances into new products whether the work is performed by power-driven machines or by hand, whether it is done in a factory or in the workers' home and whether the products are sold wholesale or retail' (United Nations, 1968).[9]

Apart from this introduction and a final, short summary the chapter contains four main sections. The first presents an overview of manufacturing industry development; from there we proceed to unpack the region as regards trade, especially the intra-regional flows in Southern Africa. The third section presents a sketch and a discussion of SADCC's industry programme, and in the fourth a similar, albeit shorter, exercise is performed regarding SADCC's trade programme.

3.2   Manufacturing industry in Southern Africa

In 1990 one tenth of the world population lived in Sub-Saharan Africa,[10] but the proportion of global manufacturing output produced there was one hundredth by the end of the 1980s (Overseas Development Institute, 1986, p.1). Sub-Saharan Africa's share of world manufactured exports fell from 0.5 per cent in 1970 to 0.3 per cent in 1988 (Riddell, 1993, p.4).[11] With the steep rise in manufactured exports from Asia and continued economic stagnation in Africa, the share of Sub-Saharan Africa is likely to have been reduced even further in the beginning of the 1990s. This would be in line with the drop in Sub-Saharan Africa's share of world gross domestic product, falling from 1.4 per cent in 1970 to 0.8 per cent in 1991 (World Bank, 1993a, table 3, p.242).

Within Sub-Saharan Africa the share of the SADCC countries can be put into perspective by the following table:

Table 3.1
Share of manufacturing value added in Sub-Saharan Africa, 1984 and 1989

Country	1984	1989
Zimbabwe	7.8	7.4
Zambia	4.8	6.4
Rest of SADCC	6.1	7.5
SADCC total	18.7	21.3
Nigeria	28.0	16.4
Kenya	6.0	4.9
Rest of Sub-Saharan Africa	47.3	57.4
Total	100.0	100.0

Sources: 1984 data: UNIDO, 1986a; SADCC, 1985e: 1989 data: Riddell, 1993; World Bank, 1991a, 1992a, 1993a; Direcção Nacional de Estatística, 1992[12]

SADCC's share of around 20 per cent of manufacturing value added is somewhat larger than its proportion of Sub-Saharan population – 17 per cent – would suggest,[13] thus, confirming the impression of Southern Africa being slightly more industrialized than the rest of Sub-Saharan Africa. It is also worth noting that Zimbabwe is ahead of Kenya – the East African industrial hub – in both years under scrutiny. In fact, Zimbabwe is only surpassed by Nigeria, which has the advantages of foreign exchange earnings from oil-exports, and a domestic market of 24 per cent of Sub-Saharan Africa's population. However, these overall dimensions must be compared to the size of industrial value added in South Africa. This may illuminate the immense difficulties of both the original objective of SADCC in the 1980s of reducing dependence on South Africa, and the strategy of the 1990s of integrating South Africa into the organization after the installation of a democratically elected government in Pretoria.

Table 3.2
**Manufacturing value added in Zimbabwe, SADCC, Nigeria and
Sub-Saharan Africa in relation to South Africa, 1989 (ratio)**

Ratio between Zimbabwe and South Africa	1 : 15
Ratio between SADCC total and South Africa	1 : 5
Ratio between Nigeria and South Africa	1 : 7
Ratio between Sub-Saharan Africa and South Africa	1 : 1.1

Sources: calculations based on the same sources as for table 3.1

All four ratios in the above table are a token of the enormous relative weight of South Africa in industrial production in Africa. Most strikingly – South Africa's manufacturing value added is larger than the total for the rest of Sub-Saharan Africa. It is seven times larger than Nigeria, the Sub-Saharan African giant in nearly all kinds of statistical comparisons, and apart from being substantially more potent than SADCC combined, it surpasses the SADCC's industrial hub, Zimbabwe, 15 times. This is an indication of how easily the SADCC countries can be dominated by South African industry, but is certainly also a reminder of the potential of a gigantic market place and an easy supplier in the SADCC countries' back yard.

However, for the analysis of the development of SADCC's industrial programme it is important to know the intra-SADCC distribution of manufacturing industry. Table 3.3 (overleaf) gives the details.

The dominant share of regional manufacturing value added held by Zimbabwe is evident. Zambia comes in as a convincing number two with nearly triple the share in relation to number three in both years. Zimbabwe and Zambia together represent about two thirds of SADCC's manufacturing value added.[14] The relative smallness of the industrial sectors in Lesotho and Namibia are apparent, but also the relatively large percentage for Swaziland is noteworthy. So are the decreasing shares of Tanzania and Mozambique's manufacturing value added, mostly due to factory closures and low capacity utilization in the 1980s.

We now turn to another measure for the role of the manufacturing sector – the proportion that manufacturing value added constitutes of Gross Domestic Product (GDP). In the World Bank's study on Sub-Saharan Africa *From Crisis to Sustainable Growth* (1989, p.109) it is stated that '... manufacturing remains mostly small, stagnating at around 10 per cent of GDP ... between 1965 and 1987'.[15] However, in the mid-eighties the SADCC average is estimated to be around 15 per cent, according to *SADCC Macro-Economic Survey 1986* (SADCC, 1985e, p.104), and this magnitude is confirmed by Ridell (1993, p.4) for 1989. Thus, SADCC's above average level of industrialization in comparison to the rest of Sub-Saharan Africa is verified.

Table 3.3
Distribution of manufacturing value added among the SADCC countries, 1984 and 1989 (per cent)

Country	1984	1989
Angola	3	8
Botswana	3	3
Lesotho	1	1
Malawi	6	4
Mozambique	6	3
Namibia	–	2
Swaziland	4	11
Tanzania	9	3
Zambia	26	30
Zimbabwe	42	35
Total	100	100

The figures behind the percentages are in current US$ and official exchange rates

Sources: calculations based on the same sources as for table 3.1

However, SADCC's 15 per cent are no match for South Africa's 24 per cent or East Asia's 33 per cent proportion of manufactured value added to GDP, but SADCC comes close to the average in South Asia of 17 per cent (World Bank, 1991a, table 3, p.208). Table 3.4 focuses on the large differences between the individual SADCC countries concealed in the 15 per cent.

Table 3.4
Share of manufacturing value added in Gross Domestic Product among the SADCC countries, 1989

Angola	4
Botswana	4
Lesotho	14
Malawi	11
Mozambique	10
Namibia	5
Swaziland	25
Tanzania	4
Zambia	24
Zimbabwe	25

Sources: see table 3.1

It is clear that three countries range far above the others – Swaziland, Zambia and Zimbabwe. A quarter of their respective gross domestic products originates from manufacturing industry. Its share is more than double the Sub-Saharan Africa mean of about ten per cent. They are on a par with South Korea and the Indian Ocean export success country – Mauritius. Zimbabwe's manufacturing sector is by far the most developed, diversified and integrated among the SADCC countries. It produces above 6000 different products (Riddell, 1993, p.14) and has substantial metal, engineering and chemical sub-sectors. Zambian industry is also diversified, but mostly characterized by basic processing of minerals before export and import substituting consumer goods industries. In the 1980s the latter reached very low levels of capacity utilization (40–50 per cent) (ibid., p.15), because the foreign exchange revenues from copper production dropped sharply. Although being the smallest country in terms of territory and population Swaziland possesses a relatively advanced manufacturing industry with processing of agricultural products, production of wood pulp and consumer goods. In the 1980s it has to some extent benefited from the relocation of foreign and South African investments from South Africa to avoid international sanctions.

Three countries cluster on or around the Sub-Saharan African average – Lesotho, Malawi and Mozambique. In Lesotho manufacturing production is small, but so is the rest of domestic production as well, and therefore manufacturing gets a relatively prominent share.[16] In all fairness, Lesotho also experienced some growth in the manufacturing sector in the 1980s linked to the giant Highland Water Project and to export-oriented foreign investment. Malawi has for its size a relatively well developed manufacturing sector mostly linked to processing of agricultural products and production of consumer goods. Before independence in 1975 Mozambique had a relatively well functioning manufacturing sector, but it depended on Portuguese manpower, and production dropped dramatically when most Portuguese left in the mid 1970s.[17] There was some recoupment of production in the late 1970s and beginning of the 1980s, but in the 1980s manufacturing was negatively affected, especially by the foreign exchange shortages.

The remaining four countries – Angola, Botswana, Namibia and Tanzania have shares of manufacturing value added that correspond to half or less than the Sub-Saharan Africa average. In Angola the history of manufacturing is very much like the one in Mozambique, only with less foreign exchange problems, but more havoc caused by the war, and the relative heavy weight of oil production in the economy pushes the share of manufacturing downwards. In contrast manufacturing industry in Namibia is indeed diminutive, consisting nearly exclusively of a narrow range of consumer goods industries. In Botswana manufacturing industry is larger; it incorporates meat processing before export, production of consumer goods for the local market and some export production, but its share is dwarfed by the dominant mining sector. Tanzanian manufacturing is plagued by lack of foreign exchange, low capacity utilization (20–30 per cent) (Riddell, 1993, p.15), and the economy is characterized by the large peasant-based population.

The overview below of the distribution of manufacturing industry by sub-sectors in the individual SADCC countries and in South Africa provides an important illumination of the strengths and weaknesses of the respective manufacturing sectors.

Table 3.5

Sub-sectoral composition of manufacturing value added among the SADCC countries and South Africa, 1987 (per cent)

Country/Sector	1/2	3/4	5/6	7/8	9/10	11	Total
Angola	30	18	11	18	22	1	100
Botswana	54	9	2	6	6	23	100
Lesotho	71	13	3	8	3	2	100
Malawi	34	17	9	31	6	3	100
Mozambique	41	23	8	15	11	2	100
Namibia	65	9	8	13	3	2	100
Swaziland	58	2	14	14	10	1	100
Tanzania	34	21	11	14	18	2	100
Zambia	35	11	8	23	22	1	100
Zimbabwe	33	15	9	18	23	1	100
South Africa	14	9	12	27	37	1	100

Sectors: 1 and 2 – foodstuffs, beverages and tobacco; 3 and 4 – textiles, clothing, leather and footwear; 5 and 6 – wood, wooden products, furniture, paper, printing and publishing; 7 and 8 – nonmetallic minerals, chemicals, rubber and pharmaceutical; 9 and 10 – metal and metal products, machinery and transport equipment; 11 – other or not classified

Source: rearranged from Riddell, 1993, p.10

One can note in the above table how the countries with a higher percentage of manufacturing value added to GDP and with more diversified and integrated industrial sectors – South Africa, Zimbabwe and Zambia – tend to have a more equal sectoral distribution of industry, and especially larger portions than the rest of the countries in the sectors 7–10, which include metal and engineering sectors. Conversely, the countries with only rudimentary industrial sectors tend to have most manufacturing industry concentrated in the sectors 1–2, typically food and beverages for the local market, and processing of agricultural products before export. Note Namibia and Lesotho with 65 and 71 per cent respectively in these sectors. The sectors 3–4, textiles, clothing, leather and footwear, have traditionally been the basis on which industrial development 'took off', supplying both the domestic market and building up exports. The figures indicate that the countries have some potential, but, apparently, no specific positions of strength in these sectors presently. Mozambican textiles and clothing industry will be more closely analysed in chapter 5. In contrast, a country such as Mauritius that in the 1980s and in the beginning of the 1990s experienced an industrialization based on the export of clothing to the world market had 59 per cent of its manufacturing value added concentrated in the sectors 3–4 in 1987 (Riddell, 1993, p.10).[18]

For some of the Southern African countries it has been possible to establish how much manufactured imports cover domestic consumption of manufactured goods. Although the information relates to trade, and as such is to be treated in the next section, the data are included here as they are highly relevant for understanding the type of industrial set-up we find in the SADCC countries and South Africa.

Table 3.6
Imports of manufactured goods as a percentage of domestic consumption of manufactured products,* 1980 (percentage)

South Africa	20
Zimbabwe	27
Zambia	35
Tanzania	56
Malawi	60
Swaziland	90
Botswana	90
Lesotho	96

* Imports divided by domestic consumption (production less exports plus imports) x 100

Sources: for the SADCC countries; UNIDO, 1985a, table 2.6, p.29: for South Africa: Riddell, 1993, table 4.4, p.20

The relatively low level of manufactured imports in relation to consumption is significant for South Africa and Zimbabwe. They are the token of an import-substitution strategy that on its own terms has been reasonably successful. However, huge inter-sectoral differences also exist there, with higher import-ratios for the more technologically advanced products and lower ratios for simpler manufacturing found in, for example, the sectors 1–4 (see table 3.5). The extremely low coverage of home consumption from domestic production is evident in Lesotho, Botswana and Swaziland, although the growth in consumer industry in the three countries in the 1980s has probably modified the picture somewhat. Still, the saying that the three countries consume what they do not produce and produce what they do not consume holds a good deal of truth.[19] Regarding exports of manufactured goods, they will be dealt with in more detail in the next section especially in relation to the region; suffice it to mention here that they constituted for the SADCC countries only around 10 per cent of total manufactured production in the mid 1980s (SADCC, 1986c, p.13). In South Africa slightly more, around 12 per cent, of manufactured production was exported in the 1980s (Riddell, 1993, pp.9 and 18). The interesting thing is that the figures are so close. They point to the dominance of import substitution and lack of international export experience as well as competitiveness in the whole of Southern Africa. Both figures were far below export ratios in countries such as South Korea and Malaysia, which exported 30–40 per cent of manufactured production (ibid.) in the same period. Thus, the foreign exchange needed to run and expand the manufacturing sector in Southern Africa is not generated in the sector itself, but has to come from the export of minerals, agricultural produce or foreign investments and other transfers. A closer look is taken below at how the financial flows behaved in the 1980s.

Industry needs constant investments to be maintained and grow. A relatively high percentage of investment will consist of imports from abroad of machinery etc. This requires access to foreign exchange. The same applies to the import of fuels, raw materials and intermediary goods, purchase of expertise from abroad, license fees etc. In the 1980s most SADCC countries had to turn to external transfers to finance this, because of the drastically reduced receipts from commodity exports and still higher debt service ratios and the bias of industry towards the internal market. However, what happened was that external commercial bank lending dried up after the debt crisis gained force in the beginning of the decade. Private direct investment, portfolio investment and export credits were also drastically reduced.[20] Only Angola and Botswana still received substantial foreign investment due to Angola's oil sector and diamond mining in Botswana.[21] Some investments also continued to flow to Swaziland and Lesotho, whilst Mozambique, Tanzania, Zambia, Zimbabwe and Malawi experienced stagnating or negative private flows. On a global scale Africa only received two per cent of private foreign direct investment to all sectors in the period 1986–92.[22] OECD has registered the below total net transfers of all types of finance and net disbursements of official development assistance (ODA) in constant (1990) prices and exchange rates to Sub-Saharan Africa in selected years.

The stagnation in net financial transfers at 15 billion US$ over the period can be observed. This covers a decline of 20 per cent in the first half of the 1980s, then a substantial increase to 17 billion US$ in 1990, which, however, falls back to the 15 billion US$ a year later. Comparing this to disbursement of net official development assistance (ODA) gives the added information

81

that in all the years except 1980 ODA is higher than net financial transfers. This means that only in 1980 did investments and loans add to the transfers to Sub-Saharan Africa. After that year the outflows, in the form of disinvestment, interests and loan repayments have reduced what was made available by ODA. This was especially severe by 1985 where an inroad of a quarter of ODA was made by negative balances in other types of financial transfers. Thus, in the 1980s the SADCC countries' industrial planners were faced with a situation where their own resources were exhausted and all kinds of foreign capital – except for ODA – avoided or directly fled the continent. The pervasive position and dependence on aid can be illustrated by the fact that in 1991 the percentage of ODA transfers in GDP was a staggering 70 per cent for Mozambique, 40 per cent for Tanzania and around 20 per cent for Lesotho, Malawi and Zambia (World Bank, 1993a, table 20, p.276). Moreover, there were strings attached to the aid. Substantial increases to any given country would normally be made dependent from the major donors side on the country undertaking an agreement with the IMF and the World Bank on stabilization and structural adjustment measures – a structural adjustment programme. We shall revert to the structural adjustment programmes, and how they influence regional industrial development in chapter 5.

Table 3.7
Net financial transfers* and net disbursement of official development assistance to Sub-Saharan Africa in 1980, 1985 and 1991, billion US$ (1990 prices and exchange rates)

	1980	1985	1990	1991
Net financial transfers	15	12	17	15
Net official development assistance	12	16	18	16

* Net financial transfers are defined as total net resource flows minus investment income payments (interest and dividends). Total net (resource) flows include official and private grants (including technical cooperation), direct investment and total long-and short term loans minus loans repayments

Source: OECD, 1992, table 17 (A–25) and table 39 (A–51)

A radical proposal to mobilize capital for investment was provided by the American economist A. Seidmann in the beginning of the 1980s.[23] She suggested that taking control over trade, banks and basic industries – 'the commanding heights' of the economy, mostly owned by foreign companies – would provide the SADCC countries with up to 25 per cent of GDP in hitherto hidden or drained investable surplus for the region that inter alia could be used for building up regional poles of growth industries in each SADCC country. My own view on this line of thought is that it is not anchored in the realities of conditions in Southern Africa. Apart from technical questions about the calculation of the 25 per cent, the whole process of making them available for concrete investment projects is not clearly spelled out. Moreover, state control over trade, banks and basic industries would undoubtedly alienate major western donors and effectively bar foreign private investment and technology transfer. It would be extremely difficult to avoid becoming a pariah in the international community, and a successful development outside the world market seems impossible with Southern Africa's extensive dependence on international trade. Add to this the impossible demands the proposal would put to the administrative capacity and capability in the region, and the nonexistence of political alliances, which could form the basis for the strong political will and determination that would be required. The inevitable result of such an analysis is negative, and the proposal was doomed even before being seriously considered.

Much critical analysis of the time seems to play down the fundamental question that far too little investable surplus was created by everyone – national and foreign companies alike in the 1980s. There may also be a tendency to underplay the fact that the countries were in a much better position than just after their independence, to benefit from foreign investment; not least because the level of education had been raised, and governments had the capacity to establish conditions and incentives which maximised linkages to the rest of society and reaped benefits in the form of technology transfer, introduction of new management techniques, knowledge of export possibilities etc.

Will investment capital for manufacturing sector development be more readily forthcoming in the 1990s? Regarding concessional flows, it is likely that the amounts of ODA for Africa will be more restricted, due to cuts in public sector spending in donor countries and the competition from the new countries in Central and Eastern Europe and Asia. Concerning private foreign direct investment it has picked up in Latin America and Asia in the beginning of the 1990s. The general investment climate there – including the political situation and growth perspectives – is regarded as better than in Africa, although the majority of African countries have established favourable investment regulations and incentives. Moreover, the little foreign investment that will be landed in Africa is unlikely to uplift the manufacturing sector. The United Nations' *World Investment Report 1993* (p.54) puts it this way:

Africa's main attraction for foreign investors is still its natural resources ... Given slow economic growth and the small size of the domestic markets in most of Sub-Saharan Africa, foreign direct investment in manufacturing remains limited. This is despite a liberalization of the regulatory framework, and the establishment of 'one-shop' investment centres in several countries.[24]

Among the SADCC countries Angola would probably be the only one to benefit substantially from this trend, provided that the civil war comes to an end. It is of special interest for this book that the negative impact of the small size of domestic markets is mentioned as a major problem, or phrased positively: the need for market sharing arrangements is singled out as a key factor for manufacturing industry development. The World Bank's *Global Economic Prospects for the Developing Countries 1993* agrees that natural resources will be the reason for most foreign investment in Africa, and that the 'majority of countries will have limited access to this source of financing ...'. The World Bank further mentions that a better functioning infrastructure would facilitate foreign investments (World Bank, 1993b, p.65). SADCC's priority of infrastructure development fits well into this.

We can now turn to the manufacturing industry growth rates that the countries in Southern Africa experienced in the period 1974–81.

Table 3.8

Rates of growth in manufacturing value added in the SADCC countries and South Africa in the 1970s and 1980s (per cent)

	1974–81 (A)	1980–89 (B)	(B) – Adjusted for population growth
Angola	-14.4	5.0	2.4
Botswana*	6.1	5.3	1.9
Lesotho	5.3	13.4	10.7
Malawi	6.2	3.1	-0.3
Mozambique	-11.6	-3.5	-6.2
Namibia	2.5	2.5	-0.6
Swaziland^	0.3	3.8	1.3
Tanzania	-6.6	-1.6	-4.7
Zambia*	-6.4	2.5	-1.2
Zimbabwe	-1.4	2.6	-0.9
South Africa	4.5	0.5	-1.9

* 1974–81 percentages are based on current prices
^ Population growth rate for Swaziland is the author's estimate

Sources: for 1974–81: UNIDO, 1985a, table 2.5, p.23; for 1980–89: Riddell, 1993, table 4.3, p.12. For population growth rates: World Bank, 1991a, table 26, p.254

Manufacturing industry in all SADCC countries experienced high growth rates in the late 1960s and early 1970s. However, it is evident from the above table that from 1974 onwards a process of deindustrialization or negligible growth characterizes the majority of countries, most pronounced in Mozambique and Tanzania, but also noticeable in Zambia, Zimbabwe, Angola, Malawi, and South Africa. From 1974–81 United Nations Industrial Development Organisation (UNIDO) estimates the weighed average of the SADCC countries growth of manufacturing industry to be -5 per cent (UNIDO, 1985a, table 2.5, p.23). This can be conveniently compared to the seven per cent annual growth rate that the World Bank in the 1989 Sub-Saharan African study *From Crisis to Sustainable Growth* (1989, p.109) indicate as a desirable and realistic figure for manufacturing growth. The difference of 12 per cent between reality and goal was probably somewhat narrowed in the 1980s, but negative overall manufacturing growth is likely to be continuing in the beginning of the 1990s.[25]

Summing up the contents of this section, Sub-Saharan African manufacturing production is diminutive in a global perspective. Within Sub-Saharan Africa Nigeria is clearly in front, but with 20 per cent of manufacturing value added, SADCC's per capita share is above average. However, with South Africa's entry on the scene, SADCC is dwarfed with only one fifth of South Africa's manufacturing value added, which is even larger than what the whole of Sub-Saharan Africa's amounts to. In SADCC the dominant role of Zimbabwe is evident with around 40 per cent of manufacturing value added; Zambia comes in second and Swaziland third ; Botswana, Lesotho, Namibia possess in absolute terms small manufacturing sectors, but their share of manufacturing value added approaches that of larger countries such as Mozambique and Tanzania because of the crisis in the latter countries industrial production in the 1980s.

The shares of manufacturing value added in GDP give the same pattern as above with Zimbabwe, Zambia and Swaziland in the forefront with around 25 per cent – on a par with successful middle income developing countries. The remaining countries cluster around or below the Sub-Saharan average of ten per cent.

A sub-sectoral view of the SADCC countries and South Africa illustrates how countries with the largest and most developed manufacturing sectors have industry evenly spread out in all subsectors, including chemical, metal and machinery, while the countries with less developed manufacturing sectors are dominated by food and beverages industries. The leading manufacturing producers, South Africa and Zimbabwe, are able to supply around 80 per cent of consumption of manufactured products from domestic sources, whilst a quite opposite situation is found in Botswana, Lesotho and Swaziland that only receive around 5–10 per cent of consumption from local production.

A picture seems to be emerging of some rather successful import substituting countries, South Africa and Zimbabwe, with diversified manufacturing sectors, a middle group of still import substituting, but less successful countries, Zambia, Tanzania, Mozambique, Malawi and Angola, and then a third group of countries, constituted by Swaziland, Botswana, Lesotho and Namibia that are more open and export orientated but all except Swaziland have rather small manufacturing sectors. However, the groups are mostly introduced for illustrative purposes and the boundaries between them are not rigid. Zambia might be said to be floating between the first and second group, and Malawi between the second and the third. Moreover, it is often overlooked that Botswana, Lesotho, Namibia and Swaziland are only fully open economically inside SACU, which is precisely intended to shield production in the area from world market competition.

Focus is then turned on the re-investments and new investments in the SADCC countries. The 1980s are characterized by lack of own funds especially in foreign exchange for investment, as export earnings dwindle and debt service payments rise. At the same time private foreign investments, commercial lending and export credits turn negative. Most SADCC countries, and Sub-Saharan African countries in general, were basically left with only two possibilities. Either to stop all external payments and purchases and consequently break most ties with the international community, or try to seek increasing amounts of concessional financing, ODA, and debt forgiveness. None of them chose the first option. Inevitably, the second was followed, and the international community responded by increasing ODA transfers, accompanied by demands to the receiving country of celebrating structural adjustment agreements with the IMF and World Bank. However, for some SADCC countries the chosen path meant that dependence on ODA grew to alarming heights. On a global scale foreign direct investment seems to be set to rise in the developing countries as such in the 1990s, but the available analyses are pessimistic regarding Africa and especially the manufacturing sector's ability to attract investment under the prevailing conditions.

Finally, the growth rates of the SADCC countries in the 1970s and 1980s are presented. They confirm the impression of deindustrialization, stagnation or negligible growth. When the growth rates are adjusted for population growth, seven of the ten SADCC countries show negative manufacturing industry growth rates in the 1980s.

Thus, there is little doubt that the model for manufacturing industry growth that the countries directly or indirectly had applied since their independence has failed. It was based on building up import-substituting industries behind protected tariff walls, quantitative import restrictions or the like, and it was geared towards supplying the home market, though in some cases exports to the region did develop. A common problem was the lack of incentive to make production continuously more effective, as there typically was no competition on the internal market from other producers or imports. Manufactured exports were low, and imports of inputs for production and investment had to be financed by the foreign exchange surplus from other sectors. As these, in turn, contracted in the late 1970s and 1980s, other restrictions and controls grew to prominence. Capacity utilization fell with the reduced availability of imported raw materials, intermediate goods and spare parts. Rational planning was made a mockery by the reduction in foreign exchange allocated to industry for imports of inputs to production, and by the cumbersome, complicated and protracted procedures for obtaining the little there was available. Centralized control over prices and wages, internal sales and exports added to this. The exchange rate was not used in macroeconomic management. Thereby prices of imports remained low to the benefit of political elites and their urban constituencies, purchasing cheap imported consumer goods, but exports became even less competitive, and there was no price incentive to produce for external sales or substitute foreign inputs to production with materials of local origin. This situation was similar in countries where the manufacturing sector was dominated by the private sector as in Zimbabwe and Malawi, and in countries where the state controlled large parts of manufacturing industry as in Zambia and Mozambique. State involvement, however, tended to be fortified as neither local nor foreign private sources wished to expand or invest. Many of the various measures might be justified as perfectly logical steps from responsible governments faced with diminishing receipts that had to be given priority. For manufacturing industry, however, they created an overall business environment that was not favourable for production, investment or exports.

A downward spiral had begun and there was no indication as to where it would stop. How could the countries react? With inspiration from Riddell[26] four possible avenues, open for the African governments, can be sketched. First, they could chose to follow the same strategy as before, merely adjusted according to the available means, and continue to assist expansion of manufacturing industry wherever possible. Second, they could give up any intervention in the manufacturing sector, but keep the overall economic system of protection and controls intact. Third, they could revamp the overall economic system, and let the manufacturing sector readjust on its own to the changed circumstances through the signals of the market. Fourth, they could seek actively to assist the adjustment process of the manufacturing sector to the changed international circumstances, emphasizing the importance of raising productivity, enhance efficient use of resources and increase competitiveness. The overall economy should also be reformed towards a market based system, but in a more selective and phased way in comparison to option three.

My hypothesis is that SADCC's initial industry and trade programme was basically an attempt to follow the first option, trying to identify possibilities on a regional level that might further the existing model and alleviate the crisis. However, more or less simultaneously in the individual SADCC countries a parallel process was taking place, shifting policies towards option three, based on structural adjustment programmes agreed with the IMF and the World Bank, facilitating increased financial transfers to the country in question. The result of the coexistence of these strategies will be more evident after the discussion later in this chapter about SADCCs industry and trade policies. First, below, the facts about the existing regional trade flows in Southern Africa are presented.

3.3   Trade in Southern Africa

To get the topic into its proper dimension from the outset, we must remember that Southern Africa's share of world manufactured exports was only 0.3 per cent in 1988, and in addition the whole of Sub-Saharan Africa only represented around one per cent of total world exports (Melo and Panagariya, 1992a, p.16ff.)[27] in 1990.

Looking at the SADCC countries as a block, their visible trade balance with the outside world is characterized by a huge deficit in the 1980s. Hard data are scarce, but the knowledgeable and outspoken Zimbabwean economist A.M. Hawkins (1992, p.111ff.) gives the figure of an accumulated 14 billion US$ deficit in the period 1980–88, and he provides information for selected years. Imports are calculated at 7.7 billion US$ and exports at 6.6 billion US$ in 1980. Two years later SADCC's *Intra-Regional Trade Study* (1986c, table 13, p.139) noted a decline in both imports and exports, settling at 7.2 and 5.5 billion respectively, thereby widening the deficit from 1.1 in 1980 to 1.7 billion US$. By 1985 an approximate balance was reached, but at the expense of a strong contraction of imports that were scaled down to 5.4 billion US$, whereas exports only fell to 5.1 billion US$, according to Hawkins. The decline in imports and stagnation and fall in exports reflect all too well the profound crisis in the development model based on commodity exports and inward-looking industrialization. Region wide information around the turn of the decade is not available for the book, but country figures point at a clear trend towards a renewed large widening of the gap between imports and exports.[28] This is caused by the increased availability of foreign exchange through the structural adjustment programmes, accorded between most of the individual SADCC countries and the IMF and the World Bank. This has boosted imports, whilst exports, albeit increasing in some cases, are still very far from matching imports.

Around three quarters of SADCC's total external trade is with the member countries of the Organisation for Economic Corporation and Development (OECD); South Africa represents about one fifth and internal trade among the SADCC countries is below five per cent according to available data from the 1980s.[29] However, these data cover wide variations between countries and between exports and imports. The latest disaggregated, comprehensive figures are the ones below from 1984, but they are probably reasonably representative for the whole period up till the new opening between Africa and South Africa from 1990 and onwards, and they are in line with earlier analysis in the 1980s (SADCC, 1986c and Maasdorp and Whiteside, 1993).

Table 3.9
Imports and exports of SADCC and South Africa (S.A.), 1984 (per cent)

	Exports to			Imports from		
	SADCC	S.A.	Rest of the world	SADCC	S.A.	Rest of the world
Angola	–	–	100.0	0.2	–	99.8
Botswana	4.0	8.8	87.2	8.8	78.2	13.0
Lesotho	–	33.3	66.7	0.2	74.3	25.5
Malawi	8.6	7.3	84.1	11.1	40.4	48.5
Mozambique	11.7	4.4	83.9	5.1	11.7	83.2
Namibia	–	25.0	75.0	–	90.0	10.0
Swaziland	1.5	37.0	61.5	0.3	90.0	9.7
Tanzania	1.9	–	98.1	1.1	–	98.9
Zambia	4.1	0.7	95.2	7.4	21.2	71.4
Zimbabwe	11.3	18.3	70.4	7.0	19.3	73.7
SADCC	3.8	9.3	86.9	3.7	36.7	59.6
South Africa	9.6	–	90.4	2.8	–	97.2

Botswana, Lesotho, Namibia and Swaziland's imports from South Africa are probably underestimated
Source: Maasdorp and Whiteside, 1993, p.14. Calculated on the basis of data from Lewis, 1987

I shall start with some general comments to the table; then look into the intra-SADCC trade flows, and finally concentrate on the SADCC – South African trade relations. On a general level, three groups can be identified. The first consists of Angola and Tanzania. They have very little or zero trade with the rest of the SADCC countries and with South Africa. The second group is made up of the SACU members Botswana, Lesotho, Namibia and Swaziland. They are characterized by their large trade with South Africa. 75–90 per cent of their imports are purchased in South Africa and for three of the countries 25–37 per cent of their exports are sold in South Africa. Only Botswana is lower due to its export of diamonds to the international market. Botswana is also the only one in the group with above average intra-SADCC trade figures, while this trade is negligible for the others. The last group, encompassing Malawi, Mozambique, Zambia and Zimbabwe, have the highest intra-SADCC trade with 4–12 per cent of exports and 5–11 per cent of imports. The level of trade with South Africa is situated between the first and second country group. It ranges between 1 to 20 per cent of exports and from 12 to 40 per cent of imports. Thus, the data suggest that in the 1980s a SADCC regional trade arrangement would be most relevant to this last group, possibly supplemented with Botswana. Nevertheless, the group have even larger trade indices with South Africa and on this basis in a post-apartheid setting it should have a substantial material interest in promoting this link either bilaterally or multilaterally, for example, in a SADCC or a PTA context. The post-apartheid scenario, obviously, also calls for a renewed view of the first group, as the military and political hindrances to trade with South Africa are removed. However, I shall now continue with the intra-SADCC flows and only thereafter return to the South African angle.

The remarkable feature of the trade between the SADCC countries is its small volume in both absolute and relative terms. Table 3.9 indicates a level around four per cent in 1984. It tallies well with SADCC's *Intra Regional Trade Study* (1986c, p.7) that calculates regional exports and imports to five and four per cent respectively for 1982. This corresponded to only about 600 million US$ out of a total trade of 12.7 billion US$.[30] The above table does not allow for an in-depth look at the relative weight of individual SADCC countries regarding the intra-regional flows. This can be illuminated on the basis of data from SADCC's *Intra Regional Trade Study* (see table 3.10).

The dominance of Zimbabwe in intra regional trade among the SADCC countries is striking. Nearly half of exports and a third of imports can be ascribed to Zimbabwe. It fits perfectly with section 3.2's identification of Zimbabwe as the leading manufacturing producer in SADCC, when combined with the below identification of manufactured products as the most important group of traded goods. At the same time the figures show that the polarization between unequal regional partners – as discussed in chapter 2 – seems to be a realistic prospect, in case the SADCC countries decided to implement a pure market integration model.

Further, the table confirms that Angola, Lesotho and Swaziland are, indeed, diminutive players on the regional scene. Tanzania's share of regional exports is likewise low, and the registered nine per cent of imports might be due to special circumstances for the years in question. This leaves us with a middle group of Botswana, Malawi, Mozambique and Zambia. For them regional trade has some, although modest, importance. Their share of intra regional exports is between 6 and 19 per cent and for imports between 9–19 per cent.

Table 3.10
**Relative weight of the SADCC countries in intra regional exports
and imports, 1982–84 average (per cent)**

	Exports	Imports
Angola	0.8	4.3
Botswana	19.2	18.5
Lesotho	0.0	0.1
Malawi	8.6	9.4
Mozambique	5.7	9.4
Namibia	–	–
Swaziland	2.9	1.1
Tanzania	1.6	8.7
Zambia	14.3	17.4
Zimbabwe	46.9	31.2
Total	100.0	100.0

Namibian data are not available

Source: SADCC, 1986c, table 1.2, p.10

The overwhelming Zimbabwean participation in intra regional trade and the position of the middle group is reflected in the identification of the most important trade flows in the region in the period 1979–84 (SADCC, 1986c, p.11ff.):

From:		To:
Botswana	–	Zimbabwe
Zambia	–	Zimbabwe
Zimbabwe	–	Botswana
Zimbabwe	–	Malawi
Zimbabwe	–	Zambia

The highest levels of trade has been reached between Zimbabwe and Botswana. Four trade flows have been fluctuating between high and medium level: between Zambia and Malawi, Malawi and Zimbabwe, Zambia and Tanzania and between Zimbabwe and Mozambique.

It is interesting to note that the highest levels have been reached between neighbouring states with easy physical access to each others markets. Moreover, trade between Zimbabwe and Botswana and between Zimbabwe and Malawi were in the period under scrutiny covered by agreements, almost

91

complete free trade among the countries.[31] However, that free trade conditions alone are not enough to boost trade can be seen by the smallness of trade between Malawi and Botswana, which also celebrate free trade between themselves, and by the practical nonexistence of trade between Botswana, Lesotho and Swaziland, all inside SACU.

The commodity composition of trade can give useful information as to the background and potential of regional trade. Below are figures for SADCC trade in 1984.

Table 3.11
Commodity composition of intra SADCC trade, 1984 (per cent)

Commodity section:

Food and live animals	22.7
Beverages and tobacco	1.7
Crude materials	5.2
Fuels	16.0
Animal and vegetable oils and fats	2.0
Chemicals	7.8
Manufactured goods, by materials	33.8
Machinery and transport equipment	5.6
Misc. manufactured articles	5.2
Total	100.0

Source: SADCC, 1986c, table 20 c, p.147

The important observation here is that manufactured products of the last four commodity sections make up more than half of the intra regional trade, while their share of total exports, as stated earlier, is estimated to be only around 10 per cent. The other two significant categories are food products with around a quarter, a quota bound to vary depending on weather conditions in the individual countries, and trade in fuels, typically re-export of oil products. The dominant position of manufactured goods is highly relevant for considerations regarding the design of a possible trading arrangement that could make the region a strategic centre for gaining export experience, as well as making the necessary adjustments to the product, organization of production and technology before exposure to the world market.

Concerning the internal balance of the SADCC trade, not surprisingly, a surplus was accumulated by Zimbabwe and to a lesser extent Swaziland in the period 1982–84. The remaining countries experienced negative balances. Of the total intra regional trade two-thirds was balanced bilaterally. Had some kind of multilateral clearing of payments existed, it would only have been able to match an additional ten per cent of the intra regional trade. The rest would have had to be paid in cash (SADCC, 1986c, p.15).

Trade of the SADCC countries with the rest of the PTA only accounted for 0.5 per cent of imports and 1 per cent of total SADCC exports in 1982 (ibid., calculated from table 13, p.139). The main trading partner is the most industrially developed country in East Africa – Kenya, and the main trader among the SADCC countries is Kenya's neighbour – Tanzania. However, it is the very low level of the trade that is really significant, and it confirms, at least at that time, the existence of a natural division regarding trade between a northern and a southern part of the PTA with Tanzania in an uncertain middle position.

We can now make a closer scrutiny of trade between the SADCC countries and South Africa. This may be approached both from a SADCC and a South African angle. Here the SADCC side of the relationship is first in focus. To this end reference is made to table 3.9 above. There, 1984 figures revealed that 9 per cent of SADCC's exports went to South Africa, and 37 per cent of their imports originated in South Africa. This is broadly in line with SADCC's calculations based on 1982 data that reached 7 and 30 per cent (ibid., p.7) for the same correlations

Thus, as a group the SADCC countries had relatively strong, but unbalanced ties to the South African economy – imports by far outmatched exports; in 1982 by 6:1, and almost the total trade deficit towards the world of 1.7 billion US$ was accumulated by trade with South Africa, whereas trade with the rest of the world more or less balanced. This may be seen as a continuation of a pattern, where the SADCC countries used their traditional surpluses in commodity trade with the rest of the world for purchases in South Africa, mainly of manufactures; but in the 1980s the surpluses had turned to deficits, because of the reduced receipts from commodity exports.

However, again the overall figures cover wide inter country heterogeneity, as was briefly touched upon above. Table 3.9 reveals that Angola and Tanzania have no trade links with South Africa. The SACU member countries have extremely high indices especially for imports from South Africa, but exports to South Africa are also substantial for all except Botswana. The latter's exports behave more like the remaining group of countries: Malawi, Mozambique, Zambia and Zimbabwe. They vary from one per cent in Zambia to 18 per cent in Zimbabwe. The latter country's exports are of special interest not only because of their size, but also because of their composition. Data from 1983 indicate that more than half of the value of exports to South Africa consisted of manufactured products,[32] and in 1992 manufactured exports made up 47 per cent of Zimbabwean exports to South Africa.[33] Especially textiles, clothing, shoes and furniture from Zimbabwe find a market in South Africa. South Africa is the largest supplier of imports to Zimbabwe with around 20 per cent of total imports.[34] Zambia receives the same share of imports from South Africa, whereas Malawi gets 40 per cent and Mozambique 10 per cent import needs covered by South Africa in 1984.

One might argue that in order to get a more realistic overall statistical picture of SADCC's trade ties with South Africa, the two countries that in the mid 1980s had no trade at all with South Africa – Angola and Tanzania – should be excluded from the statistics. Conversely, one could also find arguments for the standpoint that the SACU member countries should be left out, because they are in reality part and parcel of a larger South African domestic market. Depending on the constellation, the percentage share of trade for SADCC as a group with South Africa will increase or decrease.[35] However, statistics as such are not that important. What is really interesting is that by excluding these countries the remaining countries provide a focus on the success or otherwise of SADCC's initial goal of reducing dependence on South Africa, because in comparison to the SACU countries they are not bound to a comprehensive trade treaty with Pretoria, and in contrast to Tanzania and Angola they actually do have some trade with South Africa that could be targeted for a reduction and attempts to switch, for example, to other countries in the region. The group is likewise worth highlighting when future trading arrangements with a democratic South Africa are discussed, because they lack an overall framework for enhancement of trade although some bilateral arrangements exist, and at the same time they are traditional, and geographically close, trading partners of South Africa and both sides know each other's market relatively well. The position of Tanzania is difficult with one leg in the northern and another in the southern part of the PTA, but if peace comes to Angola, there is a great potential for expansion of trade with South Africa on the basis of Angola's high purchasing power, due mainly to its oil production and diamond mining.

We can now switch the approach and try to analyse the trade from a South African angle. Here we have the added advantage of enabling the presentation of some more recent data. Generally, analysis of South Africa's trade with Africa is extremely difficult, because in the period 1986 to 1991 statistical information on trade with African countries was kept secret by the state for strategic reasons, as a result of the international sanctions. At the time of writing the present book, the South African government had not begun revealing the figures. However, in 1991 some trade data were leaked to the press. They showed that South Africa traded with all but two African countries in 1990 although the trade sanctions had not been lifted (*Finansies & Tagniek*, 1991). Moreover, trade was on the increase. Maasdorp writes in 1993: 'South Africa's trade with Africa expanded rapidly in the last few years – by 40 per cent in 1989, 22 per cent in 1990 and 25 per cent in 1991' (Maasdorp and Whiteside, 1993, p.16). The following table gives a break down of the figures from 1990.

Table 3.12
South Africa's trade with main groups of countries in Africa, 1990
(million South African Rand (S.A. Rand))

	Exports	Imports	Total
SACU	8861	1440	10301
Rest of SADCC (6 countries)	2426	563	2989 *
Rest of PTA (10 countries)	349	27	376 *
Rest of Africa (excl. SADCC/PTA)	1294	123	1417 *
Total Africa	12930	2153	15083 *
Total of all countries	60929	44125	105054
SACU as per cent of total	14.5	3.3	9.8
SADCC incl. SACU as per cent of total	18.5	4.5	12.7 *
Africa as per cent of total	21.2	4.9	14.4 *

* Minor corrections have been made by the author to ensure internal consistency of the table
Source: *Finansies & Tagniek*, 4 October 1991 and 15 May 1992 (here quoted from Maasdorp and Whiteside, 1993, p.15)

Several features in the above deserve to be mentioned. Starting from the top the large exports from South Africa to the SACU markets are worth noting. They are remarkable taking into consideration the smallness of the economies of the countries in question, and point at the potential of intensified trade with other larger countries. Conversely, trade with Africa outside Southern Africa is minimal in 1990. Sanctions surely play a role and there is obviously a potential for an increase, if South Africa remains competitive, and the African countries have sufficient economic demand. It is also worth focusing on SADCC's 19 per cent share of South Africa's exports and 13 per cent share of total trade. The latter is precisely double the figure for 1984 (table 3.9). The large imbalance between South African exports to the SADCC countries and it imports from the same group was mentioned above, and the situation has not changed since 1984. The ratio is still 6:1 in favour of South Africa. Moreover, the lion's share of imports from Africa originates in the other SACU countries. Outside SACU Zimbabwe is totally dominant as an exporter to South Africa, although Malawi and Mozambique come in as minor suppliers. Zimbabwe also takes the larger part of South Africa's non-SACU exports to Africa, but Zambia, Mozambique and Malawi each receive between half and a third of the Zimbabwean amount in 1990. The country information is based on the following data:

Table 3.13
South Africa's trade with the SADCC countries, 1990 (1000 S.A. Rand)

	Exports	Imports
Angola	49 551	59
Botswana*	3 836 790	181 920
Lesotho*	1 578 190	81 850
Malawi	378 309	81 130
Mozambique	432 151	30 388
Namibia*	1 866 960	495 260
Swaziland*	1 569 590	681 250
Tanzania	10 319	2 580
Zambia	494 350	6 582
Zimbabwe	1 061 801	441 553
Total	11 286 831	2 002 572

* The figures for the SACU countries are approximates
   Sources: Finansies & Tagniek, 4 October 1991, Economist Intelligence
   Unit, 1992a and Economist Intelligence Unit, 1992b, here quoted from
   Maasdorp and Whiteside, 1993, p.15

While the table as such has been commented on above, there is an important qualification regarding the commodity composition of the South African exports. Again manufacturing industry is in the forefront, as highlighted in the following quotation from a SADCC Macro-Economic Study conducted by C. Chitepa of Malawi and R. Davies from South Africa (1992):

> ... this trade [South African exports to non-SACU Africa] accounts for nearly a third of all manufactured exports ... Trade with SACU partners is estimated to involve manufactured goods of a roughly similar value. Among the main products making up this trade are steel products, chemicals, paper products, foodstuffs, motor vehicles and mining equipment.[36]

Once more the prominence of the manufacturing sector illustrates the potential of combining the enhancement of this sector with the challenge of expanding regional trade, and encountering a framework in which this can be done in order to secure overall growth of the economy.

Let us end up this section on trade with a comparison of the level of intra regional trade in Southern Africa with other regions of Africa and with the world. Taking Sub-Saharan Africa as a whole, the World Bank (1991b, p.55) has in a 1991 study estimated intra regional trade to six per cent of the total trade of the countries in 1983. Again this covers wide differences between countries and to a lesser extent between regions. Below is provided an overview of the main regional groups in Africa and selected regional organizations from other continents.

Table 3.14
Intra regional trade of selected regional organizations, 1983
(percentage share of total trade)

CEAO	9
ECOWAS	6
MRU	1
UDEAC	3
PTA	7
SADCC	4
Andean Pact	6
LAFTA/LAIA	11
CACM	23
ASEAN	14

Abbreviations: CEAO: West African Economic Community (Communauté Economique de l'Afrique de l'Ouest); ECOWAS: Economic Community of West African States; MRU: Manu River Union; UDEAC: Central African Customs and Economic Union (Union Douanière et Economique de l'Afrique Centrale); PTA: Preferential Trade Area for Eastern and Southern African States; SADCC: Southern African Development Coordination Conference; LAFTA/LAIA: Latin American Free Trade Association/Latin American Integration Association; CACM: Central American Common Market; ASEAN: Association of South-East Asian Nations
Sources: all except SADCC: Mansoor, 1992, p.424: for SADCC; table 3.9
(1984 data)

During the 1980s the levels indicated are not likely to have changed significantly for the majority of the groups, except for two: ASEAN and CACM. In 1990 ASEAN registered an increase of 19 per cent of intra-regional trade, as a share of total exports. Conversely, in the same year trade among the CACM countries decreased to 14 per cent of total exports. The approximate corresponding level for the European Community is two thirds and for the US–Canadian Free Trade Area one third of total exports in 1990 (Melo and Panagariya, 1992a, p.16ff.), The apparent message of the table is that SADCC is at the very low end, both in the world and in Sub-Saharan Africa. It is within this fragile framework that the attempts were made in the 1980s to enhance regional trade and boost industrial development with a regional perspective. This is the focus of the next sections. However, as the data exclude South Africa, they are obviously not representative for the physical and geographical realities of Southern Africa. Simple addition in table 3.9 tells us that the SADCC countries received more than 40 per cent of their imports from the region and sold 13 per cent of their exports in the region in 1984. Moreover, the above scrutiny of the South African side of the equation revealed how trade with SADCC had doubled in importance for South Africa, reaching 13 per cent of total trade in 1990, with a steep upward trend in the following years. Chapter 5 on Mozambique confirms the increased weight of trade with South Africa in the 1990s. This places Southern Africa in the forefront among developing nations in Africa and Latin America regarding regional trade, and indicates the relevance and expediency of finding a formula able to fortify this in a post-apartheid scenario, making it an asset in relation to manufacturing development, and avoiding evident risks of polarization, and of an unequal distribution of costs and benefits that the exceptionally strong positions of Zimbabwe and especially of South Africa entail.

3.4   SADCC's industry programme

SADCC's industry programme originates from 1981 whereas a trade policy first was formulated in 1986. I shall deal with the two areas separately and take industry first. The attempts of SADCC to define and implement an industrial policy can conveniently be divided into three periods. However, only the first two periods will be dealt with here. The first covers the period 1981 till 1988; it is characterized by the many and diverse investment projects that SADCC presented for foreign funding, combined with some work done on industrial rehabilitation and industrial services. The second period stretches from 1988 till 1992; it is marked by a scrapping of the investment projects and a triple focus on industrial services, improvement of the investment climate and creating a framework for the establishment of regional industrial projects. Further, we see an increasing emphasis on the enterprise sector and the market as the driving forces of industrial development and a corresponding contraction in the role of planning and state intervention. In August 1992 the new Treaty transforming SADCC to SADC was approved, and the work in the industrial sector naturally turned to the elaboration of the umbrella protocols that would govern interaction within the area.

The discussion of how to formulate an industry programme for SADCC was initiated already in 1980. Tanzania was given the responsibility of drafting a plan, and subsequently submitted a proposal, which was approved by the member states at SADCC's Council of Ministers Meeting in Blantyre, November 1981. Five objectives were identified for the sectoral development; they were later condensed to the following three.[37]

1   Reducing external dependence on imports of industrial products and inputs from outside the region, especially from South Africa.

2   Increasing the size, scope and diversity of the industrial sector both nationally and regionally.

3   Increasing the linkages within the national and regional economies as a means of creating an integrated and self-reliant economy.

In an attempt to specify these rather vague guidelines, a meeting of SADCC Ministers of Industry in Arusha in September 1982 laid down the following specific criteria for the selection of industrial projects (SADCC, 1985b, p.2).

(a) The ability of the project to meet internal consumption and have a surplus for export, particularly to the SADCC region.

(b) The need for such a project to obtain raw materials within SADCC.

(c) The possibility of transporting raw materials and products within the SADCC region.

Additional specific requirements were that there should exist a funding gap in foreign exchange; that the project should be bankable (economically viable), and that it should have a reasonable implementation period. These criteria should enable a distinction between purely national and regional industrial projects. They were, however, still broadly framed and did not fulfil their objective, as later became evident.

The inherent strategy was to become self-reliant – by import substitution – in relation to industries that satisfied the demands within the listed basic needs areas: food, clothing, housing, health, water and power supply, transportation and education.[38] First nine, and in 1984 a further seven, industrial subsectors were defined as having priority in the programme. In addition, the original programme stressed the development of core industries in the region. The latter had a long term perspective of creating and expanding heavy industries like iron and steel, engineering industries and basic chemicals. Moreover, the plan underlined the need for simultaneous development of a regional trade programme, but this was deferred for future action. The theoretical background for the industrial strategy as such seemed to be the author C. Thomas, and his advocacy of an industrialization based on production of goods that fulfilled basic needs, using basic materials being transformed in industries with maximum forward and backward linkages.[39]

In late 1982 a Council of Ministers of Industry was established to direct the sector, and to support their work an Industrial Officials Sub-Committee was created. Tanzania retained the responsibility for the SADCC Industrial Coordinating Division (ICD – later SITCD, SADCC Industry and Trade Coordinating Division), which functioned as a special unit within the Tanzanian Ministry of Industries and Trade (SADCC, 1986d, pp.1–7; SADCC, 1984c, p.1). Like other SADCC sector secretariats, the main tasks of the ICD were to elaborate proposals for the sectoral strategy, to guide the selection of regional projects and to facilitate donor support for the projects. When a donor had made a commitment to the financing of a specific project, implementation was a bilateral issue between the donor and the country in which the project was located. In each member country an Industry Contact Point was created within the respective Ministries of Industry. After approval from the Council of Ministers, 88 projects – 33 for studies and 55 for capital investment were presented to the Maseru Consultative Conference in 1983. Total project costs of the 1983 programme were about US$ 1500 million with a foreign exchange component of approximately 80 per cent (SADCC, 1984d, p.47).[40] The response from the donor and investor community seemed rather reluctant and up until December 1983 commitments were about US$ 240 million (SADCC, 1984c, p.1). An 'Industrial Projects Implementation Workshop' was held in Harare in January 1984. The workshop was very well attended – also by businessmen – and gave rise to high expectation by SADCC of additional pledges[41] that, however, for the larger part did not materialize.

Since 1984, two additional areas were increasingly emphasized: industrial support services and industrial rehabilitation.[42] The latter in fact, in 1986, became the area of highest priority within the industrial programme. In August 1985, a workshop was held in Arusha on regional industrial rehabilitation. Criteria were defined for a selective rehabilitation of industry. Eligible were: industries which utilized indigenous resources; industries which had export possibilities; priority basic needs and core industries.

In undertaking rehabilitation projects, account would be taken of existing and potential inter-linkages between the industrial sector and other sectors, especially agriculture and transport. Priority in rehabilitation was given to cement and cement products, fertilizers, leather and leather goods, oils and fats, and textiles. Studies were initiated for these sectors. SADCC was aware that rehabilitation without careful analysis in relation especially to the import content of investment and current inputs for production, might simply be a waste of resources. This was discussed in SADCC's Macro-Economic Survey from 1986, which perceived rehabilitation as a chance of adapting the industrial sector to the scarcity of foreign exchange: 'The point we are making here is that rehabilitation should be used to contribute to effecting the desired structural change instead of attempting to revive every industrial capacity which has deteriorated' (SADCC, 1985e, p.155).

The industrial support services included the following elements (SADCC, 1987a, p.6ff.):

- standardization and quality control;
- research and development;
- engineering design and other product development activities;
- management and skills development services;
- industrial consultancy services;
- intra-regional industrial linkages/information exchange;
- investment policies and mechanisms – harmonization;
- small/medium scale technology development.

Concerning standardization and quality control, a SADCC expert group was established, but did not accomplish any visible tasks before 1988. National Standards bodies only existed in four of the nine SADCC countries (SADCC, 1989a, p.17). Regarding investment policies, a first compilation of national investment codes, etc. was made for the Gaborone Consultative Conference in January 1987 (SADCC, 1986e). In the remaining areas, preparatory work and studies begun. As to the core industries, preliminary surveys were made of the iron and steel and engineering industries, but in-depth studies were still to be made in these sectors as well as in the area of basic chemicals.

That left in 1987/88 priority basic needs industries as the only area of apparent practical progress for increasing industrial production in the region. Consequently, there is good reason to examine the relative success of the implementation of the programme. A survey was made by the author of this book in 1988 (Haarlov, 1988, pp.52–70). The results are summarized below. They reveal a certain ambiguity regarding the actual sums committed, the sectoral composition and country distribution.

The 1987 programme for priority basic needs industries was the one presented originally in Maseru in 1983 with some modifications and additions. In 1987, the number of investment projects was still at 55, but the total cost of implementation had increased to US\$ 1,545 million. Of this amount US\$ 1,304 million (84 per cent) were required in foreign exchange. The very low local participation reflected the reduced availability of foreign exchange, and decline in local industrial production which might have provided investment inputs; but at the same time one must not dismiss the existence of a motive from member states to reduce – even excessively – their own participation, and thereby costs of the cooperation. In the following the focus is on the foreign exchange component, not because it constitutes the larger part of the investments, but because the local part was already or should have been secured before a project was included in the programme, and reflecting that the success of securing foreign funding was decisive for the realization of the projects. The table below illustrates the status of the industrial programme as it was presented to the Consultative Conference in Gaborone in February 1987.

Table 3.15
Status of SADCC's industrial projects; foreign exchange component, 1987 (costs in millions of US$ and share of total in per cent)

Category	No.	Costs	Share of total
A1 Completed projects	4	188.4	14.4
A2 Projects under implementation	14	75.6	5.8
A3 Projects under negotiation	10	122.8	9.4
A4 Projects requiring funding	6	885.2	67.9
A5 Projects being revised	10	32.2	2.5
Total	44*	1,304.2	100.0

* A further 11 projects are deleted or suspended, thus adding up to 55 projects
Source: calculation by the author based on data in SADCC, 1987a[43]

Note can be taken of the relatively small size in terms of both number and value of the projects that were completed or under implementation. The 18 projects only represented about 20 per cent of the total project costs. Moreover, in comparison to the secured funding in 1984 of US$ 236 million mentioned earlier, only an additional US$ 28 million had been injected since then. If projects under negotiation with foreign funders were included, the categories A1–A3 still only added up to 30 per cent of the value of the projects. The major part of the programme was tied to only four capital intensive projects in category A4 that had not found any funding. Among the completed projects, just one project represented 99 per cent of the total value: the Mufindi Pulp and Paper Mill in Tanzania. In 1989 T. Oestergaard looked into the history of this project, and found that the financing of the project in fact was settled in 1977–79, and none of the local or foreign financiers considered it to be a SADCC project (Oestergaard, 1989a, p.62). If the Mufindi project's US$ 187 million are subtracted in the above table the percentage of secured funding (A1+A2) is only seven per cent and the categories A1–A3 are reduced to 19 per cent of the adjusted total project value.

We can then turn to the sectoral distribution of the projects. The following table provides an overview.

Table 3.16

Sectoral distribution of the foreign exchange component of SADCC's industrial projects, 1987 (per cent)

Sector	Share of A1–A3*	Share of all projects
Salt	3.5	1.0
Textiles	4.0	3.0
Fertilizer, pesticides & insecticides	35.5	63.0
Tractors and Farm implements	1.5	1.0
Pulp and Paper	48.5	30.0
Cement	6.5	2.0
Industrial chemicals	0.5	0.0^
Total	100.0	100.0

* See table 3.15
^ The figure is below 0.5 per cent

Source: see table 3.15

The dominance of two subsectors: fertilizers, pesticides and insecticides and pulp and paper is striking. They constituted 84 per cent of the projects with funding secured or under negotiation and 93 per cent of the value of all projects. The projects promoted in SADCC's industry investment programme within these sectors were large and capital intensive. The prominent position of the two sectors did not correspond to the expressed strategy for developing a range of basic needs industries, and they appeared to be in disaccord with the actual capabilities of absorption of the member states, and their increased emphasis on smaller, easily managed projects.

Attention can now be switched to the final parameter: the distribution of projects between the different SADCC countries. The results are reflected in Table 3.17 overleaf.

In both columns Tanzania is in the unique situation of representing more than half of the project value. Also in both columns it is easy to distinguish a number two country with a bit more than a quarter of the value: Malawi for the projects secured or under negotiation, and Mozambique for all projects. Again, note must be taken of Tanzania's dominant position in column A1–A3 largely due to the dubious SADCC project: Mufindi Pulp and Paper Mill. Malawi's strong showing in the same column was a result of negotiations over one large fertilizer project. However, even with these comments, it is clear that the table reveals a certain imbalance among the countries. In fact, Angola, Botswana, Lesotho, Swaziland and Zimbabwe are not really part of the programme, and the Zambian participation is small. Again, the distribution does not correspond to any conscious strategy judging from relevant SADCC industry sector documents. The 1980 Lusaka Declaration stresses an equitable or balanced regional development.[44] In relation to the distribution of industrial projects this could be interpreted in various ways: each country should have the same share; the countries with the least developed industrial sectors should be favoured; or the distribution should be made according to for example population, size of the economy, geographic area etc.; there could also be trade-offs taking into consideration the distribution of benefits in other sectors. However, the issue of balance in the industry programme was apparently never elaborated on by SADCC. Moreover, with SADCC's way of functioning it was up to the donors to pick and chose which projects, if any, should be promoted, and SADCC would in all likelihood not be in a position to block an investment because a given country already had received its agreed share of projects.

Table 3.17

Distribution by country of SADCC industrial projects, foreign exchange component, 1987 (per cent)

Country	Share of A1–A3*	Share of all projects
Angola	0.0	0.0
Botswana	1.0	0.5
Lesotho	0.5	0.5
Malawi	28.0	8.5
Mozambique	8.5	26.0
Swaziland	0.5	0.0
Tanzania	55.5	55.5
Zambia	3.5	7.5
Zimbabwe	2.5	1.5
Total	100.0	100.0

* See table 3.15

Source: see table 3.15

More likely and pragmatic explanations behind the unbalanced figures might be that attention to the industry programme was largest in the host country for the SADCC coordinating unit: Tanzania. Moreover, for Tanzania and Mozambique – both of which had centralized economies with a relatively high level of state intervention in industry and priorities similar to the ones reflected in SADCC's industrial programme – it was easy to shift some of their planned industrial projects from the national level to the SADCC umbrella. The opposite situation was found in the market economies of

Botswana, Lesotho and Swaziland. Zimbabwe, with its relatively developed industrial sector, probably did not see any necessity to use SADCC as a vehicle for industrial progress; on top of this, industrial development, with the exception of small scale industry, was – in spite of socialist rhetoric – nearly exclusively a private sector domain in Zimbabwe. Zambia and Malawi were placed between Zimbabwe on the one hand, and Tanzania and Mozambique on the other. The Malawian participation was a bit larger and the Zambian somewhat smaller than what could be expected from the size of their economies, and both could be coincidental. Note might be taken that the top three participants in SADCC's industrial programme – Mozambique, Malawi and Zambia – all are territorial neighbours with Tanzania. This would add a geopolitical angle to the explanations. The Angolan absence from the programme is probably mostly due to its lack of resources to become involved, because of the war situation in the country. In general its isolated position in relation to the rest of the SADCC countries also plays a role, especially before the Namibian independence in 1990.

SADCC's industry programme was criticized by academics from within the region, who felt that there was a too heavy foreign influence on SADCC's industrial programme. Writing about SADCC's industrial sector D.B. Ndlela (1987, p.56) exposed the point:

One of the main factors of the region's failure to evolve regional policies that are designed to transform the regional economy may be the overt and covert influences of the extra regional elements. This is particularly relevant in the case of the SADCC ... SADCC seems to have allowed decision-making in the selection and implementation of projects to be a domain of external technical assistance with growing involvement of direct and indirect investment by ... the transnational corporations.

The underlying understanding seemed to be that planning and harmonization from inside the region should be sufficient, and necessary for an implementation of SADCC's industrial strategy with basic needs and core industry development based on local resources. Any outside input was apparently regarded as harmful intervention. The quotation originates from a highly regarded academic publication from 1987, when the SADCC countries, as discussed above, were near economic collapse, because of the lack of foreign exchange. Therefore, it seems odd that foreign investment was rejected in its totality, instead of a qualitative discussion of the pros and cons, including ways and means of avoiding or reducing negative aspects of foreign investment, and on the other hand utilize their obvious benefits to enhance national and regional industrial development. The quotation might be seen as an expression of the extreme positions that sometimes were taken within the self-reliance, inward-looking school of thought; it was often coupled with a somewhat idealistic political analysis of the results African politicians could reach without foreign interference.

Another point of criticism was that SADCC did not go systematically or far enough in establishing a new industrial structure in the region. This aspect was pinpointed in an article by T. Mkandawire (1985, p.8ff.) in *Zimbabwe Journal of Economics* already in 1985.

> Although the industrial projects are designated as 'SADCC projects' nearly all of them are national and could have been carried out SADCC or no SADCC ... nowhere is there evidence that they are a result of clearly sectoral programming by some supranational body. Each member simply submits a list of projects which are then lumped together in a kind of regional shopping list ... There is no ranking of projects according to some regional 'social welfare function'... Nowhere is there an indication as to which projects SADCC member states would collectively fund as a matter of priority even if aid donors were not interested.

On the basis of the above analysis of sectoral composition and country distribution of projects, there seems to be a good deal of truth in the view that SADCC's industrial investment projects were somewhat haphazard. At the same time the quote reveals a misconception concerning the character of SADCC. Mkandawire is in his understanding of SADCC far beyond the regional corporation model of the organization, and well into a type of regional integration, most likely development integration, with emphasis on the 'dirigiste' element, accompanied by a centrally planned economic leaning. This was not in line with the vast differences between the economic systems of the SADCC countries in the mid 1980s, or with the growing influence of the IMF and World Bank-inspired or directed structural adjustment programmes, which directly or indirectly implied that both nationally and regionally planned industry development were on the retreat.

SADCC itself was not blind to some of the weak points of the programme. In the 1986 report on industry to the consultative conference it was stated that: 'A number of industrial projects submitted to SADCC for external funding [from member states] could have obtained such funding from internal resources' (SADCC, 1986d, p.6). This can be seen as a comment on the probably excessive dependence on foreign funds for realising projects. Regarding the selection of projects, SADCC lamented that: 'Some of the SADCC industry projects did not conform to the criteria to have the prerequisite for priority regional project selection.' Moreover, some of the project proposals were, according to SADCC, simply too poorly prepared.

The criticism from inside and outside the organization, coupled with the low level of donor response, and the changed economic conditions internationally and nationally are the elements I would single out as the main reasons behind a review of SADCC's industry sector strategy initiated in 1987/88 and finalized in August 1989.[45] The industrial projects continued to be presented at consultative conferences in 1988 and 1989,[46] but when the strategy was presented to the cooperating partners in the beginning of 1990 the scrapping of the priority investment projects was a fact.[47]

What were the main elements of the new strategy? To see this more clearly, let us recapitulate the objectives of the old one: reduction of the dependence on imports of manufactures, expansion of diversity and size of industry, creating a sectorally interlinked, integrated and self-reliant industrial sector based on local resources. The priority areas of the old strategy were: industrial rehabilitation, priority industries, core industries, industrial support services, small/medium scale technology development, investment policies and mechanisms.[48] The results were disappointing: with the collapse of the investment programme for priority industries, the sober judgement of possible practical, substantial progress in implementing SADCC's initial industrial programme must conclude that the bottom line still showed zero or just a bit above in 1989.

The new strategy[49] broadened and increased the number of objectives, and added indicative targets for a year 2000 scenario to some of them. The desired expansion of the industrial sector was codified to an annual industrial growth rate of 7 per cent, increased share of industry in GDP to 17 per cent, and the creation of an additional 0.5 million jobs in manufacturing industry by the year 2000. The objective of reducing dependence on imports was translated to a targeted fall from 46 to 35 per cent in consumption of manufactures purchased abroad by the year 2000; apart from that, import and export dependence on South Africa should be reduced, but no targets were defined. Increased production should, moreover, be achieved by elements that in reality had already been interpreted in the original objectives: increased capacity utilization, selective rehabilitation and development of a capital and producer goods industry. New among the objectives were the inclusion of the rate of savings and investments with specific targets; plus fostering of small-scale labour intensive industries and adoption of appropriate technology as well as maximum use of the domestic human resource base. Increasing the level of manufactured exports to total exports and the ratio of industrial exports to total industrial production was also new. To this was added intra-regional trade, which should reach 12 per cent in the year 2000.

According to my analysis, there were few real changes. The definition of targets were based on thorough analysis, but had little meaning, as SADCC in its capacity as instrument for regional cooperation only had the possibility of influencing a few of the elements relevant for regional industrial growth. The inclusion of savings and investment was a healthy aspect, as it indicated that SADCC no longer paid exclusive attention to physical production, and because the low levels of savings and investments were important weaknesses of industrial development. The focus on increased manufactured exports was not prominent in the presentation of objectives, but it indicated that the prior total preoccupation with import-substitution industrialization had now become somewhat modified.

An important innovation was that the relationship between the national and the regional level was taken into consideration in the formulation of strategy, and a realistic understanding seemed to dominate. It reflected the conditions of a coordination venture, where 'member states continue to design and implement their own individual industrial policies' (SADCC, 1990a, p.22), but it is the broad common ground which is really interesting, as illuminated by the following quote:

> In light of possible different policy priorities at national level, the aim of the regional industrial strategy is to establish a broad framework that reconciles national and regional interests, and to which all member states can subscribe ... In the light of the differences between countries in respect of the size of their industrial sectors, resource endowments and different stages of development; a broad and comprehensive regional strategy is required, though one in which priorities may differ from country to country (ibid., pp.22 and 45).

In relation to the innumerable possibilities of national conflicts embedded in industrial cooperation and integration, as discussed in chapter 2, the above recognition of the different national priorities and interests seemed a sound point of departure in order not to define overambitious plans.

However, what really distinguished the new strategy – at least in theory – was the inclusion of two factors: the enterprise community and market oriented macroeconomic advice to member states. Regarding the former, note that it was not yet the private sector as such which was promoted, but rather the managers of factories and mills – whether private or state – whose importance was recognized, and who according to the new strategy should have a larger say in SADCC policy implementation. The possibility of the business community also influencing policy formulation was probably quite out of the question at the time. How much larger the influence on implementation was intended to be, was not clear and probably disputed at the time, but the inclusion of the business community might at any rate be interpreted as a move away from the pervasive state dominance of industry planning that had prevailed in several SADCC countries, and which was reflected in the work of SITCD. SADCC's 1990 report on industry to the consultative conference states that the strategy 'acknowledges the role of the enterprise community as the principal vehicle for the industrialisation of the SADCC region' (ibid., p.1). This was coupled with the creation of a SADCC Regional Business Council in March 1989. It should cooperate with National Business

Councils, which existed in all countries but Angola and Swaziland, and 'intended to provide mechanisms for involving the enterprise community in the implementation of SADCC programmes' (ibid., p.2). Thus, the initial emphasis was on the business people executing what SADCC would define and not vice versa. However, characteristic of the difficulty of finding its own feet in the matter SADCC recognized that the pattern of industrialization 'depends on the perception of entrepreneurs and investors' (ibid., p.32). Here the new market orientated macroeconomic policies also came in. SADCC would influence such perceptions 'through the creation of a stable and positive investment climate, which in turn is a function of appropriate efficiently administered economic policies' (ibid.). What kind of policies were SADCC referring to? They mentioned specifically 'a system of flexible and market-oriented foreign exchange rates' (ibid., p.32ff.): 'a tariff-based system of industrial protection', avoiding non-tariff barriers and industrialization behind very high tariff walls; 'effective anti-inflationary policies', which are not elaborated, but indirectly, the statement recognizes that prices will be determined basically by market forces, and not through state price setting which had hitherto predominated in the majority of the countries. Lastly, the industrial strategy called for 'freedom from arbitrary government intervention in business decision-making'; references are made to project approvals, prices and labour relations and to avoidance of red tape and corruption. With this policy orientation SADCC must be said to have been ideologically at least on a par with, and probably somewhat more market oriented than, the mainstream of economic thinking within Governments in the region at the time.

In its new strategy SADCC maintained a mention, but not much more, concerning selective rehabilitation of industry. Industry support services were, however, shifted over more or less unchanged into the new programme, and as before the practical focus was especially on information exchange plus standards and quality control (ibid., p.49ff.), SADCC maintained its intention of establishing a 'single regional investment code' (ibid., p.43).

In SADCC's 1990 industry and trade report the priority industry investment projects are abandoned with the criticism that 'the programme itself did not sufficiently articulate the strategy, institutional mechanisms and programme framework to ensure that priority industry projects are identified, which have a regional impact in terms of sourcing raw materials inputs, and marketing finished products across national boundaries' (ibid., p.22). Consequently, in the new strategy SADCC sets itself the goal of enhancing the establishment of viable regional industries based on raw materials from the region and with access to the regional market (ibid., pp.1, 39ff., 45–9, 53 and SADCC, 1991a, pp.1 and 4ff.). In order to assess whether a project is genuinely regional or not, the strategy listed a number of criteria (SADCC, 1990a, p.53): the project should contribute towards reaching the objectives of SADCC's industry programme; it should involve more than two countries regarding input, output, investment or manpower; it should be commercially and technically feasible. However, the criteria – except for the specific mention of 'two countries' – were more or less identical with the existing ones. SADCC must have felt this and promised that more detailed criteria would be worked out and rigorously adhered to. But although these were never published, it is possible to extract more clues as to what SADCC was aiming at. SADCC wanted 'to foster cooperation through the coordination of major projects so as to ensure the exploitation of economies of scale and avoiding duplication and competition' (ibid., p.42). The regional industry projects 'should have upstream and downstream linkages with other productive sectors. The programme should give priority to intermediate and capital goods industries, while not neglecting viable investments opportunities in consumer goods and export-oriented industries' (ibid., p.45ff.), In 1989/90 SADCC, in fact, identified on this basis a number of branches and subsectors, characterized by a continued and all dominant focus on import-substituting-industrialization and local linkages. SADCC admitted that the projects typically would require heavy investment, they involved sophisticated and advanced technology, and they were sensitive to economics of scale, and needed guaranteed access to regional markets (ibid., p.48ff.), In the controlled economies of the time this required that non-tariff barriers would be abandoned for the specific products, and that excessively high tariffs lowered; that the project would be assured sufficient currency to import essential inputs; and assurances be given that the purchasers would continue buying and, equally important, had the necessary foreign exchange to do so.[50] The trade programme would include the possibility of entering into such arrangements, but the complexity of the ambition was equally clear.

To this was added the very sensible requirement, but indeed also delicate aim, of making the distribution of industry more equitable in the region. In the preamble to the new strategy, SADCC stated (ibid., p.21): 'It is essential to promote better spatial distribution of industry in the region, in order to achieve more geographically equitable industrialization'. The SADCC strategy would produce 'specific policies designed to achieve equitable distribution of industrial activities throughout the region' (ibid., p.42). SADCC would 'pay greater attention to arresting and reversing' the trend of 'polarization of industrial development' (ibid., p.45). SADCC recognized the crucial dilemma this ambition presented to the organization, since the localization of a specific project according to economic logic, might not be where the objective of equity would be met, i.e. fit into an overall pattern of balanced development:

> But if regional economic welfare is to be maximized, new industrial projects must be economically efficient. In some instances, this will conflict with the sociopolitical objective of a more equitable pattern of

regional industrialization, and some degree of trade-off between these objectives will occur (ibid., p.45).[51]

How to obtain the desired balance? SADCC seemed to have both a market-oriented and a dirigiste answer. On the one hand, SADCC hoped to ensure this through 'increased intra-regional trade, and fostering cross-border, multi-national activities such as sub-contracting and joint ventures linking enterprise sector partners from different member states' (ibid., p.21). This pure market model seemed slightly unconvincing, as the stronger partner would most likely dominate the envisaged opening up of the economies towards each other. This could, on the other hand, be contrasted with the stated intention of SADCC after due studies and consultations 'to decide on regional industrial policies, project priorities and the allocation of SADCC projects to member states' (ibid. p.45). This line of argument did not seem to be congruent with the cooperation model, where the nation state still has the last word, and it also appeared to be in contradiction to the emerging more market-oriented influence of the new strategy and in society at large.

The immense difficulties and generally negative experiences with planned or agreed regional industrial specialization of existing or new industries were discussed in chapter 2, section 2.3: 'regional cooperation' and section 2.5: 'the development integration approach'.[52] Reference is made to the complex and time-consuming planning and negotiations, and to the difficulty of obtaining among the participating states a simultaneous perception of the balance in costs and benefits of a regional industrial programme. Bureaucratic problems and delays may cover more deep rooted contradictions between countries in different stages of their industrialization, with different economic systems etc. Moreover, the possible acceptance of an economically suboptimal localization of industry is repelling when seen from an adjustment adapted market integration approach, and would be squarely against traditional advice from the IMF and World Bank, when discussing structural adjustment programmes with individual countries. Their logical argument would be that the countries are so poor that every dollar invested must receive the highest possible rate of return. Moreover, the envisaged 'ensured market' for the regional industries could easily enter into conflict with the liberalization of foreign trade that the two institutions advocated, and which – though in varying degrees and rhythms – were entailed in the market reforms under way in the SADCC countries.

To summarize the new strategy: the objectives were broadened and refined, but did not contain significant new elements in relation to the existing policy and practice. However, the prominence and inclusion of the business community was new, and so was the aspiration to advise members on conducive market oriented macroeconomic policies. SADCC maintained industrial support services as an area of priority and action; a common investment code was still the aim, whereas industrial rehabilitation was out of focus. The intention of identifying and implementing genuine regional industrial projects was the most prominent issue in the new strategy, but it was also the one which was most heavily loaded with potential problems, if an implementation should be attempted.

What then, were the results of the new strategy up to 1992/93? To take the regional industrial projects first their fate confirmed the sombre predictions. Four years after they were introduced as key elements of the new strategy not a single regional industry project had started producing or even been presented. The latest information available for this book was from January 1994, stating that 'draft proposals for the framework for the implementation' of regional industrial projects had been completed' (SADCC, 1994e, p.8). However, there were no further details as to the contents of the proposals, and no signal was given of immediate practical steps forward: rather the opposite; the draft proposals were to be included in the discussions about industry and trade protocols for the Southern African Development Community. This might well imply a serious delay if the draft plans have to be adjusted to contend with the perspective of having the highly industrialized South Africa joining the community. From 1989 to 1994 the regional industrial projects had passed through various stages: in 1991 there were reports as to 'systematic efforts made to identify regional industrial projects.' At the 1992 Consultative Conference it was revealed that the questions of preferences, obligations of host country and purchasers, and the issue of equity had not come closer to a solution. Judging from SADCC's 1993 *Industry and Trade* report it was likely that the planning approach to the regional industrial projects had been abandoned: 'The objective of the framework [for regional industrial projects] is to encourage the spontaneous development of industries by the business community'.[53] But through which type of incentives the encouragement should take place were not revealed – not even when the finalization of the draft proposal was announced in 1994.

What about the involvement of the business community – another key element of the new strategy? The main vehicle for action in this sphere was the SRBC. It was established by November 1989, but only received funds for functioning in mid 1990 (SADCC Regional Business Council, 1992, p.4ff.). Its members were the existing associations of industry and trade in the member countries. It seems to have been plagued by various problems. From the outset its relationship to SITCD and to the SADCC Secretariat was not clear. Only at the Consultative Conference in 1992 did SADCC present guidelines for cooperation (SADCC, 1992a, p.12), but these were still very vague, if not to say unclear. Perhaps the most fundamental problem was that national member organizations did not use or feel attached to SRBC, as was exemplified by their lack of payment of membership fees. In 1992 the SRBC Chairman stated : 'Most of the SADCC National Business Councils are so deep in arrears that payments will be very difficult' (SADCC Regional Business Council, 1992, p.6). Moreover, key issues were left unresolved from one annual meeting to the next.[54] An additional problem was the almost exclusive dependence on one donor – the United States Agency for International Development (USAID). The SRBC Chairman elaborated on this, and the subordinate position in relation to SADCC as such in 1992:

> What has been happening so far is that the highest policy organ, the SRBC Council, would make a resolution based on the aspirations of the business community. However, the resolutions have to be subjected to SADCC's and USAID's concurrence. ... If wishes and ambitions of the SRBC council are not respected, then we wonder which needs our organization is supposed to serve (SADCC Regional Business Council, 1992, p.5).

Finally, the duplication of efforts in relation to PTA Chambers of Commerce and Industry became more and more evident, for example regarding trade fairs and trade and investment information exchange. When the author visited SRBC in 1993 the USAID seemed on the verge of cancelling further support for SRBC, insisting on a merger with the PTA sister organization. Without this source of funds and with only a minimum of membership fees collected the future of SRBC indeed seemed bleak.[55]

We may now switch our attention to SADCC's new policy of offering advice on macroeconomic policies conducive to industrial development. As far as the author is aware this ambition never advanced beyond rather general considerations already referred to above. Even more detailed analysis and recommendations might not have succeeded in competing with the macroeconomic deliberations between the member states and the IMF and World Bank in the specific period. Independently of SADCC, the influence of market economic advice from the IMF and World Bank did, in fact, imply a substantial convergence of the macroeconomic set up in Southern Africa in the late 1980s and beginning of the 1990s. Thus, it would be a difficult case to argue that SADCC had any major impact on the harmonization of economic policies conducive to industrial development. This is an area that probably will resurface with force in connection with the envisaged SADC. The promotion of industrial services, such as common standards, will also increase in importance as markets would become more and more integrated. However, early progress would in any event have been very useful both for intra- and extra SADCC production and trade. Unfortunately, even in this relatively conflict-free area, progress was apparently slow and minimal. Therefore, in most of the many subgroups of services there is nothing or very little to report, whereas some progress has been experienced in relation to information exchange with assistance from International Trade Centre (ITC), and in the area of standardization and quality control some concrete measures have been taken with assistance again from ITC and the Nordic countries. Nevertheless, it is striking that by 1993 national standards bodies had not been established in any of the five countries that did not possess such an institution, when the activity was included in SADCC's programme in 1984 (SADCC, 1993a, p.13ff.) Regarding the possibility of reaching common investment guidelines in the SADCC region, SADCC reported in 1992 and 1993 on how investment guidelines had once more been compiled, analyzed and updated, but without any information as to tangible progress in reaching commonly defined standards (SADCC, 1992a, p.6 and SADCC, 1993a, p.4). However, one should not ignore the fact that investment rules and regulations without SADCC interference were getting closer to each other, again as a result of the IMF and World Bank advice, and the increasing realization that the region had to present itself more attractively in the international competition for foreign investment.

Let us conclude the discussion of the industry programme with a brief assessment of two elements: the Norsad fund and the SADCC initiative to establish a mechanism that could enhance cross-border investments, in spite of the scarcity of foreign exchange. They might have been important supplementary instruments in promoting industrial development, but the basic message is that both failed. The Norsad fund was part of the Nordic–SADCC Initiative[56] and its raison d'être was to provide foreign currency for joint venture companies between Nordic and SADCC firms. The joint venture companies had to be export- orientated, and could not have links with South Africa. The Norsad Fund was legally established in 1990 after protracted negotiations. However, when it was about to function in earnest, the macroeconomic environment had changed so much as a result of structural adjustment programmes, and attached balance of payment support funds, that the services of the Norsad Fund became largely superfluous. In 1993 SADCC wrote: 'Today, there exists in most member states better trade financing schemes and the problem of South Africa is on its way out. Consequently, the Fund is no longer competitive and its original mandate is in urgent need of being reviewed' (SADCC, 1993a, p.9). Thus, in the first annual report of the Norsad Fund no progress could be reported: only one out of 100 applications was approved and no money was disbursed. The report stated: 'It was soon realized that the terms and conditions specified in the Agreement and the Statutes ... were not in line with the market needs' (Norsad Fund and Norsad Agency, 1993a, p.2).[57] A review was made, and in January 1993 it was agreed to make the functioning of the Fund more flexible.[58] The requirement of export orientation was dropped, and special rules regarding South Africa would be abolished as soon as sanctions were lifted. Emphasis was put on commercial viability and the Fund was given more freedom to undertake the active promotion of joint ventures; it was to be more willing to accept risks, and to apply less stringent rules for accepting guarantees.

However, it still remains to be proved that these measures are sufficient to give the Norsad Fund a meaningful role in regional industrial development – a role that cannot be fulfilled by existing local or Nordic based industrialization institutions and development funds.[59]

We can now turn to the other additional item of SADCC's industrial programme which merits attention: the cross-border investment facility. In 1989 it was introduced in the following manner: 'In order to overcome investments across national boundaries, a study on the Cross-Border Investment Facility has been commissioned' (SADCC, 1989a, p.6). Five years later the report to the Consultative Conference in 1994 laconically stated: 'A study on the establishment of the facility has been completed but final proposals have yet to be made' (SADCC, 1994, p.14ff.). What had happened in the meantime was in fact that two studies had been made. A first study, which was concluded in 1989, and a second revised version from 1992 (Merchant Bank of Central Africa, Limited, 1992, p.[ii]). The simple idea behind the facility was to make seed capital in foreign exchange available for SADCC firms that wished to invest in other SADCC countries. The facility would be replenished from the flow of dividends and in the second study also by fees and export receipts. This was one of the precautions proposed in the second study to protect the facility from possible problems arising from currency fluctuations. Moreover, the payback period was to be a maximum of five years, and the investor should be able to ensure long term, fixed exchange rate sales. Even more conditions were set up and the construction might be considered a bit heavy and cumbersome to administer. This is admitted in the second consultancy report. It identifies two alternatives to the facility: one that restrictions on all capital movements in the SADCC countries are lifted, and second that capital movements only between the SADCC countries are allowed to flow freely (ibid., p.92). Just the mentioning of these alternatives is one more indication of how the economy in the SADCC countries changed from the 1980s to the 1990s from state control and a restrictive framework towards a more liberal economy. Consequently, mechanisms such as the Norsad Fund, and the originally conceived cross-border investment facility seemed to have lost a good deal of their logic and relevance. Nevertheless, an adopted model of the cross-border investment facility might still be necessary, and useful as free capital movements normally require somewhat more stable economies than most of the SADCC countries – even with optimistic predictions – can live up to for a number of years.

3.5 SADCC's trade programme

SADCC's trade programme may with some right be compared to a toddler that never really learned to walk. Born of the then still dynamic industrial programme of SADCC in the mid 1980s, there was a lot of enthusiasm vested in the possible qualities of the child, but these hopes were to prove difficult to fulfil.

That industry would take the first place and trade would only be added later was not quite the impression given by the Lusaka Declaration of 1980. In the document industry development was just mentioned as one among several sectors that should be studied, whereas trade held a much more prominent position. The Declaration stated:

> For trade development we recognise that many of us have existing bilateral and multilateral trade and customs arrangements. But even within these constraints we believe that there is room for substantial increases in trade among ourselves. To this end existing payment systems and customs instruments will be studied in order to build up a regional trade system based in bilaterally negotiated annual trade targets and product lists (SADCC, 1984f, p.19).

Thus, existing trading arrangements would be respected, but payment mechanisms and customs procedures were set for improvement and bilaterally agreed trade flows were expected to flourish. However, it must be noted that there is no mention of any intention of starting a market integration process by climbing the ladder from a preferential or free trade area to an economic and eventually political union, as discussed in chapter 2. There seemed to be an underlying consensus that the market integration model had caused enough failures for regional interaction and therefore should not be repeated. The traumatic closure of the East African Community in 1977 was fresh at hand and the scars of the Central African Federation were still in living memory. Nevertheless, the attitude is seldom expressed as clearly as in this quote from an unpublished document from the SADCC Secretariat in 1983 (1983a, p.1).

> To assume that expanding trade is the purpose of economic coordination is one of the two basic errors of the standard free trade area approach to economic integration. States are less concerned with trade as such than with material production, employment and economic security. The second error is to argue for an unregulated, free market approach to regional trade when, in fact, all the participating governments practice economic interventionism (even if to varying degrees) nationally ... Further, regionally as well as nationally, free markets (as opposed to managed markets) are inconsistent with ensuring an acceptable division of gains and costs.

This excerpt gives the clues to as to why production, in this case industry, is given first priority in relation to trade, and it illuminates the key parameters behind the design of the SADCC trade programme: the regulated economies and the ambition to seek balanced solutions. Against this background it was not surprising that the first initiative to activate the dormant SADCC trade profile came from the Ministers of Industry. Already in 1982 they proposed that a meeting be held to discuss the issue of trade. After approval by the Council of Ministers a meeting of the Ministers of Trade was held in Arusha in October 1983. Two reports had been prepared by the SADCC Secretariat for this meeting (SADCC, 1983a and SADCC, 1983b). They explored the subject of establishing a network of bilateral trade agreements which might later be developed into a multilateral trade system. Furthermore, they envisaged the establishment of various funds for trade financing. The reports were positively received by the Ministers. However, since the creation of SADCC in 1980, a new institution had been established that had precisely trade as its main area of action and in principle covered all the SADCC countries: the Preferential Trade Area for Eastern and Southern Africa, PTA. After decades of promotion, principally by the ECA, the organization saw the light of day in 1982. First five, then six, and in the beginning of the 1990s all SADCC members but Botswana became members of PTA. Without going into the finer details of PTA some basic features must be outlined.[60] PTA was one of the four columns or building blocks of the grand vision of a united Africa. Each area would go through several stages of integration: from preferential trading to an economic union, and in the end the areas would merge and Africa would become one economic community. These aspirations were expressed in the Lagos Declaration and Final Act of 1980 and renewed in the Abuja Treaty of 1991.[61] In all PTA's existence[62] it has struggled to make members keep to their promises of reducing trade tariffs between themselves, but serious delays in the implementation of plans have occurred. Intra-PTA tariff abolition was initially targeted for 1992, but was later postponed till the year 2000.[63] Until 1993 the tariff cuts were restricted to goods on a common list of specific interest for intra-regional trade, and the eligible products were to have been produced in factories with a majority of management positions held by nationals, and with a majority of equity capital locally owned.[64] PTA experienced some success with a central clearing house for payments between member states and a scheme for issuing of travellers cheques.[65] Useful charters on heavy vehicle transit traffic and on intra-PTA multinational enterprises were adopted, but again there were problems of adherence by members. Cooperation on policy and projects in sectors other than trade did not really get off the ground, neither did PTA's trade and development bank. In 1992 PTA launched a concrete implementation schedule for reaching the envisaged stage of a Common Market for Eastern and Southern Africa (COMESA) by the year 2000, but did not find immediate approval from all members to continue along these lines.[66] To return to the present context, what naturally worried SADCC ministers was that they might initiate something that would later turn out to be in contradiction with the PTA Treaty, and especially its stipulations regarding most favoured nation clauses, so that possible agreement between themselves would have to be extended to all PTA members.[67]

Therefore, the SADCC Ministers of Trade and Finance at their 1983 meeting in Arusha stressed that it was particularly important to 'avoid conflict with or unnecessary duplication of PTA trade development among its members' (SADCC, 1983c, p.11). They proposed a study of the issue. This was endorsed by the Council of Ministers in January 1984. In addition, the Council of Ministers requested a study of payments and clearing of trade. The studies were presented to the Council of Ministers in July 1984, but the Ministers still found that more detailed research was needed before a final decision could be made.[68] During 1985, the SADCC *Intra-Regional Trade Study* was prepared and finally submitted to SADCC in January 1986.[69] In March the same year a meeting of the Ministers of Trade was held to review the report. Sources close to the meeting revealed that the new trade measures found the firmest backing from the economies with the largest state intervention: Tanzania and Mozambique. The economically most developed country, Zimbabwe, was most hesitant, at least on the officials level, whereas Zambia, host of the PTA headquarters, was most worried about possible conflicts with the PTA Treaty. Nevertheless, the general line of recommendations of the study was adopted by the Ministers and a framework proposal for a SADCC trade programme was elaborated.[70] The proposal was approved by the SADCC Council of Ministers in June 1986. Tanzania agreed after some initial hesitation to coordinate the trade sector (SADCC, 1986h). The trade programme was for the first time presented officially to donors at the February 1987 Consultative Conference (SADCC, 1987a, p.11ff).

In the analytic background for the trade programme[71] SADCC stressed that the main reasons behind the low level of intra-regional trade were the underdeveloped nature of industry in most countries and lack of complementarity between the countries; the deficient regional transport network was another important impediment to trade; further, the lack of foreign exchange had various negative consequences: it made member countries cut down on imports and meant delayed and uncertain payments to the exporter; the length of exports credits had to be kept at a minimum, and exporting firms had difficulties in obtaining licences for import of necessary inputs for production. Moreover, companies in the region were often not familiar with each other's markets and perceived neighbours' products to be of inferior quality in relation to established OECD countries or South African suppliers; pricing could also pose a problem as the regional producers quoted to the high side, because of ineffective production, overvalued exchange rates or lack of export pricing knowledge.

This point of departure made SADCC conclude and confirm that the solution not only lay in tariff reductions or free trade. The Ministers of Trade stated that 'PTA, SACU and existing free trade and bilateral agreements fail to address the fundamental problems faced by member States ... and will, therefore, have limited incremental effect on intra-regional trade' (SADCC, 1986f, p.7). Consequently, the strategy had to be based on direct action by member Governments. At the same time, the SADCC Ministers of Trade at their 1986 meeting made a point in stressing that the SADCC countries could be blamed for not before having 'made sufficient and conscious efforts to trade among themselves.' They added that 'this attitude will need to change if there is to be a meaningful growth in intra-SADCC trade' (ibid.). This exemplifies how political will and approach were placed as the centrepiece. Enhancement of existing and new channels for regional trade would only be possible through strong political backing and sufficient capacity to influence the economic actors. Time would tell whether these requirements were to be met.

What were the main elements of the trade programme? There were four headings under which action should and could take place without coming into conflict with the PTA Treaty and other obligations:

a) system of direct trade measures and bilateral trade agreements;
b) preferences;
c) trade financing;
d) trade promotion.

a) The overall aim was to stabilize and increase existing trade flows and facilitate new ones, particularly those linked to SADCC's industry programme. Four different methods were advocated: counter-purchases, where payments could be made in goods over a period of time, provided that the involved countries perceived the exchanged goods to be of the same value, for example regarding foreign exchange content of the goods. Multi-year purchase contracts were a second possibility; they could for example stabilize fluctuating regional flows. Preferential import licensing would be necessary to make the other measures possible in countries with import controls. Product specific tariff reductions, or other financial support mechanisms, could be used as incentives for business to increase trade regionally, for example in relation to products from industrial projects. Bilateral arrangements were to be flexible and have maximum involvement of the business communities, and would depend on active promotion by joint trade commissions. Some arrangements might be in contradiction to the letter of the PTA Treaty, but as long as they were specific and limited they should be interpreted as just another way of contributing to the PTA spirit of increasing intra-African trade.

b) Regarding preferences, one proposal simply implied that the PTA members of SADCC extended the intra-PTA tariff reductions to the

SADCC countries which were not PTA members, but on a reciprocal basis. Another proposal envisaged preferences to be ceded to SADCC suppliers, when governments made purchases or donors implemented projects in the region; it might for example be a price preference of 10–20 per cent, when bids were evaluated.

c) In the area of trade financing it was proposed to establish two mechanisms: a Regional Export Credit Facility (RECF) and an Export Pre-Financing Revolving Fund (EPRF). The first would enable the SADCC countries to offer the same favourable terms of credit to regional partners as companies from the OECD countries were able to advance. The main function of the second would be to lend a company foreign exchange in order to import the necessary inputs to execute an export order. The RECF was conceived to be regional in character, whereas the EPRF would basically have a decentralized function. Funds similar to the EPRF had for some years functioned with success in Zimbabwe and Tanzania.

d) The final area of the trade programme was general trade promotion. It could include trade fairs, business visits and systematic information exchange.

What became of this programme in the years 1988 till 1992/93? In terms of practical results – very little. After going through the yearly reports on industry and trade presented at SADCC's Consultative Conferences, the publishing of a SADCC trade directory in 1992/93 and some other trade promoting efforts appear to be the only concrete positive steps taken (SADCC, 1993a, pp.1 and 18). How could this happen? It was not because the SITCD did not produce studies and proposals, hold seminars etc. On the contrary, critics would allege that they produced too much paper and talkshops – but probably these aspects only appear to dominate excessively in hindsight, because so little came out of them. Some parts of the programme became irrelevant because they depended on other factors, which did not behave as expected. Take for example the special bi- or trilateral trade arrangements and incentives foreseen for regional industrial projects. Since the latter did not advance, the trade element was blocked, too. According to the trade programme, PTA preferences ought to have been extended to the SADCC countries that were not PTA members. What happened was that the number of SADCC countries outside PTA gradually diminished, and the main problem turned out to be that the PTA members themselves did not adhere to the PTA agreements, including publishing the reduced intra-PTA tariffs. As I interpret the situation, the counter-purchases as well as multi-year purchase contracts and preferential import licensing, envisaged to stabilize and increase existing flows, fell victims to the gradual liberalization of foreign trade that took place in the same period, and the simultaneous cut back in direct government involvement in industry. Therefore, the kind of agreements envisaged would have been contrary to a key macroeconomic trend, and would have been even more difficult than before to implement. But the fact that an action might be controversial and difficult is, obviously, not the same as it being impossible or undesirable. With the right kind of interaction with the business communities, the above types of agreements might still have been possible to advance for governments in a market economic environment, and could undoubtedly in selected cases have been meaningful for trade development. Concerning preferences towards SADCC firms when tendering government and donor contracts, the Trade Ministers Committee decided in 1991 to request their respective governments to consider a system for easy access for SADCC firms to participate in tenders in the region, and to give both local and regional firms a 15 per cent price preference over foreign suppliers. Donors should untie aid and purchase more in the region. It has not been possible to detect whether this has been followed up locally, but one would suspect that any successes would have been published by SADCC (1992a, p.17) to serve as an example for others.[72]

The two trade financing facilities, RECF and EPRF were uncontroversial in relation to PTA and fulfilled obvious existing lacunas in the enhancement of trade in the region. In spite of this, they did not have more success than the rest of the programme. Already in 1988 a concrete proposal to establish EPRF was approved by SADCC (1989a, p.17). However, reports to the Consultative Conferences only announced that the existing schemes in Zimbabwe and Tanzania were expanded, while Lesotho, Malawi, Zambia formally created EPRF, but never got them fully functional, partly because of lack of funding. In Mozambique and Angola studies were only carried out in 1992.[73] The RECF was exposed to various studies, and was only approved in principle in 1991 when RECF and also RPRF were included in a proposal to establish a Comprehensive Export Financing Scheme, CEFS which would be rooted nationally but also have a regional presence. It would include loans in national currencies, guarantees and insurance, apart from the services of RECF and EPRF which would serve trade with both the regional and international markets (SADCC, 1992a, p.8ff.). However, in the beginning of 1993 SADCC was no closer to the practical implementation of the scheme. Its report on Industry and Trade stated: 'Efforts to secure funding to finance a consultancy to work out practical details for establishing the scheme are in progress' (SADCC, 1993a, p.8). A year later SADCC informed that: 'Revised terms of reference for a study have been drawn up and funding is being sought' (SADCC, 1994, p.15). In the beginning of the 1990s one might with some justification argue that – with the building up of financial markets in the SADCC countries – the two facilities and the Comprehensive Scheme would be superfluous. However, in most SADCC countries this was a medium term venture, and the type of services the facilities could have offered, would probably have had a raison d'être for a substantial period. It seems as if both the individual SADCC countries and donors were reluctant to put the issue sufficiently high on the agenda and to take the risk associated with the investment of the necessary seed capital.

Did the trade strategy change, when the industry programme was reviewed in 1989? My answer would be no. It kept the above essential features. However, a concrete target was defined of increasing the level of intra-SADCC trade from around five per cent to 12 per cent of total foreign trade, which in fact could be said to be a relatively modest goal.[74] Even so, achieving it would demand concerted facilitation and guiding from governments. Other aspects of relevance to trade, such as reducing dependence on imports of manufactured products, were mentioned above under the industry programme; likewise the industry support services which SADCC began to call the 'industry and trade support services programme' after the inclusion of trade in 1986. However, a new element emanated from a decision by the Committee of Ministers of Industry and Trade in 1992. They requested SADCC to 'design in cooperation with other regional/international organizations, appropriate, simplified, standardized and harmonized: trade rules and regulations; customs documentation and procedures; customs tariffs' (SADCC, 1993a, p.7). This must be said to be a relatively ambitious set of goals, taking into consideration the strained relations with the PTA, and the fact that the PTA felt that these matters were their exclusive sphere of action. Equally important, they were a sign that SADCC was rapidly moving towards some kind of market integration approach, but seemingly without much respect for the immense problems that were embedded in their aspiration, if the PTA's up hill struggle only to reach very limited results regarding tariffs be taken as an illustrative example.

Only a year later SADCC/SITCD came back with the honest confession that it had not been possible to advance the issue. Why? Three reasons were given: problems inherent in the legally nonbinding character of SADCC, the fact that programmes impinge on other organizations, and finally the shortage of resources (SADCC, 1994, p.1ff.). This reflected again that SADCC with the signing of the Treaty for the creation of a Southern African Development Community of August 1992 was already mentally leaving the cooperation model, and well into a sort of market integration venture, where the ambition was to establish a legally binding framework for interaction. The mention of other organizations was undoubtedly a reference to the ongoing competition with the PTA because, logically, trade in Southern Africa could not both be guided by PTA's COMESA and SADCC's new Treaty. The mention of scarce resources probably signals another problem which could turn lethal for SADCC – donors were gradually abandoning the organization, because the anti-apartheid aspect was gone, and a post-apartheid scenario in South Africa was more attractive than the hinterland. And as a consequence of an uncertainty, as to whether SADCC would be the key to regional interaction in the emerging regional order in Southern Africa. I shall briefly return to the possible future scenarios in the concluding chapter. Right now – a round up is provided of the essential features from this chapter.

3.6   Summary

The much needed diversification of the SADCC countries economies and export base, giving manufacturing industry a much more prominent position, was not achieved in the years under scrutiny. On the contrary, Sub-Saharan Africa and Southern Africa's share of world GDP and exports diminished. Stagnation and decline were catchwords for manufacturing industry development. Huge trade deficits developed towards the rest of the world, and the lack of foreign exchange became a major problem. Trade between the SADCC partners remained around 4–5 per cent of total foreign trade. Four states were identified as especially relevant for SADCC's aim of reducing dependence on imports from South Africa and expanding intra-regional trade: Zimbabwe, Zambia, Malawi and Mozambique, but no specific common measures were taken to follow up on this potential. Botswana, Lesotho and Swaziland had extremely limited room to manoeuvre due to their membership of SACU, and Angola and Tanzania did not trade much with the rest of SADCC. Among the SADCC countries Zimbabwe had an all out dominant position in manufacturing production as well as in intra-regional trade. However, if South Africa was taken into the equation, all of SADCC including Zimbabwe would be dwarfed. South Africa's manufacturing production was larger than that of the whole of Sub-Saharan Africa. Thus, from the general discussion of regional integration in the last chapter it is easy to recognize the danger of polarization around Zimbabwe in SADCC, and around South Africa, and to a lesser extent Zimbabwe in a possible new Southern African economic arrangement. The two states also fulfil the attributes of potential core states that might transfer resources to other less fortunate partner states in order to secure unlimited market access in the whole region, and achieve a higher international standing by being able to rally the whole region behind certain issues. At the same time their own developing needs will draw in the opposite direction. Interesting for designing regional trade arrangements are the facts that manufactured products constitute more than half of intra-SADCC trade, and that exports to the region are of utmost importance for certain manufacturing branches in South Africa. Compared to the low level of intra-SADCC trade, regional trade becomes relatively high, even by worldwide comparisons if South Africa is included; the SADCC countries received 40 per cent of their imports from the region and found markets for 13 per cent of exports there in the 1980s. Already in 1990 the region represented 13 per cent of South Africa foreign trade, and trade with Africa was on the increase. To its neighbours South Africa might be seen both as a source of possible domination, and as a giant market place for exports and a place for the easy purchase of imports next door. To exploit this situation without sowing the seeds of future conflicts would require a strong political will, favourable socioeconomic conditions and skilfully worked out arrangements.

For its part from the early 1980s till the beginning of the 1990s SADCC tried, under the umbrella of a cooperation approach, to further first industrial, and from the mid 1980s also regional trade development. These activities during the course of the decade did not yield any significant results. However, to establish this fact is considerably more easy than to try to explain why. In the previous chapter (2.3) we learned how excellent scholars such as Green, Ravenhill and Ndegwa all indicated that some sort of prearranged and balanced trade arrangements might have a chance of success in contrast to the market orientated arrangements that all stagnated or declined in Africa and other parts of the world in the 1980s. This was exactly what SADCC attempted. Similarly, Robson advocated that to stand a better chance of success cooperation regarding regional industries should preferably be limited to a few countries and be based on market incentives. Also this would have been possible under SADCC's industry programme, although market distortions were a problem in the 1980s. I have earlier criticized SADCC for starting out their programme for basic needs priority industries in the middle of a natural sequence: the logic of SADCC's incremental approach would rather tell policy-makers to begin with industrial support services and the harmonization of industrial policies (Haarlov, 1988, p.64). However, even after the suspension of the initial group of priority industry projects in 1989, SADCC's work with industry and trade support services did not bring about satisfactory results. We also found that trade financing facilities, which had seemed uncontroversial and highly relevant in the latter part of the 1980s were not implemented. How is it that all recommendations and efforts led to so few practical results? Probably no-one is in a position to give the final answer, but some especially relevant elements ought to be emphasized.

Perhaps the most fundamental element is the change that occurred in macroeconomic conditions and outlook during the late 1980s and beginning of the 1990s. From import-substitution, state intervention and control that had been strengthened due to the lack of foreign exchange, there was a transformation towards a more market-based, world market integrated economy, backed by concessional donor funds for import support within the framework of structural adjustment agreements between the individual SADCC country and the IMF and World Bank. Much of the industry and trade programme was formulated on the basis of the former way of functioning and when the new winds blew, some proposals became irrelevant, and others lost their attraction. As discussed earlier, SADCC seemed to attempt through its industry programme to overcome some of the limitations of the old model of industrialization through a regional outlook, but at the same time the general macroeconomic framework in the individual country changed. It is easy to imagine how this mixture of diverging strategies could lead to problems of digestion and an uncertainty as to how to proceed. This goes hand in hand with the altered international setting with the disappearance of the 'second world' around 1990, and the 'silent revolution of the market' in all corners of the world in the beginning of the 1990s.[75]

In 1980 expected support from donors had strengthened the integrative potential of SADCC by lowering perceived costs of cooperation. Continued financing by donors of almost all project costs within the transport and communication sector was an important process mechanism for SADCC, and an important reason behind the relative success in the area. In the industry and trade sector SADCC reckoned to use the same mode of functioning and cover 80–90 per cent of project costs from foreign sources. However, the model apparently could not be repeated for industry and trade. Basically, there might have been a substantial hesitation on the part of most western donors to engage in state promoted financing of industry that according to their perception was a private sector venture. Furthermore, building up an industry with minimal precautions for future functioning was far more complex than an infrastructure project. In any event, donor organizations were simply not forthcoming to support the industrial projects, and foreign investors did not step in either, as conditions apparently were still not considered sufficiently favourable. Regarding the lack of funds for trade financing I suspect that donors would not engage themselves before the full dose of liberalization was taken by the SADCC countries in order not to make parts of the old system functional, and in this way perhaps drag out the reform process.

There have also been conflicts and diverging interests among the SADCC countries which have weakened commitment to the programmes and slowed down the pace of implementation. Differences have surfaced between countries with more state intervention against more market oriented countries, and between more and lesser developed countries. The protracted process of agreeing on just a framework for the new regional industrial projects after 1989 might be seen as a token of these differences. However, the third typical obstacle discussed in chapter 2, the opportunistic nationalism, did not occur directly in the period. However, indirectly nationalism is a strong undercurrent, influencing navigation of the member states.

Chapter 2 also mentioned the importance of the integrationist technocrats and their ability to promote true regional projects which through the spillover effect might possibly function as stepping stones for further common projects. The admitted low quality of the first group of SADCC's priority basic needs industry projects is a case in point. Concerning the negotiation style of SADCC

– the minimum common dominator type – it cannot in a narrow sense be said in this sector to have withheld interaction, as not even the few agreed projects and policies were implemented. However, it is an open question if better results might have been reached by introducing package deals and trade offs, involving several sectors in SADCC; so that for example Tanzania gave some industrial concessions against advantages relating to the rehabilitation of the Das es Salaam transport corridor. This might have provided some sense of obligation – often seemingly missing – actually to implement the plans. In general, the lack of success of reaching results even in noncontroversial and low cost areas such as industry and trade services seems to confirm the hypothesis from section 2.3 that the drive to actually reach and implement agreements is relatively weak within the cooperation approach.

Cooperation in the areas of industry and trade appears to verify that identity in outlook between political leaders in the involved countries can be an important process mechanism for formulating policies and programmes. SADCC did in fact agree on various industry and trade policies in spite of differences in interests. However, at the same time, the analysis might verify that the leaders were not successful in committing state and private business, and the state apparatus in order to implement regional agreements in their home country. Thus, decisions could be adopted regionally without any effective follow up internally after the leader returned. This might be typical of OAU and ECA declarations, but SADCC cannot be said to have been immune. In a neo-functionalist terminology the situation could be described as spill around, characterized by an expansion in the scope of cooperation to other sectors, in this case industry and trade, but not succeeding in deepening the level of interaction.

This leads naturally to another difficulty which faces cooperation and integration attempts in Southern Africa – the fact that there are none or few interest and pressure groups to promote the issue with government. We registered the healthy attempt by SADCC to create and involve the SRBC, but its relationship towards SADCC and donors seemed unresolved, and its links to the national organizations appeared weak. There were no reports on trade union activities in relation to SADCC, but trade unions do cooperate over national borders in Southern Africa. However, a weak civil society is a general third world phenomenon, and as discussed in chapter 2, it merely makes cooperation and integration more difficult – not impossible. Moreover, Zimbabwe has relatively developed and articulate employers' organizations and the privatization in all former interventionist countries implies an upswing in the activities and position of national chambers of industry and commerce. In the event of South Africa being included in a regional cooperation and/or integration scheme, a new and very interesting situation will emerge, if the strong South African employers organizations, trade unions and other interest groups try to promote links with sister organizations in other countries in

Southern Africa, in order to be able to lobby decisions more effectively on a regional level.

Questions have been posed as to whether SADCCs industry and trade programme would have been more successful if commitments were binding and if SADCC headquarters planned and implemented industrial projects. The questions are relevant in theory, but at the same time largely irrelevant for any practical purposes, because even if the answers would be in the affirmative, the commitments would probably have been impossible to live up to. SADCC had consciously chosen the cooperation approach, and not a stringent development integration model, which would be required to act as proposed. I am convinced that SADCC's relative success, at least in some sectors – in a situation where other regional integration attempts stagnated or declined – was a result of the mode of cooperation, which did not impinge on national sovereignty, as discussed in chapter 2. Moreover, the economic trends pointed at less rather than more industrial planning in the individual SADCC member states. In the PTA Treaty the countries had solemnly signed and agreed to a certain schedule of for tariff reductions, but they simply did not adhere to obligations. Therefore, a looser model would seem preferable, because an organization cannot in the long run sustain consistently broken rules.

However, when all these explanatory elements have been illuminated one cannot but speculate how far the countries might have come in industrial and trade cooperation if the SADCC countries had followed up on their self-criticism from the minister's discussion of the new trade programme, and consciously taken a number of simple and low cost measures from the industry and trade programme, thus demonstrating a political will and resolve among themselves to change conditions of development through regional cooperation. To facilitate such moves the region might be said to have lacked a 'dramatic act' that forcefully could have brought home the specific advantages of industry and trade cooperation.[76] Likewise, the region missed visionary leaders with a feeling for what was practically possible at any given time. The result was that the region had no functioning buffer between the individual country and the world market, when the old models of state led, inward industrialization crumbled and demands for liberalization of the economies were put to the countries with increasing strength. The scene was set with innumerable plans and projects but all too little practical outcome. This makes it of paramount importance to analyse the regional aspect of the IMF and World Bank's policy and practice in the SADCC countries, as their agreements with governments have led to changes which are likely to have repercussions on the possibilities for regional cooperation and integration. The next chapter will focus on the regional level, whilst the following chapter will take its point of departure in the Bretton Woods institutions interaction with the individual SADCC countries, using Mozambique as an example.

Notes

1 The publication of Kuznets referred to in the quotation is *Modern Economic Growth*, Yale University Press, New Haven, Conn., 1966. The quotation as such is found in Chenery et al., 1986, pp.ix and 1.

2 Fuels, minerals, metals and other primary commodities constituted 92 per cent of Sub-Saharan exports in 1991. That was the same share as in 1970. Source: World Bank, 1993a, table 16, p.268ff.

3 Excluding oil; if oil is included the share rises to 65 per cent in the 1980s. See for example Jourdan, 1992, p.48.

4 The organization of oil exporting countries, OPEC, is normally quoted as the only exception to this, although its strength is gradually being weakened since the beginning of the 1980s. The other slightly more successful, but much less known, sales cartel is the private (raw) diamond 'Central Selling Organization', managed by the diamond production and services company 'de Beers' – ultimately controlled by the giant South African 'Anglo-American Company' – which has succeeded relatively well in controlling market supply from nearly all sources.

5 This could bring higher demand and prices to traditional African primary export goods – an income which Africa in turn could utilize to escape the commodity export trap in which the African countries are caught.

6 The lessons from the outward-looking manufacturing industrialization in East Asia are discussed in for example: Black, 1992; Leipziger and Thomas, 1993; Petri, 1993; World Bank, 1993c. The debate concerning the lessons from East Asia was typically carried out in inflexible stereotypes in the 1980s: one was either a supporter of completely free trade, rule of the market forces and export dominance, or an adherent of protection and inward-looking import substitution industrialization with heavy state involvement. The discussion and reflections in the 1990s tend to be more qualified and constructive. They try to grasp the special and country specific mix of state intervention and responsiveness to market signals that made the exceptional growth in manufacturing possible in a number of East Asian countries.

7 See for a discussion of the complex issues involved for example Gibbon, Bangura and Ofstad, 1992.

8 See for example Weiss, 1988, pp.296ff. Reference is also made to note 6 above.

9 Here quoted from Riddell et al., 1990, p.4ff.

10 Nine per cent to be exact, according to World Bank, 1992a, table 1, p.218.

11 This book (notably chapter 3) has benefited substantially from the consistent data and analysis presented in the Riddell study.

12 In this and the following tables on the dimensions and characteristics of the industrial sector in Southern Africa I have used Riddell, 1993, p.12, as the main source in order to secure consistency and coverage. The figures have as far as possible been checked with World Bank data. I have adjusted Riddell's figures for Angola and Mozambique. He puts Angola's manufacturing value added to seven per cent of GDP in 1989. I find this unlikely, as both before and after it stood at 3–4 per cent, according to his own data and to World Bank's World Development Report 1992. Thus, I use four per cent in 1989, which gives a total Angolan manufacturing value added of 309 million US$ that year. The manufacturing value added/GDP percentage of four for Mozambique stated in Riddell, 1993, p.12, is probably to the low side. World Bank's World Development Reports from 1991–93 give figures for 'industry's' share of GDP between 15 and 22 per cent for the years 1989–91. Manufacturing would constitute the larger part of this as mining is minimal in that period, and electricity and water is much smaller than manufacturing industry. SADCC, 1985e puts the share of manufacturing industry to nine per cent. My own best, rounded, estimate is 10 per cent. With a GDP of 1100 million US$ in 1989, according to the World Bank, 1991a, this gives a manufacturing value added of 110 million US$ that year.

13 The exact figure for the SADCC countries share of population in Sub-Saharan Africa was 16.6 per cent in 1989, according to the World Bank, 1991a, table 1.

14 The fall in the Zimbabwean share of manufacturing value added and the increase in that of Zambia between 1984 and 1989 are probably due to exchange rate fluctuations, and do not reflect real changes in the relative weight of the two countries.

15 Manufacturing industry's share of GDP in Sub-Saharan Africa in 1989 is put at 11 percent in World Bank, 1991a, table 3, p.209.

16 It should be noted that the income from migrant labourer's wage transfers from South Africa does not enter into gross domestic product.

17 See Torp, 1979 and 1983.

18 See also World Bank, 1992b.

19 Namibia would undoubtedly fit into this pattern, but is not included due to lack of data.

20 See e.g. OECD, 1987. Data from this publication is used for an overview table in Haarlov, 1988, table 11, p.113.

21 Regarding Botswana see for example SADCC, 1990a, p.36.

22 South Africa is not included in 'Africa'. The share of Latin America was for the same period 6–10 percent and for Asia 17–32 percent. Source: United Nations, 1993, table II.2, p.45.

23 See for example Seidmann, 1986 and the discussion of Seidmann's industrialization strategy in Peet, 1984, p.59ff.

24 'One-shop' investment centres are administrative units where prospective investors can present their proposal for investment for approval, instead of having to obtain authorizations from a range of different ministries and institutions. The investment centre will normally be obliged to answer an application within a certain time limit.

25 This trend is caused by the problems the manufacturing sector faces under the conditions of structural adjustment in Africa in the end of the 1980s and beginning of the 1990s. They differ from country to country but are typically characterized by a depressed home market, competition from cheap imports, and high interest rates on capital for investment, and on financing of import of inputs to the production process. The case of Mozambique is in focus in chapter 5.

26 See Riddell et al., 1990, p.52ff.

27 The estimate of one per cent is reached by combining the shares of PTA (0.2) and ECOWAS (0.6), and then adding 0.2 per cent as an approximate figure for the central African states.

28 See for example chapter 5 in this book on Mozambican experiences.

29 See SADCC, 1986c and Maasdorp Whiteside, 1993, p.14.

30 When analyzing intra-SADCC trade one has to take into account that precisely because of the low level of trade, the statistical information may be heavily affected by specific individual transactions of a one time only nature. For example import of food because of drought in one country or sales of electricity because of technical problems in one country.

31 The almost free trade agreement between Zimbabwe and Botswana has its roots in a similar 1956 arrangement between the Federation of Rhodesia and Nyasaland on the one hand, and Botswana, then Bechuanaland on the other. However, since 1984 conflicts of interpreting and renegotiating the treaty have regularly erupted, leading in some cases to the temporary imposition of protective tariffs from both sides. Malawi and Zimbabwe had likewise kept their open general licence policy towards each other since the days of the Federation of which they were both part. However, Zimbabwe unilaterally abandoned the agreement, alleging that the agreement was contrary to its membership of PTA in 1984, and offered Malawi the same tariff status as other PTA countries, thereby following the letter but not the spirit of PTA.

32 More precisely 58 per cent, according to the author's calculations based on data from the publication: Central Statistical Office, 1984, table 4. The export figures exclude gold sales, and manufactured products cover the Standard International Trade Classification (SITC) sections 5–9.

33 According to a table on 1992 trade between South Africa and Zimbabwe released by South African Customs and Excise Department, quoted in Financial Gazette, Harare, 15 July 1993.

34 See table 3.9 and Central Statistical Office, 1986, table 10.4.

35 See for example Haarlov, 1988, p.43ff.

36 Study made for and on behalf of the SADCC Secretariat, University of Malawi, University of the Western Cape, Bellville.

37 Regarding the originally defined five objectives, see for example SADCC, 1985a, p.4 or SADCC, 1985b, p.1. The condensed three objectives can for example be found in SADCC, 1987a, p.3.

38 Reference is made to SADCC, 1985b, p.1; SADCC, 1986d, pp.1–19.

39 Reference is made to Thomas, 1974.

40 See also SADCC, 1986d, p.3.

41 The additional pledge was calculated to US$ 378 million, according to SADCC, 1984d, p.14 and SADCC, 1984c, p.7.

42 The sources for this and the following presentation are mainly: SADCC, 1985b; SADCC, 1986d and SADCC, 1987a.

43 Reference is also made to table 11, p.56 in Haarlov, 1988. Specific comments on the table: there are no cost estimates for one project (cement–Malawi). In the source material the total sum of the foreign exchange component of the projects is indicated to be US$ 1,283,352. However, calculations project by project give the presented total of US$ 1,304, 352. The differences are located in A3 (+ US$ 1 million) and in A4 (+ US$ 20 million).

44 Reference is made to the development objective: 'the forging of links to create a genuine and equitable regional integration'. See SADCC, 1984f or Simba and Wells, 1984.

45 The new strategy was adopted by SADCC Council of Ministers in August 1989, according to SADCC, 1991a, p.1.

46 See SADCC, 1988a and SADCC, 1989a.

47 At the consultative conference in January/February 1990 the industrial investment projects were for the first time deleted. The official explanation was that the projects were drawn back for 'review'. See SADCC, 1990a, p.2. The project portfolio for the sector consequently shrunk to 12 projects, to a total value of US$ 14 million. (Distribution of projects: 1: Overall Coordination; 6: Support Services; 4: Trade Promotion; 1: Trade Financing).

48 See for example: SADCC, 1986d, p.8.

49 The following presentation of SADCC's new industrial strategy is based on SADCC, 1990a.

50 See for some of these points SADCC, 1990a, p.40.

51 Note the similarity with the quotation from Robson, 1990, p.202, cited in section 2.5 on the necessary trade offs between 'efficiency and equity'.

52 See also for example Robson, 1983, pp.25–8 and Haarlov, 1988, p.24.

53 Information on the various stages of the regional industrial projects is derived from SADCC, 1991a, p.4; SADCC, 1992a, p.4; SADCC, 1993a, p.5ff.

54 Information obtained by the author at: Interview, 1993h.

55 Reference is made to note 54.

56 References about the Nordic–SADCC Initiative can be found in note 17, chapter 2, of this book.

57 Although the Norsad Fund was legally established 31 January 1990, it only opened its head office in Lusaka, Zambia, in April 1991. Thus, the above report covers the first year of operations.

58 Reference is made to Norsad Fund and Norsad Agency, 1993b.

59 The information on the Norsad Fund and the discussion concerning its future role is partly based on: Interview, 1993i.

60 Information on PTA's background and mode of functioning can for example be found in Mwase, 1985; Ofstad, 1993; PTA, 1990; PTA, 1993b; and Takirambudde, 1993.

61 The former defined year 2000 as the year of creation of a African common market, whereas the latter after accumulating the various phases reached year 2025 for the establishment of an African economic community. See: Organization of African Unity, 1982; Organization of African Unity, 1991.

62 The brief overview is based on an interview by the author with K. Osafo, senior economist at PTA headquarters in Lusaka 1 April 1993 (Interview, 1993b). Further information has been obtained from official PTA documents: for example PTA, 1992a; and PTA, 1993a.

63 In 1993, out of 18 members of PTA only 12 had published PTA tariffs agreed in 1988; eight had published the further cuts in tariffs approved in 1990 and just six had adjusted the tariffs according to 1992 decisions. See PTA, 1993a, p.5ff.

64 See the full details in PTA Treaty, Annex III, Article 15 (PTA, 1982). These regulations resulted in constant frictions in the PTA between countries with emphasis on state led industrialization (e.g. Ethiopia and Tanzania) and countries more open towards foreign private investment (e.g. Kenya and Malawi). As discussed in chapter 2 the common list was abolished, and the rules of origin set for revision through a study in 1993. See PTA, 1993a, p.10ff.

65 See for example G. Maasdorp & A. Whiteside (1993), p.24ff.

66 The document setting out PTAs transformation to COMESA is PTA, 1992b. According to the author's interview at the PTA headquarters (see note 62) there were reports of a certain hesitation from members to proceed with COMESA, as long as substantial areas of the original Treaty were not implemented. In November 1993 the Zimbabwean President

R. Mugabe refused to sign the COMESA Treaty, allegedly because the relationship between PTA and SADCC had not been clarified, according to SouthScan, 12 November 1993.

67 See PTA, 1982. Main elements of the PTA Treaty are discussed in SADCC, 1986c, p.36ff.

68 The source for both 1984 meetings is SADCC, 1984a, p.1.

69 Reference is made to SADCC, 1986c.

70 SADCC, 1986f. The source of the inside information regarding discussions between first officials and later ministers before the adoption of a common position can for obvious reasons not be disclosed.

71 The information on the original SADCC trade programme is derived from the above mentioned sources SADCC, 1986c; SADCC, 1986f; SADCC, 1986h; SADCC, 1987a; and Haarlov, 1988.

72 In the Industry and Trade reports to the Consultative Conferences in 1993 and 1994 there was no feedback from members regarding this issue.

73 The analysis revealed that EPRF would not be feasible in Angola, while the study was not finalized concerning Mozambique, according to SADCC, 1993a, p.21.

74 SADCC, 1990a, pp.25 and 31. SADCC does not reveal how it reached the 12 per cent, but indicates that it would be a result of the implementation of the various measures of the industry and trade programme. However, there might be a larger potential if one compares imports that African countries receive from the rest of the world, to exports other African countries sell on the world market. In a World Bank analysis the intra-Sub-Saharan African trade potential is estimated to 18 per cent; see World Bank, 1991b, p.55. SADCC's Intra-Regional Trade Study from 1986 (SADCC, 1986c, p.27) indicates that on the basis of the peaks that existing trade flows had reached in recent years before the study there seemed to be a potential for at least a doubling of trade, if the trade flows could be kept close to the maximum levels attained. This would result in intra-regional trade flows of 8–10 per cent of total trade.

75 The 'silent revolution' in the developing countries was an expression used by IMF managing director M. Camdessus, when discussing the globalization of the national economies based on market principles at the annual meeting of the IMF and the World Bank, Washington D.C., 1993. See Camdessus, 1993.

76 The independence of Zimbabwe in 1980 could be seen as the 'dramatic act' that triggered off and generated the generally favourable background for the creation of SADCC, and made the countries geographically a functional entity concerning for example transport and communication projects.

4 World Bank policies for regional cooperation and integration

4.1 Introduction

We witnessed in the previous chapter how World Bank policies became ever more important for industrial development and trade in Southern Africa in the end of the 1980s and in the beginning of the 1990s. Thus, regional plans and projects that might have had a bearing on developments under earlier macroeconomic conditions, lost increasingly their relevance confronted with the policies of structural adjustment programmes accorded between the individual SADCC country and the World Bank.[1] Therefore, it becomes of utmost importance to try to identify an emerging World Bank policy on regional cooperation and integration.

Key questions for this chapter are: is the World Bank at all in favour of regional cooperation and integration in Southern Africa, judging from major World Bank publications in the end of the 1980s and beginning of the 1990s? If so, does it give uniform and clear signals? How can its approach best be characterized? How does the World Bank transform its general policies into concrete positions via-à-vis SADCC, as mirrored in World Bank interventions at SADCC's Annual Consultative Conferences? Is the World Bank's verbal support for SADCC cooperation reflected in commitments to finance SADCC activities? What is the content and type of approach found in the World Bank's Cross-Border Trade and Investment Initiative? The overall hypothesis for this chapter is that the World Bank's regional policies do not appear coherent or effective – neither regarding the general guidelines nor the operational practice.

The issues will be approached from four different angles. I shall start out by presenting the views on regional integration found in the *World Development Report 1991* (World Bank, 1991a). In this publication regional market integration is discussed vis-à-vis unilateral openings towards the world

134

market. Regional integration tends to be seen as irrelevant for Third World countries, because of their structural characteristics. This is contrasted with the line of argument in the World Bank's major publication of Africa policy analyses in the period: *Sub-Saharan Africa. From Crisis to Sustainable Growth. A Long Term Perspective Study* (World Bank, 1989). The publication will be referred to as *From Crisis to Sustainable Growth*. It contains a basic recognition of the necessity of regional cooperation and integration in Africa as one of several development priorities. Focus is then switched to the World Bank's interventions at SADCC's Annual Consultative Conferences, and to activities that the World Bank has supported in a SADCC context. Finally, there is a presentation and discussion of the above mentioned embryonic Cross-Border Trade and Investment Initiative, which the World Bank is promoting outside the existing regional organization.

4.2   Advancing unilateral trade reform

Chapter 5 in *World Development Report 1991* (World Bank, 1991a) is titled 'Integration with the Global Economy'. One of the issues dealt with is regional integration. The line of argument is based on the dichotomy of trade creation/ trade diversion, which was presented in chapter 2 of this book. The readers are informed (ibid., p.107) that when trade blocks are formed, there are in principle gains when expensive domestic products are substituted by cheaper regional goods. Economies of scale are seen as gains too, and protected infant industry will benefit from moving from a national to a regionally more competitive environment. However, there are losses as well – although these are only explained by defining trade diversion as having to accept higher priced regional products, while keeping lower priced goods from nonmembers out of reach of the consumers. The conclusion of the *World Development Report 1991* (ibid., p.107) is that: 'Even if a regional trading block can be designed to generate net gains for its members, these gains are exceeded by the benefits from unilateral trade reform.'

Thus, it is recommended to individual countries that they avoid regional solutions and instead open up towards the world market. However, it appears that the basis for doing so is purely theoretical. The argument is based on an ideal situation of universal free trade, which in theory will secure the largest benefits for all. In theory, regional integration can by definition only be the second best option, because trade is only free within the region not between the region and other parts of the world. What the *World Development Report 1991* does not take into consideration is that in practice regional integration can be the best route to take in order to move from protected national economies towards opening up for outside competition, and eventually meeting world market conditions. The *World Development Report 1991* seems to offer practical policy advice on the basis of a perfectly logical but purely theoretically drawn conclusion.

The report proceeds specifically to discuss developing country regional trade groups, or rather to present their disadvantages. We find the traditional argument that the developing countries involved produce similar products, resulting in the inability to benefit from specialization based on different skills or endowments. The discussion in chapter 2 of the book on this issue concluded that this argument is only relevant in a critique of the pure and static market integration approach. Further, the *World Development Report 1991* focuses on:

- low internal trade in the third world regions, because of conflicts in Central America and unsuccessful attempts in the Andean Pact to distribute industrial production among member states;
- high tariffs against nonmembers, limiting competition and raising losses;
- the relative smallness of markets of developing country groupings seen in a world scale.

This leads to the firm recommendation: 'Unilateral trade liberalization and multilateral efforts to free up global trade are preferable to the formation of trading blocs' (ibid., p.108).

However, should a trading block be formed the damage may be alleviated by commitment to GATT-negotiations, according to the report, and by reducing common external tariffs, preferably to the standards of the most open member. Unilateral openings towards the world market by individual countries should be welcomed. Not taken up is the argument in favour of having a certain parity between import tariffs in order to give industry reasonably similar conditions in different member countries. It will be evident from the next section that the fundamental objectives guiding the *World Development Report 1991* are not different from the ones found in *From Crisis to Sustainable Growth*, discussed below, namely reaching international competitiveness and raising return on investment. However, when trying to apply theory and objectives to reality, the *World Development Report 1991* ends up in what could be described as a rigid and negative market integration approach, while regional cooperation and integration in *From Crisis to Sustainable Growth* is seen as an organic part of the development process.

4.3   Promoting regional cooperation and integration

In the period from the end of the 1980s and to where the focus of this book ends, 1992/3 *From Crisis to Sustainable Growth* is the major World Bank strategic analysis of Sub-Saharan Africa, containing both a diagnosis of the ills of the stagnating African continent and prescriptions for a possible regaining of a momentum of growth in Sub-Saharan Africa. The study is in its own words: '... intended to help in the design of a future development strategy for each African country' (World Bank, 1989, p.2). Thus, the policies set forward in *From Crisis to Sustainable Growth* on for example regional cooperation and integration should ideally be reflected in key policy documents such as Policy Framework Papers accorded between the World Bank and an individual African country pursuing a Structural Adjustment Programme.[2]

The opening towards regionalism may be illustrated by a few quotations from the report. In his foreword, World Bank President Barber B. Conable expresses the following sentiment: 'By working together, African governments will hopefully achieve faster progress toward regional cooperation and integration, which was a central theme of the Lagos Plan of Action ...' (World Bank, 1989, p.xii). In the first chapter of 'introduction and overview' (ibid., p.11ff.) the report states:

> African leaders have long recognized the need for closer regional ties. Most African economies are too small to achieve economies of scale or specialization without trade, and their firms too new and inexperienced to compete with established overseas exporters without some protection.

Thus, it is convincingly established that in comparison to the previous section the recommendations have swung a whole 180 degrees. *From Crisis to Sustainable Growth* even rallies the rather dirigiste influenced *Lagos Plan of Action* from 1980 behind its policy advice.[3] The direct mention of the need for protection of industry is also interesting, as the Bank frankly recognizes that a unilateral and immediate opening towards world market competition would cripple African enterprises. The last chapter, presenting the proposed 'strategic agenda for the 1990s', includes regional integration and cooperation as one of seven points being highlighted for action: 'The objectives of regional integration and cooperation should be pursued with a new determination to overcome parochial concerns' (World Bank, 1989, p.192).

The chapter directly mentions areas of cooperation and integration such as rationalization of regional institutions, liberalization of trade within Africa, reduction of transport controls, facilitating intra-African payments, easing infrastructure bottlenecks, cooperating in education, science, technology, health, research, and natural resource management (ibid., p.192). Between the introduction and concluding chapter in *From Crisis to Sustainable Growth* regional cooperation and integration is dealt with in more detail both in a separate chapter, and in other chapters, when it is relevant to the subject-matter in focus, e.g. agriculture and industry. The essence is synthesized below.

It is important to recognize that the relatively positive attitude of the World Bank towards regional integration and cooperation is not born out of any sudden idealistic sympathy for the aspirations of the Lagos Plan of Action or the like. On the contrary, the approach of the World Bank is positive towards regional integration and cooperation, precisely because it has the potential for furthering objectives that the World Bank judges imperative for African economic recovery, but which are impossible to reach within the confines of a single country's market. These are:

- improved competitiveness by increasing productivity and lowering costs; both per unit produced and costs of doing business as such;
- higher returns on investment;
- improved capabilities;
- having food security not as a national, but as a regional priority.

Moreover, it is a condition for the World Bank that the regional cooperation and integration is made within a framework characterized by key features of structural adjustment policy in the macroeconomic field:

- reaching a realistic exchange rate,
- price liberalizations;
- liberalization of foreign trade in general;
- creating an enabling environment for local and foreign investment;
- minimizing deficit on the state budget.

One could, however, argue that the objectives of the World Bank, within the given framework could be reached just as well with a unilateral opening of the economy towards the world market. According to *From Crisis to Sustainable Growth*, there are two main reasons why the World Bank favours regional cooperation and integration in Africa before a world market entry. One is that trading within a regional group might be an important stepping-stone and learning ground for African business, before being confronted with the harsh conditions of world market competition (ibid., p.109).[4] Another reason and perhaps the most interesting one, is that giving priority to regional trade liberalizations is likely to appease the political resistance towards later world market exposure from interest groups that have benefited from protection and/or will be hit by factory closures and retrenchment:

> Governments, for example, fear the political costs of lost employment and output, especially in the short run, when weaker firms face retrenchment or closure, before new activity has picked up sufficiently to provide an offset (ibid., p.159)

This phasing of trade liberalization is thus a deliberate political tool, reflecting experience of delays and cut backs in reform programs, because the political context was not on the agenda as an essential variable, when formulating the adjustment proposals (ibid.).

Furthermore, the World Bank recommends that the integration and cooperation process as such shall be 'incremental but comprehensive' (ibid., p.152). The word 'incremental' implies here that it is necessary to proceed step by step from the bottom up, in order to overcome all the immense practical problems, differences of interest and past suspicion. Each step must be accompanied by a corresponding commitment from the parties involved. The word 'comprehensive' is in this context equal to 'mutually reinforcing, complementary measures' (ibid.). Thus, for example trade liberalization and infrastructure development must be implemented in sequences where one supports the other, and together they carry the process forward. On the other hand a flexible approach is advocated concerning the space and time dimensions. In a regional grouping not all the countries have to join the same cooperation schemes at the same time. Multi- and bilateral agreements can be mixed, as long as they take integration to higher standards than before. The most reluctant country should not be the common denominator. The contours of the adjustment adapted market integration approach are beginning to surface. Likewise, there are parallels to the concepts from the European debate on integration in the 1990s: 'the variable geography' in country coverage of various regional arrangements and a 'variable or multi-speed integration', indicating that subgroups within a larger regional grouping can implement agreements according to different time tables.

Turning to the content of the proposed cooperation and integration, three main areas can be identified:

- harmonization of macroeconomic policies;
- functional cooperation in various areas;
- free movement of goods, services, capital and labour.

Regarding the macroeconomic policies, a certain similarity is automatically implied by the simultaneous existence of key elements of structural adjustment programmes in the countries covered by regional integration. However, the World Bank argues that this should be carried further through harmonization efforts, e.g. concerning the exchange rate, fiscal and monetary policy (ibid., pp.12 and 162).

Concerning the functional areas of cooperation three can be singled out. One is transport, communication and services. The second is education, training and research and the third: natural resource management. Concerning the first, there are large gains to be made from improving the transport network in order to underpin trade flows. Effective telecommunications are essential to economic development, as business depends more and more on an up to date information network of worldwide trading opportunities and tendencies.

139

Electric power generation and distribution are also obvious candidates for functional cooperation. The World Bank is very keen to stress how the economic rationale and market signals must be carefully analyzed before any investment is made in infrastructure. This might be interpreted as an attempt to draw a line between its own approach and others like SADCC, which tend to give priority to infrastructure development as a condition to be fulfilled before serious trade efforts are initiated, and in the 1980s, pushes for the upgrading of certain pieces of infrastructure for strategic reasons – to avoid a South African stranglehold of member economies. Regional cooperation in services can extend from loose coordination of timetables and routing for air- and sea-transport to joint companies running for example a regional railway network. The ability to offer a financial infrastructure consisting of regional banking and insurance services will diminish the costs and uncertainties of regional trade.

Turning to the second main area of education, training and research, the gradual degradation especially of higher education in Africa over the last decade is a deplorable fact. In the short and medium term future it seems an undeniable advantage to cooperate intimately on a regional basis in order to obtain the required standards, concerning staff, libraries, laboratories etc. in many disciplines. The framework may either be a common institution or – more simply – a national institution, selling a certain number of places to regional partners, according to a mutually agreed plan on distribution of specializations. This kind of cooperation is relatively well developed among the SADCC countries within agricultural research and training. The last main area of functional cooperation was natural resource management. This comprises, according to the World Bank, such things as plant pest control and river basin management.

We can now focus on the creation of an 'enabling environment for trade, competition and factor mobility' (ibid., p.158). Goods, services, capital and labour should have the opportunity to flow freely within a given group of countries. This has, according to the World Bank, a short term perspective of doubling the present six per cent intra-African trade, as a percentage of total foreign trade. This corresponds roughly to the estimates regarding possible enhancement of intra-SADCC trade made in the mid 1980s (see section 3.5). The competition and market expansion possibilities embodied in such a move should lead to the above mentioned overall objectives of raising productivity and efficiency and a lowering of costs. It will enable the countries to 'nurture new industries supplying regional markets' (ibid., p.162). A regional integration scheme that respects market forces will be able, according to the report, even to develop 'core industries' (e.g. steel, chemical, fertilizer) (ibid., pp.187ff.), as recommended in the more state driven approach that SADCC adhered to in the 1980s.[5] However, the report stresses firmly that the regional dismantling of trade barriers should be carried out within a programme of gradually opening up toward world market competition, and that the regional protective tariffs should be relatively low in order not to allow any build up of nonviable, noncompetitive enterprises. As to the financing of trade the report does not go substantially into the subject, but mentions the possible settlement of balances through 'clearing houses',⁶ and to supplement this with private corresponding banks being allowed to hold and trade non-convertible African currencies.

From Crisis to Sustainable Growth proposes that free movement of capital and labour should be able to counteract a lack of balance in the exchange of goods, through labour remittances to the lesser developed home areas of migrant labourers and investments in these areas. The substantial political obstacles to a free flow of labour – which under the present conditions will be accentuated through the high population growth – is not reflected in the report. Neither is there a discussion of the many barriers to capital shifting location to areas far from the market place and often without sufficient infrastructure (see section 2.4). The report rightly mentions the rich variety of additional barriers to free trade other than customs tariffs. Licensing and quotas are very important as they constituted the main management tools in foreign trade before the structural adjustment programmes gradually began to change this in most SADCC countries outside SACU. Bureaucratic procedures and requirements in relation to imports and exports are typically overdeveloped, and an expansion in trade presupposes a simplification. Lack of information about suppliers and outlets in the region is another real barrier. This is often coupled with a certain non-substantiated or automatic preference for non-African products. The non-uniformity of standards also hinders trade. Several of these non-customs tariffs barriers to trade were taken up in SADCC's industrial and trade programmes, as witnessed in the previous chapter.

Finally, the report suggests that a compensation arrangement be set up in support of the economically weaker countries in the regional group. This is not a result of a sudden favouring of equality, but rather the recognition of two facts that were discussed in chapter 2. The first is that poles of industrial growth and poles of stagnation will emerge and be unevenly distributed within a regional grouping. The second tells us that the seeds of self-destruction are sown if due attention is not paid to sharing the benefits of the cooperation and integration. The report eloquently states that 'insuperable political obstruction' (World Bank, 1989, p.161) will be created if nothing is done. However, no specific proposal is presented, but it is listed as a government priority to find one, and it is mentioned that the compensation should have an automatic character in order not to fall victim of possible budget restraints in the countries that must pay. Donors could possibly contribute to financing a compensatory scheme, according to the report. The compensation schemes might in turn be part of overall regional adjustment programmes (ibid., p.162).

In relation to the earlier discussion of the 'polarization or backwash effect'[7] there are many parallels, but it is surprising that the report does not mention other methods than 'compensation' among the many possibilities that exist and are systematized in section 2.5 of this book. Would this be due to lack of knowledge, or is it a conscious avoidance of other methods that require more state intervention?

It would be interesting to try to identify the theoretical approach which lies behind the proposals in the report in relation to the general approaches introduced in chapter 2. *From Crisis to Sustainable Growth* urges the state to withdraw from industrial development, which is in opposition to the development integration approach. However, it maintains that industry can be 'nurtured' and even 'core industries' be built up in a regional integration scheme, if the right market based environment, conducive to economic growth, is present nationally as well as regionally. The regional integration will prepare the industries for full scale world market competition. It is stressed that regional trade preferences shall be accompanied by openings towards the world market. Hence, in contrast to a market integration approach no traditional customs union with high protection against competition from outside is recommended. The private sector should be given a dominant role and driving seat in economic development. Institutionally the report recommends a flexibility in the introduction of the integration measures, so that not all countries have to advance at the same pace with the same set of measures. In addition to this, the World Bank recognizes in *From Crisis to Sustainable Growth* that the weaker members of the cooperating group must get their share of the benefits accruing from the cooperation. The state sector is seen as the main actor in creating such a scheme. This also distances the report from a pure market integration approach. The integrative measures proposed are then coupled with functional cooperation whenever possible and economically advisable. All in all, the report fits very well into the adjustment adapted market integration approach. Its measures aspire to complement the ongoing national structural adjustment programmes, and there is an inbuilt institutional flexibility. *From Crisis to Sustainable Growth* even hints at the possibility of establishing 'regional' structural adjustment programmes to promote trade and capital flows as well as securing institutional strengthening and adequate compensation schemes (World Bank, 1989, p.162).

4.4   World Bank interventions at SADCC's annual conferences

The World Bank participated in SADCC's Annual Consultative Conferences in all the years in focus in this chapter:

- 1988 in Arusha. Theme: Infrastructure and Enterprise.
- 1989 in Luanda. Theme: Productive Sectors.
- 1990 in Lusaka. Theme: Enterprise, Skills and Productivity.
- 1991 in Windhoek. Theme: Human Resources.
- 1992 in Maputo. Theme: Towards Regional Integration

The World Bank's interventions at these Conferences are the prime sources for the following analysis. However, regarding the 1991 conference no World Bank intervention has been identified in the published proceedings (SADCC, 1991c). Some factual information will be drawn from World Bank's intervention at the 1993 Consultative Conference. In addition, I shall make reference to World Bank interventions at two earlier SADCC conferences, with special relevance for industrial development and trade: (1) January 1983 in Maseru, theme, Industrial Development and Food & Agriculture; (2) February 1988 in Harare, theme, Southern Africa. Opportunities for Investment and Trade.

The interventions will be analyzed from three different angles.

(1) How SADCC's approach toward regional cooperation and integration is discussed.

(2) Which recommendations are advanced regarding industry & trade development, especially in a regional context.

(3) Which concrete activities the World Bank emphasizes as its own contribution, not to the region or individual countries in general, but to the process of regional cooperation and integration.

Regarding the general approach of SADCC the following words of praise are found in the World Bank intervention in Maseru, 1983:

> We in the World Bank, for one, are heartened by the pragmatic, result-oriented spirit which has guided this organisation. We appreciate the concern to concentrate on the essentials and to focus on those matters which are amenable to regional solutions. We are indeed happy to associate ourselves fully with this approach (SADCC, 1983d, p.230).

I interpret this, as an approval of SADCC's cooperation approach, stressing the functional linkages within especially the transport and communication sector. In 1988 this attitude was reflected in an apparent willingness to include support for SADCC projects in the World Bank's lending programmes with the individual SADCC countries. Thus, the World Bank representative stated at the 1988 Consultative Conference that organizational changes in the Bank:

... should enable us to respond more appropriately to the regional dimension of development in Southern Africa, and to support SADCC's regional goals and programmes in our relationships with individual countries (SADCC, 1988c, p.225).[8]

Note that possible support to SADCC as an organization, including studies, does not enter into the discussion at this stage. However, there is a clear approval and support to SADCC's practical promotion and coordination of relevant regional development projects. After 1988 no clear statements of support to SADCC's general approach or objectives has been found. One could suspect that this is related to an uncertainty in the World Bank itself concerning the appropriate response to regional cooperation and integration efforts.

Regarding more specific policies of SADCC, it is significant that communication and infrastructure development throughout the period is applauded by the World Bank. Issues such as maintenance and the necessity to complement infrastructure with other initiatives are mentioned at the 1988 Consultative Conference (SADCC, 1988c, p.228). Concerning SADCC's own initiatives in the areas of industrial development and trade, SADCC is by the World Bank in 1988:

... commended for the important work it has begun in easing some of the immediate obstacles to enterprise development by removing some trade barriers, investigating trade-enhancing mechanisms such as export revolving funds, and improving and harmonizing investment codes (ibid., p.229).

The following year SADCC is 'congratulated on its imaginative efforts to promote and harmonize investment codes in member countries and to establish trade financing mechanisms' (SADCC, 1989c, p.207). As witnessed in chapter 3, this interpretation gave a too rosy picture of events. There was no removal of trade barriers as a result of SADCC initiatives. Investment codes were collected and published, but not harmonized. Trade financing was discussed, but no new scheme was established. After this over optimistic tune World Bank commendation of SADCC dried up completely in the following years.

At the same time the level of recommendations in the field of trade and industry intensified, although they also can be found earlier. Already at the 1983 conference on SADCC's industry programme the World Bank offered its clearly negative view on industrial development behind protective walls.

... it is essential that regional projects meet international standards of efficiency within a short period of time; otherwise it is difficult to see how Member Countries would support the operation of such ventures

144

without a complicated, costly and cumbersome system of protection (SADCC, 1983d, p.229).

The quote does not allow for much flexibility, not even regarding possible infant industry protection. After 1989 this attitude has special relevance for SADCC's attempt to establish a new focus on creating regional industries, after the priority industry investment projects were shelved (see chapter 3).

Raising external tariffs as a group in order to enhance intra regional trade was also discouraged at the 1988 Consultative Conference. Efficiency must be higher and competition increased, it is argued, if the 'high cost/low quality' syndrome is to be overcome (SADCC, 1988c, p.229). In the same year, the World Bank at the investment and trade conference presented its reasons for judging regional cooperation and integration as a necessity in Africa:

> [T]he World Bank is coming round to the view that Africa's economic future may lie in economic integration. Why? The continent is simply too sub-divided – 165 borders, 51 countries, 22 of them with a population under 5 million, 11 with a population under one million. Too many trade barriers, too much competition for the same scarce resources, human, institutional and financial. And from a business standpoint, markets that are simply too small to sustain industry and investment (SADCC, 1988d, p.77ff.).

This is certainly a convincing admission from the Bank of how it begins to see regional cooperation and integration in Africa as a precondition for doing successful business and for development in general on the continent. At the 1989 Consultative Conference regional aspects are not prominent in the World Bank intervention, but among the conditions for growth in the economies of the SADCC member states are listed regional cooperation in order to exploit mutual, complementary resources and economies of scale (SADCC, 1989c, p.207). This is squarely against the positions taken in *1991 World Development Report*, referred to above, regarding the lack of complementarity in skills and resource endowment and the relative smallness of regional markets in the Third World.

At the 1990 and 1992 Consultative Conferences, the World Bank gives the high ground to regional cooperation and integration. First a statement from 1990:

> Time has also come to accelerate plans for increased regional economic cooperation and integration in Africa. The experience of SADCC is beginning to demonstrate that the benefits of regional cooperation can be large in terms of expanded trade and markets, economics of scale, and shared resources. Again, however, ..., much more remains to be done

beyond the facilitation of investment projects by each country, to the promotion of *regionally coordinated and rationalized macro-economic policies and programmes* (SADCC, 1990c, p.42).

The World Bank representative, again, exaggerates the SADCC experience, which was blank regarding trade, markets and economies of scale, but the message follows the recommendations from the then recently published World Bank report discussed above: *From Crisis to Sustainable Growth*. The mention of 'regionally coordinated and rationalized macroeconomic policies and programmes' is in line with the possibility presented in *From Crisis to Sustainable Growth* of establishing a regional structural adjustment programme (World Bank, 1989, p.162). According to the World Bank at the 1990 Annual Conference special attention should be given to the question of removing non-tariff-barriers that are presented as the main obstacles to increased regional trade (SADCC, 1990c, p.42). This is congruent with the analysis of the adjustment adapted market integration approach.

At the 1992 Annual Conference the World Bank (World Bank, 1992e) also states its firm commitment to regional integration. The World Bank warns that costs to Southern Africa will be high, if the countries do not succeed in handling the need for increased cooperation and integration. It is, in my opinion, quite rightly argued, that the democratization process in South Africa and the establishment of trading blocks in other parts of the world, give an added impetus to identifying viable regional solutions for Southern Africa. Non-tariff barriers are once more singled out for possible immediate effective action. The general method to be used is a pragmatic, incremental and flexible one without hollow promises. It should provide the possibility of some members advancing before others, and new members being added to the group. Once more, the adjustment adapted approach seems to be the source of inspiration. In the field of functional cooperation, the World Bank proposes that, jointly owned regional operating authorities are established to cater for various infrastructure activities and public utilities. A hidden agenda behind the latter proposal probably aims at creating viable economic entities with a view to privatization at a later stage.

The World Bank stresses that this kind of regional integration demands that:

– the countries are willing to cede some national sovereignty to the regional level;
– the political will is present, and the public supports the endeavour;
– the private sector is the locomotive of integration;
– improved governance and democratization will prevail in the region (ibid., doc. 2, p.2).

All in all, it can be firmly established that the World Bank does not follow the generalized negative attitude towards regional cooperation and integration found in the *1991 World Development Report*. Conversely, in its rhetoric at SADCC conferences the World Bank encourages regional cooperation. Firstly, in support of the functional and project oriented approach and goals of SADCC; later as a promotion of central elements of the adjustment adapted market integration approach. It should be noted, however, that two politically essential aspects of the framework for regional cooperation and integration contained in the adjustment adapted approach and promoted in the report *From Crisis to Sustainable Growth* are missing. In the first place the proposal of phased tariff liberalization with priority to first opening up towards the region and only afterwards towards the world market is not presented. Secondly, the discussion of compensation is likewise apparently neglected. This is strange, as it appears to be one of the indispensable lines of argument in order to convince the majority of SADCC countries of the advisability of opening up their markets.

It is important to analyze whether the clear signals of eagerness to promote regional cooperation and integration are matched by corresponding action of a magnitude to be expected from a protagonist such as the World Bank. Unfortunately, the World Bank is not very specific at SADCC's annual consultative conferences regarding its direct support to the process of regional cooperation and integration. Apparently, it prefers to inform about the total amount of support in billions of US$ channelled by the World Bank Group to Southern Africa. This is mostly in terms of commitments – not disbursements. The latter would reveal far more about the actual impact and role of the World Bank.[9]

However, at the 1988 Consultative Conference one can find a stated intention to support the rehabilitation of four main transport corridors of SADCC: (1) the Corridor, linking the Tanzanian port of Dar es Salaam with Zambia, called the TAZARA/TANZAM: Tanzania Zambian Railway/Tanzania–Zambian; (2) the Beira Corridor, stretching from the central Mozambican port of Beira to Zimbabwe; (3) the Northern Corridor providing access for Malawi to the TAZARA/TANZAM Corridor, and finally (4) the Limpopo Corridor, taking its name from the Limpopo river, which it follows from the Mozambican capital Maputo, through Mozambique to Southern Zimbabwe. After 1988 there are no references to actual financing of these projects; only at the Consultative Conference in January 1993 did infrastructure projects resurface with an unspecified involvement in the Beira Corridor, the Malawi Northern Corridor and the Tanzania Port modernization (World Bank, 1993d, p.5).

If one turns to SADCC for information by scrutinizing the Annual Report 1990–91 (SADCC, 1991b), it reveals that the World Bank involvement reaches 10 per cent of secured financing at the Beira Port Transport System[10] and 8 per cent of secured financing at the Dar es Salaam Port Transport System, including TAZARA/TANZAM and the Northern Corridor from Malawi. The World Bank only represented 0.5 per cent of financing secured for the Limpopo Corridor, including the Maputo harbour. All in all, the World Bank had committed US$ 100 million to projects within SADCC's Transport and Communication sector. This represented 3.5 per cent of total secured funding. Thus, there seems to be a certain discrepancy between the actual rather limited investments and the World Banks rhetoric, which strongly supports the enhancement of functional linkages in the region in the form of transport and communication projects. Moreover, the comparatively restricted amounts of financing from the World Bank is surprising, as infrastructure is probably the sector in which the Bank has its greatest expertise,[11] and taking into consideration also the role as a lead donor that the Bank has in the majority of the SADCC states.

Apart from infrastructure, only studies and technical assistance are mentioned by the World Bank in 1988:

– technical assistance to the SADCC Secretariat and staff support to sector reviews;
– discussions on a programme for training of staff at sector coordinating units;
– assessment of energy coordinating unit's organizational needs;
– co-sponsoring of energy assessments for all SADCC countries (SADCC, 1988c, p.230).

At the 1989 conference there is a reiteration of technical assistance to the SADCC secretariat and sector coordinating units, and the World Bank announces a range of studies and programmes to support manpower development and underpinning for intra-regional investment (SADCC, 1989c, p.208). Indeed in 1989, the World Bank did enter into an agreement to support the SADCC Secretariat, and initiated financing of one economist and one human resources specialist at the SADCC secretariat. However, the World Bank discontinued the agreement and drew back the two specialists in mid 1992.[12]

In 1990 there is an emphasis on a pilot operation concerning the 'removal of non-tariff barriers and providing a funding mechanism for the promotion of cross-border trade and investment – especially to help stimulate exports to countries outside the regional market' (SADCC, 1990c, p.42). The relationship between this and the 1989 'underpinning for intra-regional investment' is not obvious from the intervention, but the world market bias is clear. In 1992 there is a follow-up in an expressed willingness 'to undertake, in cooperation with other donors, initiatives for practical steps towards regional integration such as promotion of economically efficient cross-border investment' (World Bank, 1992e, doc. 1, p.1). But the cross-border investment issues are apparently still being studied, now under the title 'Regional Integration Study' launched in cooperation with the EC and the African Development Bank. The study 'will seek to identify a policy framework within which cross-border private investment and direct foreign investment could flourish, to produce for the intra-regional market and for markets beyond' (ibid., p.3). However, in spite of the similarity of heading and issues of the study announced by the World Bank, it is distinct and separate from SADCC's own 'cross-border investment study', which was discussed in the previous chapter (section 3.4). At the 1992 conference the World Bank also prides itself over the near completion of region-wide studies in the areas of power development, fertilizer and airlines. A study on the working of SACU is announced as close to finalization, and the World Bank will explore ways of assisting SACU 'in achieving a more efficient trade and payment arrangement' (World Bank, 1992e, doc. 1, p.1). The relationship of this study to SADCC's reform process and preparations for a democratic South Africa on the regional stage is not made clear by the World Bank.

This section has witnessed how the World Bank in its rhetoric at SADCC's consultative conferences embraced SADCC's transport and communication programme and put its considerable weight behind the necessity to integrate the regional markets along the lines of the adjustment adapted market integration approach and the recommendations in *From Crisis to Sustainable Growth*. However, no phased liberalization or compensation schemes are presented or promoted. When it comes to practical support for cooperation and integration efforts, only a relatively modest participation in SADCC's infrastructure programme can be identified. There has been no direct assistance to SADCC's industry and trade programme in spite of the importance World Bank attaches to this area. The World Bank reinforced the SADCC Secretariat with two professionals, but discontinued this after approximately two years. Besides, the Bank lent its support to various studies of regional questions. However, it is doubtful whether the majority of the studies are properly integrated in SADCC's work programme. On this basis, it is not surprising that the unofficial view among staff at SADCC headquarters is that the World Bank mostly paid lip-service to regional integration in the 1980s and at the beginning of the 1990s.[13] The same sentiments can be found at the headquarters of the PTA in Lusaka.[14] There is a distinct feeling of being served ready-made meals from World Bank's headquarters in Washington D.C. The only possibilities for the African regional organizations seem to be either to go hungry or accept the menu without question, although discussions between World Bank representatives and people with a regional experience and responsibility might introduce the changes that could make the meal palatable for Southern African consumption.

4.5   Cross-border trade and investment initiative

This section focuses on what appears to be a more tangible result of the World Bank's cross-border investment studies initiated around 1989. The full title of this endeavour is 'Regional Integration Initiative to Facilitate Cross-Border Trade, Payments and Investment in Eastern and Southern Africa'. From now on it will be referred to as the Cross-Border Initiative. The actual launch only took place in 1992, where the empirical thrust of this chapter is ending. However, it has been found appropriate to introduce it, as it is rooted in the years studied, and links up with earlier theoretical discussions. Its importance for future developments is still an open question. The EC Commission, the African Development Bank and IMF are co-sponsors of the Initiative.[15] The objectives of the Cross-Border Initiative are spelled out as follows in a letter from the EC Commission to the Minister of Finance in Malawi on behalf of the sponsors:

> Our main objective is to identify pragmatic steps to promote cross-border private investment for production, with economies of scale and substantial employment impact, for the larger regional market as well as for the external market. The initiative also addresses the facilitation of regional trade and payments. The policy environment thereby created should be helpful in attracting the direct foreign private investment that is so essential for sustaining national investment flows and transferring technology and would also enhance the outward orientation of the economy (Commission of the European Communities, 1993c, p.1).

Concerning the formalities and institutional set up, the Cross-Border Initiative presents itself as a joint initiative between the World Bank, European Community, African Development Bank and IMF. It covers Eastern and Southern Africa, and it overlaps countries eligible for PTA membership. It alleges to have been undertaken in cooperation with the regional and sub-regional bodies concerned: ECA, OAU, Indian Ocean Commission (IOC), PTA and SADCC (ibid.). Note, however, that it is not done with and through these organizations, as envisaged in the adjustment adopted approach, which would have been logical in order to root and sustain the initiative. My own interviews at SADCC and PTA headquarters suggest that the organizations on the one hand are satisfied that the World Bank comes up with a concrete regional initiative, but on the other hand they lament that they have not been involved in its elaboration and they are sceptical as to its viability.

Technical Working Groups are set up in the countries interested in joining the initiative with the participation of both government and the private sector. They review the individual country's situation, and function as forums for the discussion of issues related to regional integration and as counterparts to the staff from the involved international organizations. By early 1993 Technical Working Groups had been created in 13 countries – Burundi, Comoros, Kenya, Madagascar, Malawi, Mauritius, Namibia, Rwanda, Swaziland, Tanzania, Uganda, Zambia and Zimbabwe. Technical surveys had been prepared for Ethiopia and South Africa. In 1992 seminars were held in Mauritius in June and in Zimbabwe in December with participation of the sponsors and of Technical Working Groups as well as consultants and regional organizations in order to discuss the findings of the Groups and identify proposals for a Common Programme of Action. The timetable was expected to be as follows: comments from the involved governments should be received in the first half of 1993, whereafter the implementation phase ideally should begin. As stipulated in the adjustment adapted market integration approach, the countries which are quick on the uptake will be rewarded. The co-sponsoring agencies state that early affirmative replies from the governments will enable considerations of financial assistance, tailored to the individual country's needs (ibid., p.2).

We may now turn to the proposed Common Program of Action as it was elaborated and presented at the end of 1992 (ibid., attachment). It contains activities in four main areas:

(a) trade;
(b) investment;
(c) payments;
(d) institutions.

(a) Regarding trade, the Common Programme of Action – loyal to the adjustment adapted approach – gives first priority as a short term measure for national governments to exempt participating countries from import licensing, foreign exchange allocation etc. In other words, it abolishes the non-trade barriers on a reciprocal basis. No independent move is proposed concerning tariffs. The countries are simply urged to implement the tariff reductions already agreed to in a PTA context. But simultaneously the common list of goods and existing rules of origin must be abolished. At the January 1993 meeting of the Council of Ministers of the PTA the common list was in fact scrapped, and a study on altered rules of origin initiated with a view to abolishing the requirements of majority local ownership and management. Thus, all goods with a minimum regional content will be eligible and there will be no discrimination against foreign-owned and managed firms.[16]

Payments for services are to flow freely in the region, for example as regards the financial sector, including insurance, transport, consultancy and tourism. Access to foreign exchange and use of PTA's travellers cheques for business and leisure travel shall be eased and encouraged.

Transit traffic charges, insurance, customs data, tariff classification, and goods declaration documents will be simplified and harmonized, building on the work PTA has already initiated. A common international standardization norm will be defined, and the countries' standardization organizations will be strengthened. SADCC's experience in this field is not mentioned.[17] It is proposed to improve trade financing through better pre- and post-shipment export credits, and the central banks are urged to allow for at least 180 days credit when firms are exporting to the region, in order to match conditions that countries outside the region can offer. Again there is no mention of earlier SADCC proposals of the establishment of export pre-financing and export credit schemes. (See chapter 3). There should be training at a national level in intra-regional trade development and firms should be assisted to take the initial steps into the regional market.

(b) Regarding investment measures, the domestic regulations will be rationalized and harmonized and the foreign investment code made public. All countries are advised to sign the PTA Charter on Multinational Enterprises and a maximum of 45 days for processing an application is introduced. However, as in the case of tariffs, the Charter is modified so that foreign-owned firms in the region will also be covered by the provisions. The countries will be able to trade each others stock-market shares, double taxation agreements will be established and all the countries will sign the Multilateral Investment Guarantee Agency (MIGA) agreement. The proposal does not seem to take into consideration that, for example, among the SADCC countries only Zimbabwe had a functional stock market in the beginning of the 1990s.[18]

Provision of investment capital has hitherto been a major stumbling block for cross-border investment, as the national banks did not want to sell the necessary amount of scarce foreign capital to the private investor and transfer it abroad. The Common Programme of Action has no solution to this, but proposes that the private sector, governments and regional organizations develop an appropriate mechanism. Once more, there is no reference to SADCC's thorough studies of the issue.[19] Persons attached to cross-border investments should automatically be granted work and residence permits in the country where the investment is made. A PTA protocol on the gradual abolition of visas should be signed and adhered to. 24 hour visits across borders should be automatically permitted.

(c) The liquidity necessary for payments of goods and services is proposed to be reduced through increased and effective use of the PTA Clearing House, and wherever possible market determined exchange rates will be used. New trade facilitating financial instruments will be developed to enable commercial banks in the different countries to create close relations, including operating of accounts in each other's currencies.

(d) Institutionally the national chambers of trade & industry and trade development organizations will improve services to members such as training and trade information. The competing SADCC and PTA organizations in the area[20] shall merge, and efficient, viable regional organization with adequate private sector participation will be created to assist the national members, for example with up-to-date computerized trade information. On a regional level, trade development activities will be arranged such as trade fairs and buyer-seller meetings.

The Technical Working Groups will be maintained, according to the proposal. On the national level they will function as advisory committees for government in matters concerning regional integration. It is stated that a 'programme will be developed for them to continue the work of facilitating regional integration' (Commission of the European Communities, 1993c, p.6). The undertone seems paternalistic: someone from outside – probably the sponsors – will define the programme. Further, Technical Working Groups shall establish channels of communication between themselves and also with regional organizations. Efforts will be made to establish Technical Working Groups in all eligible countries. The concept of a string of Technical Working Groups is interesting. The Groups could be compared to the integrationist technocrats in the neo-functionalist approach. However, there is a major difference. The Technical Working Groups are not fully home grown in the region. They constitute a direct link from the sponsoring agencies such as the World Bank and EC to the heart of government service and the private sector. The link is presented as technical in nature, and as such politically neutral or non-biased. However, this can presumably not be upheld in the long run as the subject-matter with which the Groups are dealing is highly political and at the centre of current debates in the countries. This would be in line with the discussion in chapter 2 of the concept of 'premature politization' of regional issues, which according to the neo-functionalist approach, often blocks or at least complicates a sequence of regional integration measures with high 'spillover' potential.

The existing regional organizations are urged to facilitate the implementation of the Common Programme of Action, for example by allowing nonmembers of the PTA to settle their regional trade through the PTA Clearing House and to sign the PTA Charter for Multinational Industrial Enterprises. The Cross-Border Initiative takes account of 'ongoing studies on the rationalisation and harmonisation of the regional institutions in Eastern and Southern Africa and the Indian Ocean' (ibid., p.7). Thus, a certain neutrality in relation to the future set up for regional cooperation and integration is attempted, but the extended utilization of PTA agreements and rules as building blocks, seems to indicate that the sponsors tend to favour the PTA – if existing regional organizations are at all relevant to the Cross-Border Initiative.

Summing up this section, the Cross-Border Initiative is in a sense refreshing as it tries to distil and apply to Southern and Eastern Africa some of the main content of the adjustment adapted market integration approach and the recommendations contained in *From Crisis to Sustainable Growth*. Moreover, the Initiative tries to go beyond and across the apparent inability of both SADCC and the PTA significantly to advance regional integration in the beginning of the 1990s. However, this last aspect is probably also the greatest weakness of the Cross-Border Initiative: the lack of anchorage in the existing organizations and the absence of firm backing from credible political groups or persons in the relevant countries. Thereby the 'ownership' of the Initiative is put into question: is it something imposed from outside or does it have a genuine African content? If the latter question cannot be answered positively the Initiative is likely to be blocked through a premature politization. Thus, the Technical Working Groups will have no chance of influencing governments to implement the proposals. Consequently, the Initiative might end up as one more idealistic attempt to push regional integration forward. Such a fate is underpinned by the absence of discussion about compensation or other measures to assist the least developed countries to improve their position. Thus, at the time of writing, a pessimistic interpretation as to the possibilities for the success of the Cross-Border Initiative is the most plausible outlook. However, possible efforts especially by the World Bank to integrate the Initiative in its negotiations with the individual countries over structural adjustment programmes, might to some extent alter this perspective.

4.6   Summary

The ambition of this chapter is twofold: (1) to identify the World Bank's general approach towards regional cooperation and integration in Southern Africa, and (2) to assess how the general approach has been transformed into policies and practice towards SADCC. The answer to the first question turned out to be ambiguous. In *World Development Report 1991* a narrow and restricted market integration approach is found. With such a point of departure the World Bank's representatives should discourage or at least refrain from supporting regional integration ventures. A very different approach is detected in *From Crisis to Sustainable Growth* from 1989. Regional cooperation and integration are seen as an organic and indispensable part of the development process in Sub-Saharan Africa. Functional cooperation is strongly supported. The arguments on market integration run to a large degree parallel to the adjustment adapted market integration model; for example, as regards the political motivation to seek regional solutions before a full world market exposure. It is hoped that the regional opening will ease economic hardship as well as build up supportive groups for outward oriented growth. The political factor is also paramount in the discussions of why it is necessary to counteract the polarization process. In *From Crisis to Sustainable Growth* the envisaged institutional set-up is flexible as to geographic coverage and the timing of measures. State intervention in industrial development is to be avoided, but at the same time it is asserted that industries could be 'nurtured' on a regional market.

Turning to the second question, the actual positions taken by the World Bank at SADCC's annual Consultative Conferences show an initial strong verbal support for functional cooperation. Later the Bank representatives in their interventions promoted key elements of the recommendations contained in *From Crisis to Sustainable Growth*. However, the emphasis appears to be more on the liberalization of markets and promoting private investments in general, than sketching a convincingly phased opening first towards the region and later in relation to the world market. Also, there is a conspicuous absence of any mention of the need to compensate weaker regional states. Thus, although the messages from the World Bank representatives are much closer to *From Crisis to Sustainable Growth* than to *World Development Report 1991*, they are still somewhat blurred. This impression is fortified when analyzing the comparatively rather limited World Bank support even for the infrastructure projects. Some technical assistance was provided to the SADCC Secretariat to further the process of regional cooperation and integration as such, but for a relative short period. Various studies were financed but not all seemed to be well coordinated with SADCC. No support has been given to SADCC's industry and trade activities. The Cross-Border Trade and Investment Initiative was also somewhat ambiguous. On the one hand, it is a bold attempt to promote in practice some of the elements of the adjustment adapted approach. On the other hand, the Initiative has a series of weaknesses, not least the lack of local ownership or anchorage, which make plain sailing unlikely in the years ahead. This is underpinned by the lack of mention of polarization and ways to counteract it. Thus, this chapter's initial hypothesis appear to be confirmed: the World Banks signals on the regional level are neither regarding general outline nor concerning the actual policies and action consistent or effective. This is an argument for the necessity to shift the focus to the country level, and there possibly detect the consequences for regional cooperation and integration of the World Banks agreements with the individual countries on structural adjustment programmes.

Notes

1   Reference is made to the discussion in chapter 1 on the limitations of the book, which for both pragmatic and professional reasons, argues for leaving out the IMF and concentrating on the World Bank in relation to structural adjustment programmes in Southern Africa.

2   The Policy Framework Paper is an agreement on the main macroeconomic and sector policies, accorded between the borrowing country on the one hand, and the World Band and IMF on the other. The "ownership" of the document is ideally and formally placed with the borrowing Government, and it demonstrates the country's commitment to the programme. The World Bank and the IMF only assist in its elaboration and sanction its contents. The Policy Framework Paper is the basis for IMF's board to approve loans and payment of tranches from IMF's Enhanced Structural Adjustment Facility, ESAF. However, in the shaping of the pap*er the World Bank plays a* key role and the World Bank puts its authority behind the paper and ties up its own action on the agreements in the Policy Framework Paper.

3   See Organization of African Unity, 1982. In the 1980s the World Bank's policy analysis and advice are normally seen as being at odds with the recommendations of the Lagos Plan of Action from 1980. See for example Browne and Cummings, 1985.

4   Note the similarity with Miksell's, 1963, promotion of protected regional markets in order for exporters to gain experience and discipline, as discussed in section 2.4.

5   Reference is made to chapter 3 of this book.

6   Regarding the 'clearing house' of the PTA, information can be found through the references in note 60, chapter 3.

7   Reference is made to section 2.4 in this book.

8   At SADCC's Consultative Conference in Gaborone a year earlier the World Bank also expressed a very positive attitude to SADCC: 'I would like to reaffirm the Bank's full commitment to SADCC. We believe your goals are important and timely, and your determined efforts worthy of strong external support.' Re SADCC, 1987c, p.225.

9   Overall lending figures to the SADCC countries was at the January 1992 consultative conference estimated to be US$ 1 billion a year (World Bank, 1992e, doc. 1, p.4). Later figures have shown that total direct World Bank lending to the SADCC countries reached US$ 1.5 billion out of US$ 4 billion to Sub-Saharan Africa as a whole. World Bank's global lending stood at more than 21 billion in 1992 (World Bank, 1992f, p.176, table 7–1. Note that both IBRD loans and IDA credits are included). If one focuses on net disbursements from the World Bank to Sub-Saharan Africa the total in fiscal year 1991/1992 reached US$ 783 million. If the

SADCC countries receive the same percentage of this amount, as they constitute of total lending to Sub-Saharan Africa in 1992, a disbursement figure for the SADCC countries of US$ 294 million is attained. To give an impression of the magnitude of this amount, net disbursement of Official Development Assistance (ODA) from all donors to the SADCC countries excluding Angola and Swaziland totalled US$ 4.2 billion in 1991. Corresponding ODA figures for Angola and Swaziland totalled US$ 177 million in 1989. Later ODA data are unfortunately not available. Sources: World Bank, 1994, p.198ff., table 19. The figures for Angola and Swaziland refer to the year 1989. They are sourced from UNDP/ World Bank, 1992, p.294, table 12–2. This crude estimate suggests that the World Bank provides somewhere between 5–10 per cent of net disbursement of ODA in the SADCC countries in the beginning of the 1990s. This deserves further investigation, which space unfortunately does not allow in this book. However, it fits well with the later observations of the World Bank's relative limited concrete support for SADCC projects. It also serves as a pointer to the exaggeration of the actual importance of the World Bank in financing Southern African development that is widespread both among supporters and critics of the World Bank in the region.

10   Other larger donors for the Beira Port Transport System are the European Community with 17 per cent, Italy with 21 per cent and the Nordics with 24 per cent of total secured funding which at that stage stood at US$ 413 million. Re. SADCC, 1991b.

11   See for example World Bank, 1994.

12   Interview made by the author in March, 1993 with Emang Maphanyane, Senior Economist at the SADCC Secretariat from the mid 1980s till the end of 1992. Re. Interview, 1993a.

13   Interview, 1993a.

14   The author's own interview at PTA headquarters in Lusaka, April 1993. Re. Interview, 1993b. The PTA has even produced introductory documents regarding possible cooperation between the organization and the IMF and the World Bank. Re. PTA, 1991; PTA, 1993c. However, no serious two-way discussion had been initiated, according the above PTA source.

15   See Southern African Economist, 1993.

16   Reference is also made to the discussion of these issues earlier in the book: sections 2.6 and 3.5.

17   Reference is made to last chapter's discussion of SADCC's mostly futile attempt over a decade to assist the establishment, and to strengthen the functioning of standards bodies in the member states.

18 There are efforts in other SADCC countries, notably Botswana, to float shares locally and establish real stock markets, but this is likely to be at least a medium term venture.
19 Reference is made to section 3.4 of this book.
20 SADCC Regional Business Council and PTA Federation of Chambers of Commerce and Industry.

5   National structural adjustment programmes and their consequences: The case of Mozambique

5.1   Introduction

Whereas in the previous chapter World Bank policies and action were treated on a regional level, this chapter will focus on the national structural adjustment programmes, arranged bilaterally between the IMF/World Bank on the one side, and the individual SADCC member states on the other. Mozambique has been chosen as a country example which allows for a more in-depth analysis than an examination solely of regional trends would have permitted. Among the two Bretton Woods institutions I shall maintain the previous chapter's focus on the World Bank.[1]

At the heart of structural adjustment programmes are the policies guiding external macroeconomic relations - avoiding imbalances, liberalization versus protection etc. They are coupled with structural changes in for example industry. These policies are at the same time key variables in any attempt to foster greater regional integration in trade and industry. As a growing number of SADCC countries in the 1980s and early 1990s entered into structural adjustment programmes, the discussion in relation to a possible enhancement of regional trade and industrial production becomes increasingly inadequate without contemplating the contents and effects of these programmes.[2] Thus, the aim of this chapter is to scrutinize the consequences of structural adjustment programmes on manufacturing industry and trade, especially in a regional perspective. This provides, furthermore, an opportunity to analyse the consistency of World Bank policies, when the focus moves from a regional to a national level.

Do the PFPs[3] that constitute the common platform of the government in question and the World Bank exhibit any references to regional cooperation and integration within trade and industry? If so, which approach and policy do they reflect? In the case of an answer in the negative, relevant questions would be: how do the agreed policies influence the countries' chances of enhancing regional trade and industry development; how can the framework be characterized that has been indirectly created for regional economic interaction and what are the preliminary experiences?

Among the ten SADCC countries, the six non-SACU members are the most interesting for the purpose of the present book, as the trade regime of the four SACU countries is, by and large, covered by the customs union treaty which is not altered by structural adjustment programmes, at least not in the short and medium term.[4] Five of the six - non-SACU - SADCC members have in the 1980s or in the beginning of the 1990s initiated structural adjustment programmes. The exception is Angola, which was in a special situation, because of the high foreign exchange receipts from oil sales, the internal war situation as well as the close ties with the Soviet Union and hostility from the United States in the 1980s. However, from 1987 onwards Angola implemented successive home grown restructuring and austerity programmes.[5] Tanzania did the same in the period 1981-86 after brief overtures with the IMF in 1980.[6] After serious initial disagreements, the local programmes in fact paved the way for a stand-by arrangement with the IMF in 1986, and in 1987 a Structural Adjustment Facility was in place to back up the implementation of the new Economic Recovery Programme. There have been more controversies, for example about the depth of devaluations, but the programme has continued up until the time of writing, although at a relatively modest pace.[7]

Zambia has the longest and most turbulent history with the IMF and the World Bank.[8] It started out in the beginning of the 1970s with stand-by facilities and loans accompanied by various economic reform packages. However, with the collapse of the world market price of copper, the non-viability of Zambia's import-substitution industrialization, the steady decline in economic conditions, high inflation, under-financed foreign exchange auctions, and unemployment, tensions rose between the government and the World Bank in the first half of the 1980s. In 1986 the 'riot-threshold' was passed, and violent demonstrations and strikes broke out in the copper-belt[9] in protest against the price rise of basis food items. In 1987 Zambia introduced its own modified reform programme.[10] However, without World Bank approval other donors held back, and hard currency generation was insufficient, although debt payments were reduced to ten per cent of export revenues. Consequently, a new deal was struck between the government and the World Bank around 1990. It was never fully implemented before the multi-party elections that brought the Movement for Multi-party Democracy to power in 1991. In the following two years structural adjustment was pursued with a vigour and commitment not before seen in the region.[11]

Zimbabwe did not join the club of countries with World Bank sanctioned structural adjustment programmes until 1990. Discussions had been held for several years during the 1980s, but massive divergencies evolved around the

160

admissible level of public budget deficit, and the phasing of import liberalizations. After 1990, especially the high level of inflation and the negative social developments have been controversial political issues in the debate in Zimbabwe about the structural adjustment programme.[12] In Malawi the first stabilization package undertaken with the IMF dates back to 1979 and up until 1987 three structural adjustment programmes were agreed with the IMF and the World Bank. In 1987/88 Malawi was together with Mozambique one of the first countries to benefit from IMF's Enhanced Structural Adjustment Facility (ESAF) with a substantially larger concessional element[13] than a 'normal' stand-by facility. However, in the beginning of the 1990s donor opposition to the continued one-man/one-party rule in Malawi circumscribed severely external funding of both the structural adjustment programme and other foreign financed projects.[14]

In Mozambique the move towards a more liberal orientated economic policy was formally initiated at the Fourth Congress of the ruling party, Front for the Liberation of Mozambique (Frelimo) in 1983. This Congress stressed the need for decentralization, incentives to stimulate peasant family production, and that priority be given to small projects as distinct from the grandiose scale or 'gigantismo' of the former projects which consumed the major part of available development financing.[15] This was followed up by membership of the IMF and the World Bank in 1984. The following year some price liberalizations were initiated, and at the beginning of 1987 the government introduced the Economic Recovery Programme, known by its Portuguese acronym PRE (Programa de Rehabilitação Economico). During 1985-86 the contents were negotiated with the IMF and the World Bank, but disagreements still existed regarding the final version, when the government presented its plan. The controversy concerned essentially the phasing of price liberalizations and devaluations, allocation of foreign exchange and level of support to the private sector.[16] However, PRE was accepted by IMF and the World Bank, and is reflected in the first Policy Framework Paper 1987-89 agreed between these institutions and the government in May 1987. Thus, IMF approved an ESAF for Mozambique of US$ 16 million in June, and in May and August the World Bank agreed to loans totalling US$ 135 million (Hanlon, 1991, p.122). Mid 1987 the first Consultative Group meeting was held in Paris between the government, World Bank and the main donors.

As already mentioned, the rest of the chapter will concentrate on one country, Mozambique. In terms of methodology this will allow the analysis to be more specific when scrutinizing empirical developments, than would have been the case, if the analysis had covered the whole region. On the other hand the concentration on one country weakens the ability to generalize findings. However, the purpose is not to establish sweeping generalizations across the region, but rather to substantiate key aspects of a structural adjustment programme in the region that may illuminate important issues of the book, and indicate areas for further research. Mozambique has been chosen because - as one of the larger SADCC countries - it has had a stable, relatively well defined cooperation with the World Bank within the time frame of the book' main focus. Moreover, Mozambique has experience with a good deal of the key elements of structural adjustment programmes.[17] In addition, Mozambique has been a strong supporter of regional cooperation and integration since its independence. The internal war situation in Mozambique in the 1980s and early 1990s might be said to discredit it as a 'typical' country example. However, manufacturing industry, which is central to regional trade enhancement, is located in the larger cities that remained relatively unaffected by the war. The prime focus is on the period 1988-91.

In the next section, consecutive Policy Framework Papers will be analysed after a brief background note on developments from 1980-86. This is followed by an overview of economic performance by Mozambique under structural adjustment. The ensuing topic is trade - how imports and exports have developed with special emphasis on the region. Subsequently, foreign investment and industrial development are highlighted, and an attempt is made to substantiate the observations with a discussion of developments within one industrial branch - textile and clothing.

5.2 Regional aspects of policy framework papers

5.2.1 Background

In the first half of the 1980s Mozambique had been caught in a vicious circle of dwindling hard currency exports and service earnings on the one hand, and an ever increasing inability to import incentive goods for agriculture, inputs and spares for industry on the other. This was intensified by South Africa's destabilization policies, Mozambique National Resistance (Renamo's) acts of sabotage and destruction of infrastructure in the countryside,[18] and was further aggravated by policy failures of the ruling Frelimo party government, especially the over-optimistic belief in the country's short term ability to construct large projects and benefit from them.[19] Moreover, the government had little success in reversing the situation once that political decision had been taken, due to insufficient resources and the sluggishness of the state apparatus in transforming policy into action. Furthermore, economic policy was characterized by a belief in the state as the all dominant engine of development. Well-meaning but, under the circumstances, idealistic policies of creating tolerable conditions for the whole population were implemented through administrative plans and control. This left little space for creativity, incentives and adjustments.

The seriousness of the situation can be illustrated by the rate of growth in Gross Domestic Product 1980-86:

Table 5.1

Mozambique – growth rate of Gross Domestic Product (GDP), 1980–86 (per cent)

1980	1981	1982	1983	1984	1985	1986
4.7	0.9	-3.3	-12.9	-2.2	-10.4	-2.0

Source: Government of Mozambique, 1988

With about 2.5 per cent annual population increase the decline per capita is naturally even more accentuated.

The Balance of Payment position illustrates how the trade deficit persists, service receipts fall, and interest and other payments multiply. The result is an ever-increasing current account deficit.

Table 5.2

Mozambique – balance of payment, current account, 1980/83/86 (million US$)

	1980	1983	1986
Trade balance	-519	-505	-463
Service receipts	171	166	119
Interests & other paym.	-75	-166	-278
Current account	-423	-505	-622

Source: World Bank, 1988, p.36

The trade balance figures cover a fall both in imports and exports. Imports fell from 800m US$ in 1980 to 543m US$ in 1986. In 1986 exports had contracted to 28 per cent of their 1980 value, as indicated by the following figures:

Table 5.3

Mozambique – exports, 1980–86 (million US$)

1980	1981	1982	1983	1984	1985	1986
281	281	229	132	96	77	79

Source: as table 5.2

In 1983 Mozambique exhausted its foreign exchange reserves, and in January 1984 officially declared its inability to continue normal debt servicing. This is not surprising, taking into account the debt service ratio indicated below.

Table 5.4
Mozambique – debt service in per cent of export and service receipts after debt relief, 1980–86

1980	1981	1982	1983	1984	1985	1986
32	75	97	129	96	110	248

Source: as table 5.2

Turning to the internal balances, the state only succeeded in covering around 60 per cent of expenditures by revenues, and the public budget deficit varied from 8 to 16 per cent of GDP from 1980–86. The money stock tripled and state companies' operating losses were relatively uncritically covered by low interest bank credits (Government of Mozambique, 1988, pp.1 and 34).

It is against this bleak background – which spelled imminent collapse, and excluded a continuation on the basis of 'socialism as usual' – that the Economic Recovery Programme must be analysed.

5.2.2 Policy framework papers

The basis for the following is the PFPs[20] that are annually agreed between the government, the IMF and the World Bank. The PFPs are 'Prepared by the Mozambican Government in collaboration with the staffs of the International Monetary Fund and the World Bank', as officially stated on the cover. They are key documents for the granting of credits by the two institutions, and they constitute a basis for the annual Consultative Conferences between government and donors. The contents is typically an economic status report, perspectives for economic development and external financing requirements for the coming 2–3 years, as well as an outline of adjustment reforms, including an implementation schedule. In the midst of innumerable unilateral statements, position papers, 'aide mémoires', consultancy reports etc., they must be seen as probably the most authoritative source of information on the structural adjustment programme. Six PFPs – issued in the period from 1987–92 – are main sources for the discussion below.[21] Thus, one additional PFP is included on both sides of the main period in focus 1988–91, in order to complete statistics and not to forego important background information.

The first question to be asked is whether reference to regional cooperation and integration is included, when the external economics and industrial development are discussed and strategies outlined in the PFPs. The firm answer is no. It has not been possible to find any reference to the region, apart from sporadic mention in relation to the transport and communications sector.[22] I have likewise not succeeded in identifying any mention of the programme of cooperation in industry and trade within SADCC, or of the PTA obligations – for example tariff reductions.

Consequently, it is necessary to establish the framework that is indirectly created for regional cooperation and integration in trade and industry. This is ventured by identifying the relevant measures of the programme within the areas of external economic relations and industry/enterprise development.[23] The following two broad fields of intervention will be taken up:

1   exchange rates, allocation of foreign exchange, as well as tariffs and export promotion;

2   prices and distribution, management independence, credits, privatization and rehabilitation of industry, as well as industrial development strategy.

However, before going into these in detail, they must be put into perspective by presenting the goals of the programme. In the 1987 PFP (Government of Mozambique, 1987, p.1) the following triple general objectives are stated:

–   stabilization;
–   more effective resource allocation;
–   growth.

The direct mention of the growth objective is interesting, as it is sometimes omitted when discussing the goals of structural adjustment, because it is seen as an automatic result of reaching the two other objectives. However, it can also be noted that the growth element is not qualified, for example in relation to the distributional or environmental effects of growth. Stabilization is the typical domain of the IMF, and refers to the removal or reduction of the deficit on the external account, and an elimination or minimization of the fiscal deficit. Action in these areas tends to be seen as short term in nature, and as a precondition for success in the two other areas. The agenda behind external stabilization is to facilitate a resumption of repayment of international debt as well as maintain or re-establish other normal relations with the international financial institutions. The reduced fiscal deficit will limit the money supply and ideally lower the level of inflation. The more effective resource allocation is usually the field of operation of the World Bank, and covers the transition of the economy from various forms of distortions in relation to an ideal market economic model to a situation where the economy functions according to market signals. To 'get prices right' and be 'guided by the relative prices' are the important catch words of this approach. The policies are normally seen in a somewhat longer perspective than the stabilization measures, and involve a wide variety of changes – legal, institutional, even physical – in a diverse range of areas: finance, commerce, industry, agriculture etc. The indirect agenda behind this is the greater integration of the given country into the world market. The distinction between stabilization and effective resource allocation is analytical and cannot as such be applied mechanically to reality. A given measure in a structural adjustment programme may very well contribute both to stabilization and to effective resource allocation.

The above threefold aims could form the basis of any structural adjustment programme in the Third World. The more country specific aims formulated in 1987 for the Mozambican programme are the following (ibid., p.4 and Government of Mozambique, 1989, p.5).

a) Reverse the decline in production and restore a minimal level of consumption and income for the population, especially in rural areas.
b) Curtail domestic financial imbalances and strengthen the country's external payments position.
c) Establish the conditions for more rapid and more efficient economic growth in the medium and longer term when the security situation and other exogenous constraints to the programme have eased.

In the 1989 PFP the following two aims were added:

d) Reintegrate official and parallel markets.
e) Restore orderly financial relationships with trading partners and creditors.

In 1991 these goals had been redefined as an overall aim of ' achieving financial viability and to overcome the extreme poverty ... through the restoration of sustainable economic growth' (Government of Mozambique, 1991a, p.2). The programme is intended to foster 'growth and employment in the private sector, reduce imbalances, particularly in the public sector, while raising public sector efficiency and lowering external imbalances by stimulating export activities' (Government of Mozambique, 1992, p.3). To achieve this, restrictive fiscal and monetary policies are stressed, ensuring adequate credit to the economy and promoting stable prices.[24] Institutional capacity building is to be strengthened and there will be a deepening of the reforms concerning the liberalization of the exchange rate, trade and price regimes, acceleration of the privatization of public enterprises and further financial sector reforms. Living conditions in the rural areas are to be improved and targeted measures will support households that are 'beyond the scope of current growth strategies' (Government of Mozambique, 1992, p.3). Thus, there is not much in the 1991 formulation of aims and means that cannot be covered by the initial goals. However, the social dimension which since 1989 the government has insisted on including, is contemplated, but only in a restricted form as indicated by the expressions 'extreme poverty' and 'beyond the scope of current growth strategies'. Important for the analysis given below is the emphasis on privatization and on restrictive monetary policies.

Moreover, in all the years of structural adjustment the government and the World Bank have set explicit goals regarding the foreseen rate of growth and inflation, and stipulated that export of goods and services are expected to cover an increasing part of imports and service payments. I shall come back to the objectives and their implementation later. First, I shall present a scrutiny of the above mentioned measures of special relevance for regional cooperation and integration within trade and industry.

5.2.3 Exchange rates, allocation of foreign exchange, tariffs, export promotion

Exchange rate adjustments – normally a euphemism for drastic depreciations of an overvalued currency – is the archetypical measure of a structural adjustment programme. It is intended to contribute both to stabilization and transformation towards a market economy with effective resource allocation. It stabilizes the external imbalance by discouraging imports, as they become more expensive, and stimulates exports that become cheaper for foreign customers and/or more profitable in local currency for the exporter. It helps to bring about a more effective resource allocation by setting a more realistic price on foreign exchange, by gradually creating a currency market, and it should encourage the use of domestic resources. In 1986, the last year before the introduction of the structural adjustment programme, the official rate of exchange was 1 US$ equal to 40 meticais (mts), whilst the price for a dollar on the black/parallel market reached 1600 mts – 40 times the official rate. In January 1987 the meticais was devaluated to a fifth of its value – so that 1 US$ corresponded to 200 mts, and in June the same year IMF insistence led to a further drastic depreciation to 400 mts a dollar. The rates under PRE are shown in table 5.5

The gap between the official and parallel rate is clearly diminishing in the period under scrutiny. Until the end of 1989 the exchange rate was determined through a fixed rate towards the US$, and the period was characterized by periodic rather large devaluations. In the 1990s the metical was pegged to a basket of currencies, and devaluations have been smaller and carried out routinely on a monthly basis. The latter method is much less disruptive to the economy than the former which made sound company planning virtually impossible (Interview, 1993c). In October 1990 a secondary market for foreign exchange was created with rates between the official and parallel market. Here the exchange rate was in principle decided by demand and supply.

167

Individuals could freely sell foreign exchange and buy up to certain limits for personal use and for imports. Companies were later included in the system. They could sell their export retention rights (see below) and receipts from non-traditional exports. Imports were only subject to an import licence and to a small negative list of goods. This move ended with the integration of the secondary and official exchange rate in April 1992. Thus, a market had been established, but its fragility is obvious, as its functioning depends on the availability of untied donor funds to supplement Mozambique's own foreign exchange earnings. Tied funds would be sold with a discount of eight per cent in relation to the market rate. The Mozambican government estimated in 1991 that donor funds between US$ 300–350 million were needed annually (Government of Mozambique, 1991b) to make the new system work. However, that year a delay and reduction of promised aid hampered industrial growth in the country, making the prospects for the new system somewhat bleak.

Table 5.5
Mozambique – official and parallel foreign exchange rates, 1987–92
(Meticais value of 1 US$)

Rates	1987	1988	1989	1990	1991	1992
Official (1)	292	529	745	929	1434	1990
Parallel (2)	1095	1185	1500	2115	2150	2765
1 as per cent of 2	27	45	50	44	67	72

Note: Official rate' is the one quoted by the National Bank of Mozambique, whereas the 'parallel rate' is the one to which foreign exchange takes place outside the officially sanctioned system
Sources: calculations based on: International Monetary Fund (IMF), 1992, 1.6 and Abreu and Baltazar, 1992

The exchange rate policy is intimately linked to the allocation of foreign exchange and the import system.[25] Before the above mentioned new 1992 system a variety of administrative measures had been in place to distribute the scarce foreign funds in the PRE-period. Firstly, there was the export retention scheme, introduced already in 1984, which secured exporters a part of their export earnings to be used for necessary imports without having to go through the cumbersome procedures of applying for a foreign exchange allocation. In 1987 the World Bank supported the creation of a foreign currency Market Fund that distributed foreign exchange to importers of various consumer goods. The number of products that could only be traded through state trading corporations were reduced to just a few. Individuals did not need any authorization to import goods for own funds up to a value of US$ 500. Imports valued above US$ 500 would automatically be granted import licences, when purchased for the importers own foreign exchange.

In 1989 the System for Non-Administrative Allocation of Foreign Exchange (Sistema Não-Administrativo de Alocação de Divisas – SNAAD) was introduced. It came after the IMF had unsuccessfully tried to convince the government to start up an auction programme for foreign exchange, like the one in Zambia that fared so badly.[26] Through SNAAD, companies could import raw materials and spares for a number of industrial branches without having to apply for an import licence. SNAAD covered five branches in 1989, including clothing, growing to more than ten in 1991. However, SNAAD never really achieved the intended function of opening up the economy and making imports more effective, because few funds were put at the facility's disposal (US$ 20–30 million yearly) and then at irregular intervals, which was greatly damaging to the Mozambican enterprises. Moreover, administrative rules were established to avoid fraud, which made it difficult to distinguish SNAAD from the Office for Coordination of Import Programmes (Gabinete de Coordinação de Programas de Importação – GCPI) that administered the mostly tied aid import support programmes and still required import licences. The 1987 Policy Framework Paper stated that in the unavoidable interim period in which administrative allocations of foreign exchange would continue, government should 'ensure that resources are channelled to firms with high domestic value added and with efficient import substitution possibilities' (Government of Mozambique, 1987, p.10). No mention has been found in the PFP's of the possibility of earmarking a certain percentage of the import licences to imports from other SADCC or PTA countries. This has been recommended by both organizations and implemented in Zimbabwe, although on a small scale.

Tariffs had been unchanged since colonial days (*Bolletim Official de Moçambique*, 1964) until they were modified in 1988 and 1991. The 1988 legislation – only implemented in early 1989[27] – contained basically a rationalization of legislation with fewer product categories, reduction of applicable rates and exemptions, plus the introduction of ad valorem rates.[28] The 1991 reform implied a harmonization with international nomenclature and an emphasis on the economic role of tariffs in the economy. This includes considerations about (Government of Mozambique, 1989, p.8):

- tax revenue needs;
- industrial priorities and protection to promote efficient sectors;
- the impact on consumption; and
- the relationship with other aspects of the trade regime, for example foreign exchange allocation.

The result was the introduction in 1991 of only six ad valorem rates, increasing with the level of industrial processing, with the exception of capital equipment, and with a maximum of 35 per cent. Moreover, the turnover tax was made applicable to imports, too, and made equal for domestic produce and imports.[29] The new rates are:

- 5 per cent: essential goods;
- 10 per cent: raw materials;
- 15 per cent: intermediary semi-processed products;
- 25 per cent: finished intermediary products;
- 10 per cent: capital equipment, machines and equipment;
- 35 per cent: consumer goods – both durable and nondurable (Weinmann, 1991, p.58).

To this shall be added a general, across the board, 7.5 per cent import tax that the Mozambican authorities apply for fiscal reasons.[30] The latter tends to distort the picture as it constitute a relatively larger increase in the lower than the higher tariff categories. The following comments do not take the 7.5 per cent tariff into account. The new scale's unweighed average of 17 per cent is not high compared to a developing country mean of more than 30 per cent (World Bank, 1991a, p.98, table 5.3). The structure of the new rates seems sensible from an industrialization point of view with relatively low rates on raw materials, intermediary products and capital equipment. The 35 per cent tax on imported manufactures is not an extremely high rate, as it correspond to a developing country average (ibid.), and could be judged as low for a country nurturing an embryonic industrial sector. Whether or not a given rate is sufficient to make industry grow and produce more effectively or conversely overexpose it to world market competition depends on the situation in the individual branch, and on other supplementary measures including the government's strategy for industrial development. However, an initial tariff rate should – after a transition period – ideally be lowered in order to stimulate competitiveness. This could be done in phases as the World Bank proposes in *From Crisis to Sustainable Growth*, where an opening towards regional partners is the first step (see chapter 4). However, this discussion is not taken up in the Policy Framework Papers. There is also no reference in the Policy Framework Papers to the agreed gradual reduction of tariffs between the PTA member countries towards 0 per cent intra-regional customs duties in the year 2000, or to the special arrangement that Mozambique has obtained of reducing only by all in all 10 per cent before year 2000 (Interview, 1993d and PTA, 1993a, p.6). Winding up the issue of tariffs, the questions of inefficiency in customs administration and smuggling must also be mentioned. Both are widespread in Mozambique. By moderate efforts to increase efficiency the effective tariff collection, compared to total imported value, increased from 12 to 18 per cent in 1991–92 (Government of Mozambique, 1992, p.5). Smuggling is much more difficult to quantify, but undoubtedly takes place on a large scale from neighbouring countries and by sea from for example Dubai. Unrecorded border trade is generally estimated to 10–15 per cent of total trade in Africa (Interview, 1993b), and is probably higher in the Mozambican case.

Export promotion has not either been targeted towards the SADCC or PTA region, according to the Policy Framework Papers. The measures have been few and general in nature. The export retention scheme was expanded to cover all non-traditional exports, but its retention rates were reduced. Moreover, the state monopolies within foreign trade were gradually abolished and ordinary firms were allowed to trade abroad.[31] With a view to enterprise rehabilitation the 1991 Policy Framework Paper stresses (Government of Mozambique, 1991a, p.10):

> [I]n view of the relative small size of the domestic market and the likely continuation of limited internal demand in the medium term, priority is being given to the rehabilitation of large-scale enterprises in sectors with high export potential

However, nothing seems to be done to put this policy into practice. This inability to promote exports from manufacturing industry is all the more surprising when taking into consideration the overall aim of letting exports of goods and services cover a larger part of imports, and the fact that non-traditional goods have been the fastest growing export product group after the introduction of PRE, but at the same time operating on very thin ice, as will be evident below. The Policy Framework Papers do not even mention simple things such as Mozambique's participation in trade fairs in the region, financing of regional market surveys and market exploration visits and attempt to start up a quality and standardization office that could facilitate regional trade.[32] Nor is there any discussion of the important 1989 trade agreement with South Africa (see below) that allows for some Mozambican exports to enter South Africa with an import tariff of only three per cent within certain limits as to volume and value. We may now turn to the remaining items that constitute the framework for regional economic interaction within trade and industry.

5.2.4 Prices and distribution, management independence, credits, privatization and rehabilitation of industry, industrial development strategy

The question of decontrolling prices was one of the major issues in 1987, when the PRE was introduced. 44 products were subject to fixed prices and the majority of the rest were under a system of ex-post reviews of possible price changes – known as 'conditioned' price setting. By the end of 1988 fixed prices were only applied to 25 products and many product prices were completely set free. In manufacturing industry just three product groups remained with fixed prices: beer, cigarettes and soap. In the beginning of 1992 all three had been transferred to the 'conditioned system' and later in the year the Policy Framework Paper could announce that:

> [F]ixed prices are now limited only to basic necessities including food aid, staples, fuels, and utilities ... The conditioned price system, currently applied principally to domestically produced industrial goods, will be phased out by end-June 1993, except for products subject to monopolistic conditions (Government of Mozambique, 1992, p.4)

The distribution system was dominated by state trading monopolies before 1987. Encatex was the state-owned wholesale company for textile and clothing. It bought everything the factories produced and sold it to the retailers, other ministries, agricultural commercialization companies etc., according to a prearranged plan. However, the latter was never fulfilled in the 1980s, because of the constant drop in production. This and other monopolies were abolished in 1987 and already in 1989 the Policy Framework Paper stated:

> ... Government has over the two years opened up domestic trade allowing increased competition with other enterprises in domestic and international markets. In particular, private enterprises have been permitted to participate in most trading activities reserved to public corporations (Government of Mozambique, 1989, p.3)

Thus, the structural adjustment programme has succeeded in creating markets in these areas, where before there were none, and has established the possibility of 'getting the prices right' as well as achieving a more effective resource allocation. The question that remains to be posed is whether markets function sufficiently well to be trusted with the main allocating tasks in society. This is to be doubted. I shall not go into the disputed decision of abolishing the low-cost subsidized general rationing system in Maputo and Beira in 1989 and the attempt to reintroduce targeted subsidies in the beginning of the 1990s.[33] However, the political consequences of the undisputed fall in living standards for ordinary wage earners and the increase in absolute poverty for more vulnerable groups, have undoubtedly implied an increased disruption of the social fabric and an alienation of a large part of the earlier coalition of forces behind the government.[34]

Increased management autonomy is an indirect consequence of several of the other PRE measures, such as the above price liberalizations and opening up of domestic and international trade for the individual company. The abolition of state subsidies to all but a handful of strategic and war-exposed companies, has also emphasized the management's independence and responsibility. However, for the large number of state owned and worse, 'intervened'[35] companies, there is still a grey zone of submission and dependence. It functions often indirectly and on a personal level, because managers may be shifted etc. by decision of the relevant sector ministry. However, it is the author's impression from interviews with industrial leaders in 1993, that there is a profound feeling of far greater autonomy and also a greater job satisfaction than before 1987.[36]

The increased autonomy of the companies, moving away from direct state subordination, has meant an increased demand on the individual company's liquidity and a dependence on the banking sector for loans. However, in order to curb inflation tight monetary policies have been adopted in the structural adjustment programme. This has implied credit ceilings and high interest rates. Thus, in the banking sector the companies may be met by the impossibility of expanding credits, because overall credit ceilings accorded between the government and IMF have been fully subscribed.[37] If funds are available, interest rates are very high. From the beginning of 1989 to the end of 1991 interest on a one year bank loan rose from 22 to 35 per cent and a year later interest had jumped to 45 per cent. The latter should correspond to a real interest rate of around 20 per cent (Direcção Nacional de Estatística (DNE), 1992 and Interview, 1993g). The high rates have the laudable purpose of facilitating positive interests on deposits and they should assist in curbing inflation. However, the negative side effects on productive activity are indisputable. It is impossible to quantify the foregone welfare improvements which the seemingly prohibitive high interest rates have caused; nevertheless that this is a major problem, can be confirmed by industrialists and government officials.[38] Representatives of the World Bank are aware of the problem, but stick to the restrictive credit policy from fear that to relax it will accelerate inflation (Interview, 1993g).

At the same time a common picture emerges among Mozambican enterprises that by 1990 they had exhausted whatever funds they had possessed for the self financing of investments, and for overcoming a liquidity crisis. Consequently, in the 1990s they have increasingly had to rely on bank loans for financing the ever growing amounts they have to pay in local currency for imports. This is money that they will only gradually get back after transforming the imports to saleable products. The result was stockpiling in harbours of imported goods ordered by companies, but which these companies were unable to pay for, because they had not sufficient money for countervalue and custom duties, and they could not afford the expensive bank loans. This kind of experience makes firms very cautious of importing inputs for production, which in turn leads to lower production levels. New investments are reduced, as both industrial entrepreneurs and well established companies

173

have little chance of fulfilling their obligations to the banking sector.[39] The competitiveness of Mozambican industry on the export market in the region and elsewhere will naturally suffer, and the ability to compete with imports will likewise diminish. The World Bank (1991c, p.3) admits the negative influence of the financing conditions in a background paper

> The poor performance [of public enterprises] is primarily because of outmoded or damaged equipment and technology, lack of skilled workers, *high debt and liquidity problems, tight credit ceilings in the banking system which deny enterprises access to necessary working capital*, [my emphasis] and insecurity in areas that supply raw materials.

It seems strange that the parties involved are not engaged in an effort to secure low interest capital for promising projects and industries that have proved their effectiveness in practice. In South Korea this was done on the basis of a company's export performance. The lack of an overall strategy, defining priorities for industrial development is strongly felt.

The questions of enterprise rehabilitation and privatization within PRE are interlinked with, and constitute an important part of, the potential for Mozambican industrial performance on the regional market. Right from the outset of the PRE programme, in the PFP of 1987, a review was on the agenda of some 25 industrial and 15 agricultural enterprises, and the 1988 PFP announced that in the middle of that year recommendations regarding possible rehabilitation, disinvesture or closure would be forthcoming. However, in 1993 it could be observed that the process had not really taken off, but rather entered into a vicious circle of inaction, as the World Bank did not want to go ahead with investment and rehabilitation without a preceding financial reorganization and privatization, and both these processes have dragged out. Consequently, in 1993 the World Bank concentrated on a smaller number of already private enterprises (Interview, 1993g). However, it seems strange that the World Bank should not have the power to insist on, and the government a willingness to go through with, an early economic reconstruction of the original enterprises. Moreover, the World Bank should have the capacity and the flexibility to start rehabilitation before a possible privatization instead of blocking progress.

The impasse created is probably a symptom of underlying political divergencies between the World Bank and dominant parts of the Frelimo party on the issue of privatization in the late 1980s. The development agenda of the World Bank urges it to maximize the role of the private sector, but for example in 1988 the central committee of Frelimo states:

> Our strategic orientation remains:
> – to develop the state and cooperative sectors;

- to integrate and develop the family (peasant) sector and encourage it to organize cooperatives or other forms of collective production;
- to involve all other productive sectors, viz. the private and mixed sectors, with the patriotic duty of rehabilitating the country's economy (SIDA, 1988, p.17).

The intention of letting the state sector and collective form of ownership play a leading role is evident from the above. The private sector will simply be complementary. However, this position was steadily undermined by the increased orientation towards Western countries and the embrace of a free market economy, which was directly enshrined in the new constitution of 1990.[40] A contributory factor was also the ever more frequent examples of state companies becoming plagued by corruption and decay.[41]

The table below gives an overview of the situation regarding enterprise ownership in 1989.

Table 5.6
Mozambique – overview of ownership of enterprises, 1989

	No.	Per cent
State owned enterprises	114	20
'Intervened'* enterprises	140	25
Private or mixed enterprises	321	55
Total	572	100

* The status 'intervened' indicates that the state had to take the company over, because it was abandoned by the former owners, but a corresponding legal status was never established

Source: World Bank, 1991c, p.3

From 1987–92 about 120 mostly small and medium scale enterprises were privatized, 17 have come under mixed ownership, and 48 are under 'concession contracts' (Government of Mozambique, 1992, p.7). This will further increase the dominance in numbers of private or mixed companies, but if data were available for the relative weight of the enterprises involved,[42] the picture would be reversed, and the state owned and intervened firms would dominate. The PFPs confirm the impression that not much progress was made regarding the privatization issue in the first three years of the PRE programme. Only around 1990–91 did the government have its first legislative framework in place[43] and the World Bank stepped up its support for a key technical unit in the Ministry of Finance[44] that would prepare larger enterprises for privatization, and for corresponding units in sector ministries dealing with smaller and medium level companies. A high level interministerial committee, chaired by the Prime Minister, was created to oversee the work.[45] The enterprises were grouped in three categories. 1) Strategic companies and public utilities that remained statal. They will be assisted to function effectively in a market economy; 2) non-strategic and nonviable companies that will be closed; 3) the commercially oriented companies that already are, or potentially can be made, economically viable. They will be included in a privatization process that on a case to case basis can imply direct sale of the whole company, joint ventures, management contracts, leasing, management buy-out, selling public shares to the highest bidder, selling a prearranged part of the shares to management and workers[46] and the remaining to a foreign or local private entrepreneur.

The privatization process will undoubtedly proceed in the coming years. Neither the Frelimo party, the government, the state apparatus or organized workers have the ideological conviction or resources to work for anything other than a handful of key companies remaining in state hands. At the same time the privatization process will be cumbersome and probably drag out. Why? Firstly, the qualified personnel to manage the process is very limited both at central and sectoral level,[47] and it is an enormous task, because accounts have not been closed for years, inventories have not been made, and the legal status in many cases will have first to be established. Secondly, the investable surplus among individuals and companies is severely depressed. Only traders with import-export businesses are accumulating substantial capital, but they probably regard industry as too risky and difficult. Interest from outside the country is limited, although much depends on developments in South Africa. From there one can expect interest both from the very large investors such as Anglo-American (cashew processing, Pande natural gas) and Gencor (coal mining), fishery companies such as E. Johnson (prawns), and smaller firms, for example owned by the more than 700,000 strong Portuguese community. Companies in Portugal are also on their way back, probably not on a large scale, but supported by the Portuguese state that has opted for a debt for equity swap, so that there will be shares for billions of meticais for Portugal.[48] Thirdly, the option of letting management and/or workers take over part of the shares does not seem to be pursued with any vigour by the state; and no special scheme appear to exist which could encourage local entrepreneurs to take over the privatized firms. The final outcome is impossible to estimate with any certainty. The privatization process can easily end up in being very prolonged: management and workers will be demoralized, production will fall and maintenance neglected. In fact, we are likely to experience the opposite of the envisaged 'dynamism' that an increased role of the private sector ideally should create (World Bank, 1991c, p.2).

Some of the concrete problems might be said to reflect a general dilemma facing African countries in the midst of market reforms: the indigenous or national bourgeoisie is non existent or very small, but precisely because the state political power is occupied by others, the effort to support the evolvement of a national private sector is often half hearted. In the authors view a viable development policy must be able to combine the dire need for foreign capital, technology and market access with national participation and ownership of larger parts of the private sector. The latter will in turn enable the creation of an African anchor class which, as I. Mandaza puts it, 'can develop into an economic and political power block ... in a national democratic framework'.[49] This new social force is expected to have the development of the nation as a prime focus in contrast to the earlier ruling elite's exclusive preoccupation with and dependence on the state or on foreign companies.

Mozambique's arrangements concerning regional trade and investment, not least with South Africa, will naturally also influence the interest in investing in the companies under privatization. The same can be said about the whole strategy that the Mozambican state has for industrial sector development. It has been mentioned above how various PFPs contained recommendations to give priority to companies with high value added production, with products that substitute imports or have an export potential. These could be interpreted as weak hints of an underlying strategy. However, the general approach that filters from the PFPs is that the various measures under the structural adjustment programme – exchange rate adjustment, free price setting, opening up of internal and external trade etc. will create an umbrella under which industry will thrive and grow, allocate efficiently, and therefore develop exactly the products that are economically viable to produce and are competitive internally and externally. In the author's view, this line of argument must under the prevailing circumstances in Mozambique be characterized as idealistic and most likely self-defeating.

The government side, in terms of industrial policy formulation, has been handicapped by a seemingly never ending UNIDO/UNDP project on 'Industrial Policies and Institutional Adjustments'. It was initiated in 1989 and should have been concluded in 1992, but continued into 1993. A range of detailed sub-sectoral studies have been elaborated, but kept secret until they can be presented as a package to government together with overall medium and long term recommendations on industrial strategy. In the meantime the country lingers along without any benchmarks for future industrial development. By way of example, in 1992 it seemed certain that the government was just about to introduce Export Processing Zones (EPZ)[50] in order to stimulate capital inflow, exports, employment etc. However, in 1993 no progress had been made and it appears that the proposal was stopped in the higher echelon of government. This would probably not have happened if EPZs were part of a fully fledged national industrial policy. Furthermore, one cannot expect the World Bank Office in Maputo to take the lead in relation to developing manufacturing industry, as the view found there was that Mozambique was probably only apt for some agro-, semi-processing industries linked to crops such as sugar, cashew and tomatoes (Interview, 1993g).

To sum up the analysis of the PFP, it was not possible in any of the measures constituting the key elements of the economic framework for external trade and industry development to find references or arrangements, which took into account the special conditions, opportunities and in some cases, obligations related to the regional economic interaction or regional organizations.

One may ask what kind of framework for regional cooperation and integration is created by relevant parts of the structural adjustment programme? On the positive side feature some new general opportunities for industrial growth and exports: through facilitation of the import of inputs for production, access to foreign exchange, increased management autonomy, permission to trade externally, and through a favourable exchange rate for exporters. On the negative side, there is the vulnerability caused by very high effective interest rates, an industrial rehabilitation that has not really got off the ground, a difficult as well as prolonged privatization process, and a lack of an industrialization strategy in which these, and other issues such as tariffs and export promotion could be incorporated.[51]

5.3 Achievements of the structural adjustment programme

There are three dimensions to assessing the degree of success of PRE in achieving the goals set up for the programme, as discussed in the beginning of 5.2.[52] To recapitulate briefly, there is first the overall objectives of stabilization, effective resource allocation through market signals and growth. Secondly, there is the application of these to the specific country, resulting in the following aims that were later somewhat- but not substantially- reformulated. However, the government would probably argue that to point (a), there should be added a more direct focus on reducing poverty in the country.

a   Reverse the decline in production and restore a minimal level of consumption and income for the population, especially in rural areas.
b   Curtail domestic financial imbalances and strengthen the country's external payments position.
c   Establish the conditions for more rapid and more efficient economic growth in the medium and longer term when the security situation and other exogenous constraints have eased.

d   Reintegrate official and parallel markets.

e   Restore orderly financial relationships with trading partners and creditors.

The third dimension is the annually established goal regarding growth rate and level of inflation plus the non-quantified objective of increasing the percentage that exports of goods and services cover of imports and service payments.

It is not possible in the limited space of this book to go into a detailed discussion of achievements in the various areas. It would also be somewhat out of line in relation to the overall issues of the book.[53] Therefore, only the following short discussion and presentation of growth, inflation and export coverage will be included in order to gain a more comprehensive picture before discussing Mozambique's performance regarding external trade and industrial production.

Regarding stabilization the picture is mixed. The external imbalance continues unabated, as we will see below, but the massive inflow of donor funds and debt relief has meant that the country can afford this in the short run, and has resumed an orderly relationship with its creditors. That the debt to the multilateral organizations is simultaneously growing, is another worrying side of the coin that will not be elaborated upon here. Concerning the internal public budget balance, there have certainly been expenditure cuts which hit sectors such as education and health hard, especially in the first years of PRE, and tax collection has been improved. Nevertheless, revenue only covers current expenditure, while the entire investment budget is donor financed.[54] Inflows of donor funds constituted as much as 66 per cent of GDP in 1990 (World Bank, 1992a). It is obvious that stabilization based on the country's own resources can by no means be achieved in a short term perspective neither externally nor in relation to state expenditure. Turning to the effective resource allocation and reliance on market mechanisms, developments are much more difficult to measure, but undeniably a process in that direction has been initiated and many obstacles have been removed. However, the imperfections of markets are present in all spheres, and the difficulty of the World Bank and government to recognize this, and intervene appropriately, is pronounced. The growth part of the overall objectives will be taken up below. This will also cover the country specific point 'a' presented above. The question of imbalances indicated in the country specific point (b) has been illuminated when discussing the stabilization objective. The answer to point (c) depends on one's evaluation of the reform process. Some of the most important market orientated reforms, their advantages and shortcomings were discussed above in 5.2. The objective of integrating the parallel and official markets raised in point (d) is close to being fulfilled. The all pervasive black market of commodities of the 1980s is gone, and the integration of the secondary and official rate in 1992 has implied that the parallel exchange

179

rate just reflects simple speculation, and the possibility of purchasing foreign exchange to buy goods in a neighbouring country, and smuggling these goods to Mozambique without paying customs duties. Point (e) as stated above is also accomplished, but the result has been achieved on the basis of borrowed funds and time. We can now turn to the more quantitative targeting of goals.

The growth targets are set out in the annual PFP. Below is an account of how the real GDP growth rate developed after the introduction of the PRE and the projections made in the PFPs.

Table 5.7
Mozambique – Gross Domestic Product; real growth rate and targets, 1987–92 (per cent)

Year	1987	1988	1989	1990	1991	1992
Real	4.4	5.5	5.4	1.3	2.7	-1.4*
Target in PFP						
1988		4	4	4		
1989			4	4	4	
1990				5.6	6	6
1991					5	5

* Estimate
Sources: Government of Mozambique, 1988; 1989; 1990a; 1991a; 1992

Thus, targets set up for 1988 and 1989 were a bit conservative and real growth rate surpassed 5 per cent. GDP growth of 4–5 per cent is seen by the World Bank as a necessary minimum in order to reverse economic decline, start improvements in living conditions within a reasonable time-frame and avoid a major human catastrophe in Africa.[55] However, in the years 1990, 1991 and 1992 the PFPs were too optimistic about the prospects for growth, and achievements are substantially lower than the desired levels. In 1990 a difference of up to 4.3 per cent can be found between reality and a target set the same year, and in 1992 the difference between the target set the year before and real growth is 6.4 per cent. The poor performance in the 1990s is especially stark, when adjusted for population growth (table 5.8).

There are naturally many factors that should be taken into account when interpreting these figures – both concerning natural conditions such as drought, the military situation and concerning specifics around the implementation of the adjustment programme. Likewise, the contribution of the different sectors varies from year to year. However, the overall trend is clear. It spells out a reasonable recovery at the end of the 1980s, and on the other hand, stagnation and decline in the first years of the 1990s.

Table 5.8
Mozambique – GDP growth adjusted for population growth, 1987–92 (per cent)

1987	1988	1989	1990	1991	1992
1.8	2.9	2.8	-1.3	0	-4.1

Sources: the previous table for GDP growth rates and Direcção Nacional de Estatística (DNE), 1992 for population growth rates

The second variable for which the structural adjustment programme sets up targets is inflation rate. It is once again possible to follow objectives and reality from 1987–92.

Table 5.9
Real and projected rate of inflation, 1987–92 (per cent)

Year	1987	1988	1989	1990	1991	1992
Real	163	50	42	49	33	35
Target in PFP						
1987	15					
1988		15				
1989			30	–	10	
1990						10

Sources: Direcção Nacional de Estatística (DNE), 1992 for 1987 inflation rate; Government of Mozambique, 1992 for inflation rates 1988–91, and Interview, 1992g for inflation rate in 1992. Targets are sourced from Government of Mozambique 1989, 1990a, 1991a and 1992

Once more objectives and reality do not match very well, nor does the ability to make projections substantially improve over the period. However, a slight downward trend can be observed in the overall rate of inflation. Nevertheless, it is clear that the relatively strict monetary policies followed in the period were insufficient to bring the inflation rate down significantly, and that the foreseen supply response to the PRE measures have not been forthcoming to the extent expected. Increased domestic production (probably the only lasting solution to curb inflation) did not materialize, as revealed by the above growth rates.[56]

We may now turn to the third parameter of PRE success – increase in the part that exports of goods and services cover of imports. This is at least how it was formulated in the first years of the programme in the PFPs. In 1991 and 1992 the PFPs want exports to be measured against the total deficit on the external current account. The latter has the advantage of also including service expenditures, such as interest payments on loans, transfers of dividends etc. However, this multitude of variables may also be said to blur the picture. Below we see the results of both methods.

Table 5.10
Mozambique – percentage of imports covered by exports of goods and services, 1988–91

1988	1989	1990	1991
35.3	33.6	34.2	40.6

Source: Direcção Nacional de Estatística (DNE), 1992

Table 5.11
Mozambique – external current account deficit as a percentage of export of goods and services, 1988–91

1988	1989	1990	1991
253	281	263	193

Source: Government of Mozambique, 1992

Both tables show more or less the same picture of no improvements in the first three years of the programme, whereas in the last year a small move in the intended direction can be observed. Export of goods and services covers around one third of imports, and the external current account deficit corresponds to 2–2,5 times the value of exports of goods and services. The slight improvement in 1991 may be linked both to an improved export performance, and to lower imports than expected, as donor financed import support funds did not reach the anticipated levels.

Thus regarding growth, the general impression is that the initial relatively correct projections and successes were reversed in 1990–92. Concerning inflation the constant prophecies of a low inflation rate could not be fulfilled, and as to the external balance, exports of goods and services still have a very long way to go before catching up with imports and service payments out of the country. Taken together the situation regarding the direct targets is tantamount to stagflation with continued large external deficits in the beginning of the 1990s. They indicate that the PRE policy mix is not fully adequate in relation to the economy's needs, and spell out the necessity to be aware of additional and corrective measures that might move Mozambique along a more secure growth track.

5.4   Trade

The trade pattern is of central interest for evaluating possibilities, advantages and disadvantages of regional integration. Below, an account is given of how it has developed under the PRE policies. The level, content and origin of imports and the amount, type and destination of exports will be analysed with special reference to the African countries. As done earlier in the book, I must stress that illegal and nonregistered border trade is not included in the analysis.

5.4.1 Imports

First, the magnitude and composition of imports. An overview is presented in the table below.

Table 5.12
Mozambique – imports, major categories, 1986–90 (million US$)

Category	1986	1987	1988	1989	1990
Consumer goods	231	247	281	330	338
Raw materials	157	185	216	248	255
Spare parts	68	92	101	87	84
Equipment	87	118	138	143	201
Total	543	642	736	808	878

Source: Direcção Nacional de Estatística (DNE), 1992

Note the 40 per cent increase in overall imports from 1986 to 1990 made possible by the inflow of import support funds under the PRE. Estimates for total imports in 1991 and 1992 are US$ 899 and 911 million, respectively (International Monetary Fund (IMF), 1992, p.80), i.e. only moderate increases from the 1990 level – probably due to the delays and non-fulfilment of donor pledges. The division between the different categories have generally been around 40 per cent for consumer goods, 30 per cent for raw materials, 10 per cent for spares and 20 per cent for equipment. In the consumer goods category a staggering three-quarters is made up of food imports, and about a third of

183

the raw materials is oil products. Also, under the category of equipment, one-third is used for imports of vehicles, including trucks and buses. Both regarding food and non-food consumer goods the countries in the region can be expected to contribute relatively significantly. Cloth for retail sale or processing constituted a quarter of non-food imports in 1990 and had a value of US$ 22 million. The origin of imports in broad categories of countries is:

Table 5.13
Mozambique – origin of imports, 1986–92 (per cent)

Origin	'86	'87	'88	'89	'90	'91	'92
OECD Countries	60	65	57	50	71	60	58
Socialist Block*	17	10	13	14	7	5	1
Africa^	16	20	25	33	18	28	34
Others	7	5	5	3	4	7	7
Total	100	100	100	100	100	100	100

* The Socialist Block covers former Soviet Union, former socialist Central and Eastern Europe, China, North Korea, Cuba and Vietnam
^ Including South Africa
Sources: the figures from 1986–89: Direcção Nacional de Estatística (DNE), 1992. The 1991 data are from International Monetary Fund (IMF), 1992. Figures from 1990 and 1992 are based on the author's calculations from Ministério do Comércio, 1993a. All information from 1989–92 is based on issued import licences

In the PRE period the OECD countries have remained with around 60 per cent of total imports, and the category 'others' has been relatively stable and low – approximately five per cent. However, the two remaining categories have experienced drastic changes in the period. The socialist block of countries have been practically eliminated, falling from 17 per cent in 1986 to one per cent in 1992,[57] which reflects the economic collapse of the Soviet Union, Central and Eastern Europe and the end of their special relationship with Mozambique – e.g. relatively cheap deliveries of oil from the Soviet Union. The second spectacular development is the dramatic rise in the slice of imports purchased in other African countries, including South Africa. They more than doubled and constituted a third of all imports at the end of the period. In the next table an attempt will be made to decode the contents of the Africa category.

Table 5.14
Mozambique – imports from major African suppliers, 1986–92
(distribution in per cent)

Country	'86	'87	'88	'89	'90	'91	'92
South Africa	64	68	60	70	83	86	84
Zimbabwe	11	12	17	8	6	4	7
Others	25	20	23	22	11	10	9
Total	100	100	100	100	100	100	100

Sources: calculations based on the same sources as in the previous table

The dominance of South Africa is evident in all years, and the spectacular rise in the share of African countries in Mozambique's imports is accompanied by an increase in South Africa's share of about a third from 1986–92. In money terms imports from South Africa grew from around US$ 50 million in 1986 to more than a quarter of a billion US$ in 1992 (Direcção Nacional de Estatística (DNE), 1992 and Ministério do Comércio, 1993a). Imports from Zimbabwe reached a peak with one-sixth of all African imports in 1988, but dropped to 5–10 per cent of imports from Africa from 1989–92. Imports from other African countries seem to have stabilized around 10 per cent. For selected years it is possible to go beyond these figures and establish the more detailed regional trade flows. 1982 is included in order to put the more recent data into perspective (see table 5.15, overleaf).

Besides the strengthened South African position, the overall picture is one of negligible trade with both the non-SADCC countries of the PTA and with the rest of Africa. Within SADCC imports from Tanzania and Botswana have been nearly totally eliminated in the period, and the share of Zimbabwe is halved, whereas Swaziland has risen from zero to a level of 6–10 per cent. However, it is probable – conservatively estimated – that half of the imports from Swaziland in reality are re-exports from South Africa.[58] Thus, close to 90 per cent of the African imports derives from South Africa.

To sum up the regional aspects of imports, the African share of Mozambique's imports has grown significantly in the 1980s and in the beginning of the 1990s; within Africa, South Africa has an all dominant role with nearly nine tenths of the total value. The remaining African trade is conducted with the SADCC countries whereas imports from the rest of Africa are insignificant.

Table 5.15

Mozambique – imports from African countries, 1982, 1990 and 1992

(distribution in per cent)

	1982	1990	1992
SADCC total	27	17	14 *
– Angola	1	0	0
– Botswana	6	1	0
– Lesotho	0	0	0
– Malawi	1	0	0
– Namibia	–	–	0
– Swaziland	1	10	6
– Tanzania	3	0	0
– Zambia	0	0	0
– Zimbabwe	15	6	7
Rest of PTA	2	0	2
Non-SADCC/PTA Africa	–	0	0
South Africa	71	73	84
Total	100	100	100

* The SADCC countries only add up to 13 per cent in the table, as the last per cent is subdivided into negligible portions between the countries with '0'

Sources: 1990 & 1992: Calculations based on Ministério do Comércio, 1993a. 1982: SADCC, 1986c

5.4.2 Exports

Attention may now be turned to Mozambican exports. For a start, the focus is on total exports and the distribution between the various export products over the years (tables 5.17, 5.18 and 5.19).

The rise from the extremely low level of 1986 to 1991 is a spectacular 105 per cent. Thus, it can be argued that the economy has responded positively to the various indirect stimuli of exports that PRE contains, although the picture is modified by the fact that exports had not reached the 1981 level of US$ 281 million after six years of PRE policies. In 1992 exports are contracting to a level below the 1990 figure, reflecting the above discussed negative GDP growth, a fall in industrial production, reduced catches of shrimp, and the impact on export crops of the devastating drought that year. The yearly ups and downs are evident from table 5.17.

Table 5.16
Mozambique – total exports, 1986–92 (million US$)

1986	1987	1988	1989	1990	1991	1992
79	96	103	105	126	162	117

Sources: 1986–91: Direcção Nacional de Estatistica (DNE), 1992. 1992: Ministério do Comércio, 1993a (preliminary estimate)

Table 5.17
Mozambique – annual variations in the level of exports, 1986–92 (per cent)

1986	1987	1988	1989	1990	1991	1992
3.3	22.5	6.2	1.7	20.6	28.4	-28.2

Sources: calculations based on the sources of the previous table

Table 5.18
Mozambique – main export products, 1988–92 (million US$)

Product	1988	1989	1990	1991	1992
1 Prawns	44.1	39.4	43.4	60.8	53.4
2 Cashew nuts	26.5	20.0	14.3	16.0	17.0
3 Cotton	4.9	7.4	8.7	8.8	8.7
4 Sugar, copra, citrus, timber, tea*	12.3	11.5	14.5	18.1	12.2
5 Petroleum Products	4.4	9.5	10.2	7.2	1.9
6 Minerals, inc. coal & gold	1.1	0.9	1.1	0.8	7.6
7 Fishery products	3.4	2.5	6.1	3.9	2.6
8 Manufacturing	4.1	7.6	9.0	30.0	11.6
9 Others	1.9	6.0	19.1	16.8	1.4
Total^	103.0	104.8	126.4	162.3	116.5

* The products are placed in decreasing order of export-value
^ If the summing up of the products does not reach the exact total, it is due to the necessary rounding off of the figures

Source: calculations based on Ministério do Comércio, 1993a

It is of special interest for the purposes of the present book to turn to the composition of exports (table 5.18) in order to illuminate how industrial exports have behaved in the PRE period. However, this is only possible in the period after 1988.

Throughout the whole period the products of unrivalled dominance are prawns and cashew nuts. These constituted on average 56 per cent of exports. The strong performance has to be seen against the background of the relative weakness of traditional agricultural export crops, but even in the boom years for export, viz. 1980/81, prawns and cashew represented more than a third of all exports.[59] However, the prawn yield has probably reached its maximum sustainable limit, and cashew nut collection is, likewise, unlikely to increase significantly before a prolonged period of tending and replanting trees. The world market prices have in the period been relatively stable, but increased world market supply is likely for both products. The third and fourth category of traditional agricultural export crops have contributed modestly in the period, as a result of drought, the instability in rural areas, and the need to rehabilitate e.g. sugar and coconut plantations. The potential for increased production is at hand, but world market prices are gloomy. However, investments have been made in cotton production, which is reflected in the doubling of production. Exports of petroleum products in this period and earlier, have reached substantial levels, but are typically re-exports of oil imported to Zimbabwe. Mozambique is under-prospected in relation to minerals; thus, mineral exports have an undisclosed potential. However, already with coal mining in Tete province and gold production in Manica a substantial contribution to foreign exchange earnings can be expected in the future.[60] The non-prawn fishery products are mostly specialized items such as lobster, sea-cucumber and products from the shark. Mozambican Indian Ocean waters do not have the same potential as the Atlantic for mass catches of e.g. pilchards or horse-mackerel. Therefore, only some export-diversification on relatively modest levels can be expected.

The two last categories, manufacturing and 'others' both belong to the non-traditional exports. The category 'others' contains a variety of items from scrap iron to live crocodiles. 'Others' reached very high levels in 1990 and 1991, and some of it might reflect an inability to register correctly the exported product in the relevant category. Together, the non-traditional exports in category 8 and 9 constitute nearly 30 per cent of exports in 1990 and a staggering 47 per cent in 1991. Leaving 'others' aside, the most impressive growth in exports is found within the manufacturing sector in the period under scrutiny. This can be illustrated by able 5.19 overleaf..

Taking the two extremes 1988 and 1991 a nearly fivefold increase is shown in manufacturing's share of total exports. The drastic decrease in 1992 is equally evident, but matches a general decline in industrial production in that year. We can now focus on the country distribution of overall exports. Table 5.20 should be able to shed some light on this.

Table 5.19
Mozambique – manufacturing sector exports, 1988–92 (per cent of total exports and yearly growth)

	1988	1989	1990	1991	1992
Per cent of total exports	4	7	7	19	10
Growth from previous year	–	85	18	233	-61

Source: the previous table

Table 5.20
Mozambique – export to main destinations, 1987–91 (per cent)

	1987	1988	1989	1990	1992
OECD countries	73	70	60	52	54
Socialist Block*	18	13	15	4	5
African Countries^	5	7	7	8	13
Others	5	10	18	36	30

* The Socialist Block covers former Soviet Union, former socialist Central and Eastern Europe plus China, Cuba, North Korea and Vietnam
^ Includes South Africa
Source: Direcção Nacional de Estatistica (DNE), 1992

The table reveals significant changes in all four country categories. One can observe a high, but declining share of the OECD countries, diminishing from three-quarters to half of the export value. The Socialist block is drastically reduced in the period with the disappearance of GDR and dissolution and economic crisis of the former Soviet Union. However, it is likely that China will still import selected products, but on a limited scale. The share of the African countries have grown more than two and a half times in the period, and provisional data indicate that it has increased to 15 per cent of exports in 1992 (Ministério do Comércio, 1993a).[61] As the African share of exports is especially relevant from the perspective of regional integration it is further examined in the next tables.

Table 5.21
Mozambique – exports to Africa, major markets, 1987–91 (per cent)

	1987	1988	1989	1990	1991
South Africa	88	78	73	87	70
Zimbabwe	12	10	15	3	26
Others	–	12	12	10	4
Total	100	100	100	100	100

Source: calculations are based on Direcção Nacional de Estatistica (DNE), 1992. Figures from 1988 are corrected on the basis of more detailed primary data from Ministério do Comércio, 1993a

As in the case of imports, South Africa is totally dominant within the African group of countries. The average share of South Africa is 81 per cent in 1988–91. This leaves the rest of Africa with 19 per cent, and in relation to total exports they have varied between 0.6 and 3.8 per cent in the same period. Zimbabwe is the dominant trading partner, but other African countries combined surpass Zimbabwe in 1988 and 1990. The following table gives a more detailed overview of the position of Africa in Mozambican exports, and adds information from the record export year 1981,[62] to put the PRE data into perspective.

In relation to the previous table, table 5.22 reveals the imports of Mozambican goods by four additional African countries: Angola, Malawi, Tanzania and Swaziland – all SADCC member states. Apart from some exports to the rest of DTA in 1981, exports to the rest of Africa is nonexistent or too small to be accounted for. In the beginning of the 1980s attempts to increase trade with Angola and Tanzania were made by the Mozambican state through bilateral trade agreements. In the case of Tanzania it developed into celebrating the 'Rovuma Free Trade Area' with reciprocal accounts for trade clearing in each other's National Banks. However, unsettled balances made the agreement inoperational in the mid 1980s. The goods exported from Mozambique to Angola and Tanzania were typically manufactures – cloth, tires, watches etc. Concerning exports to Malawi one primary, traditional export product dominates – coal from the mines in Tete province bordering on Malawi. Swaziland imports a more varied, but traditional range of Mozambican export products such as cotton, cashew nuts and citrus for re-export. Mozambican exports to South Africa are also dominated by traditional exports, especially prawns, copra, cashew nuts, oil from copra and cashew, and timber. Nevertheless, there are manufacturing exports too, for example tires and glass products.

Table 5.22

Mozambique – exports to African countries, 1981, 1988–91

(distribution in per cent)

	1981	1988	1989	1990	1991
SADCC Total	67	22	27	13	30
– Angola	1	2	6	–	–
– Botswana	–	–	–	–	–
– Lesotho	–	–	–	–	–
– Malawi	8	5	5	5	2
– Namibia	–	–	–	–	–
– Swaziland	3	5	1	5	2
– Tanzania	5	–	–	–	–
– Zambia	–	–	–	–	–
– Zimbabwe	50	10	15	3	26
Rest of PTA	15	–	–	–	–
Non-SADCC/PTA Africa	–	–	–	–	–
South Africa	18	78	73	87	70
Total	100	100	100	100	100

Sources: 1981 figures: SADCC, 1986c. 1988–91: Ministério do Comércio, 1993a

Having dealt a great deal in percentages in the above in order to create an overview of developments, it is probably appropriate to end up with the hard currency deficit faced by Mozambique in relation to its trade with Africa.

Table 5.23

Mozambique – export–import balance with Africa, 1987–91

(millions US$)

	1987	1988	1989	1990	1991
Exports	5	9	7	10	20
Imports	127	183	270	198	255
Balance	-122	-174	-263	-188	-235

Sources: Ministério do Comércio, 1993a; Direcção Nacional Estatistica, 1992; International Monetary Fund (IMF), 1992

The bulk of the deficit is with South Africa, but it is certainly also present in trade with Zimbabwe and Swaziland. This imbalance is, indeed, an important political variable and part of the framework for Mozambican decision-making on regional integration. South Africa has made one concession in response to the imbalance. As mentioned above a range of Mozambican export products are allowed into South Africa with only three per cent customs duty. Regarding the other SACU members, the agreement has only been approved by Botswana, but not by Lesotho and more important not by neighbouring Swaziland.[63] The agreement contains one section on mostly traditional primary exports quantified in tons; the other section on non-traditional manufacturing industry exports gives maximum ceilings indicated in US$, totalling US$ 6.7 million all in all. This is not much in the overall picture, but could prove significant as a stepping-stone for promoting industrial exports. Textiles and clothing are included in the agreement with an upper limit of US$ 2.4 million and tires and tubes have a ceiling of US$ 1 million per year. When the quotas are fully utilized Mozambique, on the basis of the large trade deficit with South Africa, will have a good case for demanding a rise in the export ceilings. However, pressure from employers' associations and growing unemployment in South Africa, will make for very tough negotiations and uncertain results. Obviously, confronting South Africa alone on this issue stands a much lesser chance of success than if effective coordinated regional action was employed. The acceptance of the other PTA countries to limit Mozambican customs tariff reduction to a total of 10 per cent before year 2000, whilst they in principle follow the route towards intra-regional tariff elimination, can be seen as a possibility for Mozambique to redress the imbalance in relation to these countries, if they comply with the agreed schedule. However, as discussed below, the advantage might be temporary, and neighbouring Swaziland is as a SACU member state exempted from implementing the PTA tariff reductions.

However, what is of interest are not only the deficit with Africa and the ways and means to counterbalance this; their percentage of overall trade is equally worth noting. This reveals that trade with Africa in the period 1988–91 on average represented 25 per cent of all Mozambican external trade. This is five times the level of intra-SADCC trade in the 1980s, and is high by any Third World regional comparison. It calls for a special role in macroeconomic policies, and the 25 per cent gives Mozambique and SADCC countries in a similar position a firm interest in a dialogue with a democratic government in South Africa on how substantial trade links and other forms of cooperation can develop.

5.5   Foreign investment and industry

5.5.1   Foreign investment

The depressed levels of foreign direct investment nearly all over Southern
Africa in the 1980s was discussed in chapter 3. Direct foreign investment in
Mozambique reflects this trend. The following table gives the figures year
by year.

Table 5.24
Mozambique – private foreign investment, yearly amount, 1987–91 (millions US$)

1987	1988	1989	1990	1991
3.4	4.5	3.4	9.2	22.5

Source: Economist Intelligence Unit, 1992c

From 1987–89 around US$ 4 million are invested yearly. This figure more
than doubled in 1990, and increased again twofold in 1991. The 1987 figure
corresponds to 0.5 per cent of GDP, while in 1991 it reaches two per cent of
GDP. Thus, the general level is not high, but might increase in the future if
the 1991 figure sets a trend, and the military-political situation permits. It
also requires that the government takes a firm decision regarding the possible
establishment of the above-mentioned EPZs. The uncertainty on this point
probably makes a number of prospective investors wait until the position is
clearer. Apart from the unsettled EPZ issue, Mozambique was in 1984 one of
the first countries in Southern Africa to introduce a liberal investment code
with attractive incentives for the investor. In 1992 Mozambique signed the
MIGA agreement on protection of foreign investment.[64] In the same year, in
an attempt to assure possible investors of the wisdom to invest in Mozambique,
the Director of the Investment Promotion Office went so far as to draw
attention to 'Mozambique's full circle return to the emphasis of pre-
independence economic policies' (Economist Intelligence Unit, 1993, p.21).
However, the policies, rules, regulations and incentives are only one part of
the overall investment climate in a country. The very low internal demand,
the lack of a regional trade agreement, the absence of an industry development
policy and the war have undoubtedly dampened investment. Furthermore,
legislation left a relatively wide space open for the administration to stipulate
the exact conditions for a given investment. This was probably not the most
appropriate solution. It is the author's impression that the investment office
had its fair share of the same problems as the major part of Mozambican

state administration, viz. the lack of trained manpower and financial resources, delays in decision-making, and, moreover, it was being exposed to foreign firms trying to pay their way through the system.

The value of approved projects is US$ 406 million between 1985–1991. Only 5.7 per cent of this, or US$ 23 million is earmarked for the manufacturing industry[65] – the bulk goes to agriculture and tourism. The main investor is Britain, mostly because of the dominant agricultural joint-venture between the UK firm 'Lonrho' and the government. South Africa comes in second with investments concentrated in tourism – especially hotels in Maputo. A Portuguese bank, specializing in external relations, opened a branch in Maputo in 1993, assisting the Portuguese investment portfolio, which until 1991 came in third. Zimbabwe, more specifically the 'Cresta Group', engaged for several years in negotiations and options to invest in hotels in Beira, but apparently nothing ever materialized, probably because of the negative attitude of the National Bank of Zimbabwe to allow the necessary outflow of capital. Thus, Zimbabwean investments are minimal and no other African country has invested. Winding up investments, it is clear that they have not been large enough to significantly facilitate an outward orientation through setting international standards for production, rejuvenating industry or putting export outlets at the disposal of the Mozambican partners. Moreover, the rigidities in the SADCC countries cross-border investment mechanisms have been illustrated, as well as the tendency in South Africa primarily to go for the relatively easy service sectors with assured high returns on investments in the period under scrutiny, while only studying possible later substantial involvement in manufacturing and mining. Finally, on the part of Mozambique, key ingredients of the investment climate tended to hamper rather than promote a substantial expansion of foreign direct investment.

5.5.2 Industry

Mozambican statistics unfortunately group fisheries and industry together when economic sectors are analysed. The World Bank has also been weak on industrial information, and has tended to concentrate effort on improving statistics in other sectors such as finance and agriculture. However, it is possible to follow developments in selected years (see table 5.25). The same pattern as GDP growth can be noted, but it is just more accentuated: the increase is higher than average for the whole economy in the end of the 1980s, and the downturn in the beginning of the 1990s is more severe than the general decline in the economy.

The increase in production in the beginning of the PRE period can be explained by the sudden availability of raw materials, spares and minor equipment. In this way capacity utilization of existing factories could be relatively easily boosted from the very low level of around 30 per cent reached in the middle of the 1980s.[66] Moreover, purchasing power was high in the initial years of PRE. The sharp fall that followed is due to more complex reasons, among which the difficult liquidity and credit situation and depressed internal demand are prominent features. This move from euphoria to severe crisis which might be synonymous with deindustrialization in the 1990s, naturally influences industry's regional performance. On the one hand the search for market outlets intensifies, yet the basis for expansion seems very weak both regarding the individual company's dwindling internal resources, lack of supportive action from the state in accordance with a well defined strategy, and finally, the lack of measures for enabling and enhancing regional trade. The focus below on one industrial branch – textile and clothing – may substantiate and illustrate some of the above developments under PRE.

Table 5.25
Mozambique – growth in manufacturing industry in selected years (on the basis of constant prices in relation to previous year) (per cent)

1986/87	1987/88	1989/90	1990/91
7.4	9.7	-14.6	-9.6

Sources: Direcção Nacional de Estatística (DNE), 1989; Direcção Nacional de Estatística (DNE), 1990; Direcção Nacional de Estatística (DNE), 1991; Direcção Nacional de Estatística (DNE) , 1992

5.5.3 Textile and clothing industry

Seen from many different perspectives the textile and clothing industry is an interesting and strategic sector in the Mozambican development context. First, it adds value to a nationally grown resource, cotton, still leaving a surplus for immediate export; secondly, it produces a basic needs item in short supply; and thirdly it represents a sector which was historically at the centre of the industrial revolution in Europe; and more recently in Asia has been the key to starting the process of industrialization. Fourthly, the population growth in Mozambique and other countries in the region and elsewhere in the third world will increase demand for the sector's products. Finally, as a signatory to the Lomé convention, Mozambique has duty-free access to the European Community's market for textile and clothing products.

Textile production was the first manufacturing industry to be established in Mozambique in the late 1940s and 1950s, although Mozambique's prime role was still to deliver raw cotton to Portuguese industry and serve as a market for its products. Even in the beginning of the 1970s on the eve of colonial rule, the second largest, integrated, textile mill was constructed with

195

a relatively small finishing department in relation to spinning and weaving. Thus, competition with finished products imported from Portugal was reduced. In the beginning of the 1990s Mozambique has 11 textile and 28 clothing factories.[67] The two subsectors employ about 10,000 and 5,000 workers respectively. This corresponds to 20 per cent of the industrial work force of around 80.000 in 1990/91. They also represent approximately 20 per cent of the production value (Direcção Nacional de Estatistica (DNE), 1992). This makes textiles and clothing the second largest manufacturing sector after 'food, drink and tobacco'. Within textiles the main product is cotton cloth in various qualities for direct use as cangas (capulanas) or for further processing by industry, tailors etc. The clothing sector transforms both national and imported fabric to a range of products – mainly shirts, vests, trousers and shorts. In the last ten years production has developed in the following manner:

Table 5.26
Production value within textile and clothing industry, constant 1980 prices (billion Meticais)

	'82	'86	'87	'88	'89	'90	'91	'92
Textile	5.2	1.4	2.0	3.2	3.3	3.8	3.1	1.7
Clothing	2..2	1.1	1.4	1.5	1.8	1.6	1.4	1.3
Total	7.4	2.5	3.4	4.7	5.1	5.4	4.5	3.0

Source: calculations based on CONTEX, 1993

The above pattern reflects a high initial value in the beginning of the 1980s, a drastic fall in the middle of the decade, and from there a steep rise in production till 1990, followed by a significant fall in 1991/92. The vicious circle of lack of foreign exchange and restrictive policies in the beginning of the 1980s were discussed in section 5.2. It has also been mentioned above how PRE-financed imports of raw materials and spares facilitated increased production to fulfil the high demand for products after years of scarcity. However, production begins to decrease in 1990 for clothing and in 1991 for total production. Why is this? Several factors deserve to be highlighted:

- depressed internal demand;
- competition from second-hand clothes, clothes smuggled in, and low cost imports;
- low and unstable supply of import funds;
- prohibitive high interest rates on bank credits;
- insufficient exports.

I shall go through the items one by one. The depressed internal demand is linked up with the philosophy of structural adjustment programmes to remove the urban bias of development, and instead favour productive activities in the rural areas. Thus, in the cities real wages have dropped, food subsidies have been cancelled and unemployment has increased. However, because of the war and drought only small segments of the rural population have been able to benefit substantially from improved producer prices, better market access etc. A report by R.H. Green (1991) for the National Planning Commission on Social Dimension of Adjustment[68] estimates that two-thirds of all Mozambicans lived in absolute poverty in the end of the 1980s. This covers around a third to a half of the urban and peri-urban population and nearly 70 per cent of rural dwellers. In 1990 and 1991 the World Bank has registered a drop in consumption per capita of -4.1 and -2.0 per cent respectively (Government of Mozambique, 1992, table 1). Taken together the national market has shrunk substantially with difficult access and low purchasing power in the rural areas and widespread poverty in the cities. Moreover, the groups in the cities that have benefited from PRE-policies tend to favour imported clothes.

Concerning competition on the internal market, one can distinguish between second hand clothes, illegally imported goods and legal imports. Imports of second hand clothes made good sense in the first half of the 1980s, but they enter into stiff competition with the clothing industry in the second half of the decade and beyond.[69] The latter is a phenomenon known in other African countries as well. However, in Mozambique, imports of second-hand clothes might be said to have a useful function in the emergency stricken rural areas after 1985. Yet, what happened was that large amounts of used clothes imported under that pretext, were in reality sold in the cities.[70] Excluding emergency appeal donations the import of second-hand clothes constituted a third of all textile and clothing imports in 1989 (Weinmann, 1991, p.47ff.), and in relation to the impoverished majority of the population there is no way any clothing industry can compete with the extremely low-priced used clothes.

It is very difficult to estimate the value of illegal imports of textile and clothing,[71] but they have surely a possible edge over other products by escaping 35 per cent import tax on consumer goods plus 7.5 per cent of general import duty. Inefficiency in customs service and outright corruption contributes to this situation. As discussed above, the legal imports have been liberalized since 1987 through the removal of quantitative restrictions. This has resulted in a doubling of import value for 'cloth' in the period 1987–90.[72] The quantity of clothing imports rose 240 per cent from 1985 to 1989 (Weinmann, 1991, p.48). The competitiveness of imports of both clothing and textile products is indicative of the extremely high productivity and advanced technological level of the textile and clothing industries in the countries of origin, mostly located in South-East Asia. The Mozambican import duty totalling 42.5 per cent might in the final analysis be seen as relatively low for a country that is in the process of building up an industry. Pakistan with a much more advanced textile and clothing industry applies a tariff on imported textiles of 130 per cent and 160 per cent on clothing imports. A country such as South Korea which has left the stage of textile-led industrialization behind, but exports substantial amounts of textiles and garments, still has tariffs of 35 and 40 per cent on textiles and clothing imports (ibid., p.84). Both clothing and textile industry leaders argue that a practical, positive move to enable them to compete more effectively with imports would be to reduce the 25 per cent import tariff that they pay on finished intermediary products (Interviews, 1993c and 1993f). Regarding the regional aspect, Mozambique has till now the PTA Summit's approval of its 'ten per cent only' reduction of tariffs for imports from other PTA countries before the end of the decade. However, after the 1992 peace accord and the installation of an elected government Mozambique will probably be urged to approximate its rates to the others' agreed schedule of reaching zero per cent tariff for intra-PTA trade by the year 2000. Such a scenario might be one of the elements of an industrial strategy. It could be combined with strategic and process oriented proposals regarding tariffs for world market imports. They should ideally unite the need to pressurize local industry to improve competitiveness with industry's need to have reasonable conditions on the home market as a basis for export expansion.

The low[73] and unstable level of imports to the companies within the textile and clothing sector is another major problem. The problem reflects the far too high donor-dependence of the country. The foreign exchange that the companies plan to spend on imports in a given year, and which is matched with pledges from the donor community to the structural adjustment programme, turns out later in the year not to be available in the promised amounts. This hampers growth and compromises export orders, where timely delivery is one of the key elements. This was especially problematic in 1991, as the following table illustrates:

Table 5.27
Imports to the Mozambican textile and clothing industry, 1987–91

	1987	1988	1989	1990	1991
Million US$	8.6	18.8	24.3	21.9	10.6
Per cent of planned imports	31	54	64	88	28

Source: as previous table

In the first six months of 1991 no imports at all were effectuated, because no donor funds were available. The production result for that year would naturally be negatively affected. In 1992 a similar shortage of funds was experienced periodically, but no specific data is available at the time of writing. However, the figures in the more normal years of 1988/89, show that the industry only received 54–64 per cent of the scheduled amounts. This not only immediately affects production levels, but also investments in new equipment. The latter becomes ever more important, especially in textile production, which moves rapidly towards increasing technology dependence and capital intensive production. If donor funds are forthcoming in the form of 'tied aid', bound to be spent in the specific donor country, the companies normally have the additional drawback of having to pay more than the cheapest world market price for the given import item, because of the more limited competition for the order.[74]

Another tendency that also affected imports to the industry in a downward direction in the early 1990s is the growing incapacity of companies to finance planned imports. The liquidity situation is under so much stress that they have no cash for payment of the local currency countervalue that constantly rises with the currency depreciations of the meticais and on top of this is the import tariffs. If the companies try to raise the necessary capital in the banking sector they were likely to be rejected, because of the very tight credit ceiling, which is a key element of the structural adjustment programme. Should capital be available the interest rates are prohibitive for many companies (see also 5.2).

The last area is exports. Why has it not been possible to counteract the decrease in internal demand by increased exports? To explain this it is necessary to get an impression of both the overall level and the destinations of exports. Table 5.28 overleaf presents some key data.

First, the dramatic 17 fold increase in exports between the two poles – 1986 and 1991 – should be noted.[75] This is again an indication that industry understood the indirect message and reacted to the incentives of various PRE measures to increase exports. However, the very large exports in 1991 were made on fragile grounds. More than half went to Russia and a quarter to Bulgaria. The amounts exported were deducted from Mozambique's interstate debt to the two countries. These exports cannot, therefore, be compared to orders won on the world market. The companies were paid the local currency counterpart value to the exported amount in US$. This was fair enough for the companies, but not to Mozambique as a nation, as Mozambique typically defaulted on repayments of foreign loans or asked for and obtained debt rescheduling or forgiveness in various forms. However, Mozambique could be said to have an interest in continuing the arrangement, as it probably was a precondition for further deliveries of petroleum and other products from the two countries. In 1992 the 'debt for clothes trade' was stopped. This meant that three-quarters of the export value of the previous year was lost for the sector which had otherwise expected to continue and possibly expand the scheme. Neither Soviet Union's heir in terms of international debt, Russia, or Bulgaria would continue purchases on normal trade conditions.

Table 5.28
Amount and destination of textile and clothing sector exports, 1986–92 (million US$)

Destination	'86	'87	'88	'89	'90	'91	'92
Soviet Union*	1.3	1.5	1.8	2.8	1.5	12.1	0.3
Others	–	0.3	1.4	8.1	11.3	x	x
Bulgaria						5.3	–
Portugal						2.6	0.9
Rest of EC/EFTA						1.2	1.6
Canada†						0.2	–
South Africa						0.3	0.1
Total	1.3	1.8	3.2	10.9	12.8	21.6≈	2.9

From 1986–90 no further subdivision is possible due to lack of data
x In 1991 and 1992 there is no category 'others' in the source material
* From 1991 Russia replaces the Soviet Union
† There were some, but minor, exports to Canada in 1992
≈ In 1991 also a minor amount was exported to Hong Kong

Sources: as previous table

Thus, exports were reduced from US$ 21 to US$ 3 million in 1992. The bulk of 1992 exports consisted of simple cotton cloth, exported from the largest cotton mill to Portugal and the rest of Europe under a cooperation agreement with a Portuguese company. The export of cheap cotton cloth is in payment for the Portuguese company securing essential imports of raw materials, spares etc., provision of technical assistance and gradual renovation of the equipment of the factory. In 1992/93 the second largest textile mill attempts to enter into a similar arrangements with another Portuguese firm. For the Mozambican company it is a last resort survival strategy, as it is on the brink of collapse, due to lack of liquidity to secure the necessary imports and cover other current expenditures.

Already in 1987/88 the largest clothing factory made strategic alliances for two subsidiaries with a Hong Kong based and a Bulgarian clothing factory in the form of commercial joint venture agreements and support to quality control. At the same time investments in new equipment were made. This has facilitated exports to Europe and Canada and given the company sufficient export experience to strike export deals by itself.[76] This is the case with South Africa. The company produces jeans and shorts for two of the larger clothing retail chain stores.[77] The company was hit severely by the collapse of the Russian and Bulgarian markets, and sees South Africa as the most promising alternative, especially with the 3 per cent only tariff agreement in place. However, in 1991/92 just US$ 0.1–0.2 million worth of garments were sold to South Africa. The sales to Europe and Canada were also limited in scope. For most export orders the buyer supplies all inputs to production, and the Mozambican company must earn its money by virtue of its cheap and efficient work force.[78]

For the whole textile and clothing sector the percentage of the US dollar value of production exported in the years 1986–90 increased from two to twenty-five per cent.[79] In 1991 exports – with large increases to Russia and Bulgaria – might have touched half of the production value. Followed by a steep decline in 1992. It will probably take several years to reach just US$ 10 million in export value again. In a regional context it is likely that the sector will seek to fill out its US$ 2.4 million quota of the low tariff exports to South Africa. There the consumption of textile fibres is 6.9 kg a year per capita in relation to the approximately one kg in the SADCC countries (Weinmann, 1991, p.45). This places the Mozambican textile and clothing industry on the doorstep of a market that is three times as large as all SADCC countries together. However, competition is stiff, and in 1992 South African textile employers have successfully pressed the government to increase protection primarily towards Far Eastern producers, but the move also hurt Zimbabwean textile and clothing industry, as a renewal of the trade agreement between South Africa and Zimbabwe was not finalized at that time. Therefore, tough negotiations may be expected when and if the Mozambican state seeks to raise the low tariff export ceiling. Exports to Tanzania and Angola were made under centralized agreements in the beginning of the 1980s, for example of synthetic cloth, but ten years later industrialists claim that possibilities for exports to the other SADCC countries are few, as competition is generally tough, because they themselves produce similar products. However, in a regional free trade area, regional trade is stimulated by industries of the same nature in the different countries. Therefore, there should be exploitable possibilities in the other SADCC countries, depending on the trade regime imposed by the countries and their overall economic situation.[80]

The continuation of existing policies under PRE for the Mozambican textile and clothing industry will most probably imply bankruptcies, closure of factories, mass retrenchments etc. These are the combined effect of competition from second-hand clothes, clandestine imports and imports from high-tech East Asiatic producers, stop-go production depending on the availability of donor funds for imports, the depressed internal demand that in spite of the peace accord in 1992 will continue for years, the difficulty of financing and finally the too low level of exports to mitigate the other negative tendencies. In this situation it will be difficult to attract foreign capital to invest in private companies or take stakes in hitherto state owned firms. However, sale and privatization is the only option left for the Mozambican authorities, faced with factories that must give up production, as they cannot continue to finance imports, wages etc. Symptomatic of the crisis, in 1992/93 a bloody wild cat strike broke out in the third largest textile mill over lack of payment of wages for months, and the first clothing factory put up for sale did not attract any bidders. The closed factories' equipment and buildings will begin to deteriorate, and the trained work force disappear. PRE policies, unaccompanied by any strategy for industrial development, including regional trade within manufacturers, are apparently leading to a dead end for textile and clothing – and will take their toll, most probably in the form of de-capitalization and deindustrialization in the coming years.

Obviously, some companies will survive, but within textiles these will probably be increasingly dependent on Portuguese interests, and the latter's definition of the most optimal division of labour.[81] Other firms are likely, on a small scale, to develop niches based on efficient clothing production for export to the world market and South Africa. South African firms might engage themselves in this, and take over some of the clothing industries set for sale. Export Processing Zones, EPZs, are the 'dark horse' that might attract especially Asian capital to produce clothing for the European and US markets. EPZs might also reactivate the finalization of one of the giant development projects from the beginning of the 1980s – the integrated textile mill in Mocuba. An agreement with an Egyptian/South African consortium has been made – pending that Mocuba is made into an EPZ. However, it seems probable that a large number of African countries in the 1990s will attempt to copy Mauritius' success with EPZs;[82] a sheer oversupply of EPZs will tend to dilute and diminish their impact in the individual country.

5.6   Summary

In the previous chapter it was possible to identify how the World Bank in the 1989 key publication on Sub-Saharan development *From Crisis to Sustainable Growth* advocated that regional cooperation and integration should be high on the agenda in African development efforts. Increased regional economic interaction was seen as an indispensable part of structural adjustment, and the drive towards renewed growth, and avoidance of imminent human disaster. The theoretical background for this was found in the 'adjustment adapted market integration approach', discussed in chapter 2. However, on a regional level, verbal support for regional cooperation and integration, but relatively little concrete action from the World Bank could be found, and a recent initiative seemed not to be sufficiently anchored in the region to promise early success. Moreover, one could also find rather rigid views in official World Bank publications, which insisted on avoiding regional arrangements, and concentrated solely on unilateral openings of the economy and on global free trade. Therefore, the country focus became necessary. It should establish whether or not the World Bank in its policy dialogue and practice, together with the partner government, directly or indirectly had included regional cooperation and integration in external macroeconomic and industrial policies in structural adjustment programmes. Mozambique was chosen as the country to scrutinize and the period was set at 1988–91 with a flexible margin on both sides for including additional relevant information.

It soon became obvious that the structural adjustment programme as expressed in the successive PFPs does not have any direct and/or overall references, discussions, plans or conditions regarding the possibility of creating favourable conditions for trade, investments, industrial cooperation or the like in the region, and in this way, use the region to strengthen national development. Thus, no trace of the adjustment adopted market integration model can be identified. Neither is there any mention of how the structural adjustment programme relates to the activities, obligations and plans of the regional organizations in which Mozambique already participates. An outline is given of the different elements of the structural adjustment programme which constitutes Mozambique's external economic and industry policies in order to find out how in practice the framework created relates to and influences the regional dimension of economic development within trade and industry. Each of the measures can be characterized as general in nature. No allocation of foreign exchange is set aside for regional imports. The tariff reform does not favour the region or take into account regional obligations. Export promotion is not targeted towards the region. However, the structural adjustment programme does contain indirect incentives to increase exports, which ideally should also influence positively trade with regional partners. Currency depreciation, liberalization of prices and trade, and greater management autonomy pull in that direction too. But counteracting tendencies tend to eliminate this; they are high interest rates and low ceilings on credits, an apparent early derailing of industrial rehabilitation, a prolonged and uncertain privatization process, and the absence of a strategy for industrial development, including the role of the region. The approach that emanates from the totality of the different measures is the unilateral trade liberalization and opening up of the economy towards the world market. Moreover, the underlying strategy for industrial development seems to be that the creation of a new macroeconomic framework will automatically adjust industry towards production-levels and types of goods that are economically viable under the new conditions. This appears to confirm the hypothesis from the end of section 3.2 on manufacturing industry development in Southern Africa. Mozambique does follow the third option among the four industrialization strategies identified by R.C. Riddell (Riddell et al., 1990, p.52ff.). It is characterized by a revamping of the overall economic system and basically, letting industry on its own adjust to the market signals and forces.

Attention is turned to the overall results of the structural adjustment programme in order to understand the background for developments within trade and industry. It is found that the external and internal imbalances of the economy have been stabilized, but only thanks to greatly increased inflows of donor funds that at the same time make the country vulnerable and dependent. Market oriented reforms to strengthen effective resource allocation and indirect management of the economy as opposed to earlier direct controls have been implemented with reasonable success in many spheres of the economy. However, the very creation of markets seems to make the government and the World Bank ignore the fragility and imperfections of these, and to overlook the need for additional action by the state. The internally defined objectives of the programme have been met regarding growth from 1987–89, but thereafter targets have not been fulfilled. In the whole period the inflation rate has been much higher than forecast, and no significant improvement of the coverage of imports by export of goods and services can be observed. Stagflation appear to be a fitting expression to characterize the situation in 1991/92.

Regarding imports, Africa doubles its share and takes home one third of orders in the end of the period. South Africa is the all dominant supplier with 85 per cent. Zimbabwe still has a certain but declining part and Swaziland is on the increase. In relation to exports, Africa's share is only 15 per cent and South Africa represents 80 per cent of this. Common for imports and exports is the almost nonexistent trade with Africa outside South Africa and the SADCC member states. Mozambique's deficit on trade with Africa is substantial and could be used as leverage in bilateral or multilateral negotiations on trade arrangements. Within exports the high growth and substantial share of manufacturing exports are noteworthy, and highlights the importance of nurturing the sector. Attention must also be drawn to the fact that with the inclusion of a post-Apartheid South Africa as an equal regional partner, the percentage of intra-regional trade in total trade that can be included in deliberations of regional integration, increase drastically for Mozambique, and for the majority of the other SADCC countries as well, and they far exceed the African average of around six per cent.[83]

Foreign investments have not yet been substantial, nor have they created significant new manufacturing export possibilities for the region or elsewhere. South Africa has concentrated on easy projects and money within tourism, and Zimbabwe has demonstrated the total insufficiency of cross border investment arrangements and attitudes, and in spite of many possibilities has not come in with substantial amounts.

Industry has experienced and partaken in the economy's up- and downturns, it is just more accentuated with high growth rates in the late 1980s and steep declines in the beginning of the 1990s. Depressed internal demand and high interest rates are key problems. A scrutiny of one specific sector – textile and clothing – illustrates the severity of the crisis in which industry finds itself at the beginning of the 1990s, and illuminates how easily the contribution of entire sectors to national development can be dramatically reduced under the circumstances created by the patchwork of general structural adjustment measures and the particular circumstances of the country.

A basic problem seems to be the failure to adjust the adjustment process. Policies which according to internal structural adjustment objectives are logical and correct can very well have adverse and negative effects when applied to reality in a specific country; but even so they do not seem to be rethought, modified or changed. This is aggravated by the lack of an industrial development strategy and the absence of the regional dimension in the external economic policies.

Notes

1   Thus, I shall not attempt to identify and separate the actions of the IMF and the World Bank respectively. For my purpose, the commonly agreed documents, cross-conditionalities, and the combined impact of the policies of the two institutions are the focus of study. The main focus on the World Bank is justified by its leading role in relation to policy formulation, government negotiations and country presence in Sub-Saharan Africa. Moreover, it ensures consistency in relation to the rest of the book.

2   The consequences of structural adjustment programmes on possibilities for enhanced regional integration were typically not dealt with in their own right and in a systematic manner, when research for this part of the book was initiated in the beginning of the 1990s (see also chapter 1). The book will hopefully contribute to reverse this trend.

3   Reference is made to note 2 in chapter 4.

4   Moreover, till now, among the SACU countries, only Lesotho has undertaken a structural adjustment programme with the World Bank and the IMF. See for example Petersson, 1992.

5   In 1987 the program for economic and financial reorganization (Programa de Saneamento Económico e Financeiro) was approved, and in 1990 it was reactivated through a governmental action programme (Programa de Acção do Governo). Only in 1991 was the first World Bank loan

approved for Angola, and it was not part of a structural adjustment programme. For further information see for example Tarp, 1992.

6   Tanzania presented the National Economic Survival Programme in 1981, after the failure to agree on a programme with the IMF, as a follow up to the 1980 stand-by credit agreement. In 1982 a more coherent local structural adjustment programme was introduced, and strengthened in the 1984 national budget. See for example Stein, 1991 and Hyden and Karlstrom, 1993.

7   See note above. However, by the end of 1993 the IMF and the World Bank did freeze payments, as the government did not live up to earlier agreements on public budgets. But this was probably more a reflection of the institutional incapacity of the government and of the IMF being caught in its own over-optimistic conditionalities than a sign of new conflicts being created between the Bretton Woods institutions and the government.

8   See for example Callaghy, 1990.

9   In Hanlon, 1991, the author alleges (p.144) the existence of a so-called 'riot-threshold' in any informal World Bank policy analysis of a given country's ability to absorb structural adjustment measures that lower living standards for especially the urban population and state employees. I tend to agree that such a concept exists, and has an informal but real impact on policy making. Without entering the discussion between the World Bank and the Zambian government of the responsibility for the events one can simply observe that the riot-threshold was transgressed in Zambia in 1986. Where a given riot-threshold is situated is time and place specific. Regarding the situation of Mozambique a reference can be made to Hermele, 1992, p.180, of how the willingness of ordinary people to endure declines in living standards depend very much on their perception of how the leaders of the nation conduct themselves. If corruption and land grabbing by the higher echelon of society prevail, the limit is low, whereas a social atmosphere of common struggle and short supply of goods for everyone, also ministers, induces a spirit to withstand hardship without protests for a very long time. This psychological phenomenon has also been experienced in situations of war. The Mozambican riot-threshold was surpassed in the beginning of 1991, a period marked by strikes and demonstrations of a level hitherto unheard of in the country. However, they did not reach the Zambian level of violent action.

10   This was optimistically characterized as the 'New Economic Recovery Programme'.

11   In 1993 the pace of implementation was somewhat slowed down, due to practical, legal complications of implementing the ambitious privatization program, and as a consequence of a political weakening of the government.

12 See for example articles in *Daily Gazette*, 1 March 1993; *Horizon*, July 1993; *High Density Mirror*, May 1994; *SAPEM*, March 1994; *Southern African Economist*, 1994.

13 ESAF's financial conditions are an interest rate of 0.5 per cent, a 10 year's maturity, and a grace period of 5 1/2 years.

14 See for example Economist Intelligence Unit, 1993. An overview of the structural adjustment programmes in Malawi can be found in Chipeta, 1993.

15 On the policy shift of Frelimo in the beginning of the 1980s see for example Hanlon, 1991 or Munslow, 1984.

16 See Hanlon, 1991, p.118.

17 My reasoning concerning the other countries that makes me hesitant to use them as country examples boils down to the following: Zambia's relationship with IMF/World Bank has been dominated by stop-go policies and controversies, which makes it extremely difficult to detect the effects of the adjustment programmes; Tanzania had strong initial confrontations with the World Bank, and the rhythm of implementation has been relatively slow, making it difficult to cover all relevant elements of the structural adjustment programmes; Zimbabwe's program is too recent to provide a basis for analysis; the programme only started out in 1990 – and the upstart was marred by unexpected shocks, such as the drought in 1991. Malawi becomes a difficult example, because of the very specific political problems in the beginning of the 1990s, which restricted financing for the adjustment programme.

18 On Renamo's background, concrete actions and policies see for example Geffray, and Petersen, 1986; Gersony, 1988; Government of Mozambique, 1985; Haarlov, 1987; Hanlon, 1986; Johnson and Martin, 1986; Minter, 1989; Morgan, 1990.

19 For example dams, irrigation schemes, and a giant textile mill; and this was on top of the inputs that the state run industries, plantations and large scale agriculture required.

20 See also note 2, chapter 4.

21 The Policy Framework Papers in focus are Government of Mozambique, 1987; Government of Mozambique, 1988; Government of Mozambique, 1989; Government of Mozambique, 1990a; Government of Mozambique, 1991a; Government of Mozambique, 1992.

22 The Policy Framework Papers, naturally, have references to the service receipts from the Mozambican transport-corridors, linking the landlocked hinterland with the sea.

23 This is therefore no attempt to make an exhaustive presentation of the Economic Recovery Programme.

24 Note the apparent, and often experienced real life contradiction, between a 'restrictive monetary policy' and the availability of 'adequate credit'.

But the discussion is never ending as 'adequate' can be interpreted from many different points of view.

25 The following is mostly based on the relevant Policy Framework Papers, see note 21 above, and on Abreu and Baltazar, 1992 as well as on International Monetary Fund (IMF), 1992.

26 See Hanlon, 1991, p.135.

27 For references see *Boletim da República*, 1988; Policy Framework Papers from 1988, 1989, 1990 and 1991 (re. note 21); and Weinmann, 1991, p.58. The latter study is also integrated in the book Weinmann, 1993.

28 Rates that constitute a percentage of the value of the item in question – in contrast to a fixed sum.

29 The new turnover tax rate was 5 per cent. Domestic products had previously suffered a 10 per cent turnover tax rate.

30 Called 'Emulamentos Aduaneiros' in Portuguese.

31 Some larger firms had also had this privilege before the PRE.

32 An industrial quality and standardization office is only about to start up in 1993, six years after the introduction of PRE. Re. Interview, 1993e.

33 See for example Green, 1991 and Hanlon, 1991.

34 This is one of the main points in the interesting works of the Swedish researcher Hermele, 1990 and Hermele, 1992.

35 An 'intervened' company is normally a firm abandoned by its former owners in the mid and late 1970s. The state then took it over and ran it. However, the firm did not obtain a new legal status. This has been a major problem for efficient running of the firms and for the privatization process.

36 This transpired for example at the interviews at CONTEX, Texlom and Soveste. Re. Interviews, 1993c and 1993f.

37 The author was told at the World Bank Office in Maputo that a substantial part of the defined credit limits were filled out with old non-performing loans. Therefore, what remained for others was severely reduced. Re. Interview, 1993g.

38 This was for example a common denominator at the interviews conducted by the author in Maputo, March 1993 (Interviews, 1993, c, d, e and f).

39 At the same time only few, weak and uncoordinated measures were working to support the special demands of the small and micro enterprise sector for credits. See for example Vletter, 1992.

40 See Government of Mozambique, 1990b, articles 41 and 86 on a market economy and private ownership.

41 Corruption and mismanagement by state firm managers were often denounced by the work force that not seldom used the strike weapon to make their claims heard.

42 For example in relation to value added, turn over or number of employees.

43 Reference is made to the Decrees 18/89 and 21/89, dealing with the transfer of firms from an intervened status to the state sector as a precondition for possible later privatization, and Law on Privatization, No. 15/91 of 3.8.1991. The latter sets out the principles for state companies' restructuring, sale and distribution of shares to private owners. It also deals with improving public utilities' efficiency and accountability. For further information see World Bank, 1991c.

44 The unit was called UTRE, an abbreviation of Unidade Tecnico de Restruturação das Empresas = Technical Unit for Enterprise Restructuring. UTRE was established in 1988, under the International Development Association (IDA) financed Industrial Enterprise Restructuring Project, as the responsible entity for the rehabilitation of 13 larger industrial enterprises. In the beginning of 1992 only two rehabilitation plans had been approved for rehabilitation under World Bank credits (Madal/Copra + CIMOC/Cement).

45 The Committee was called CIRE, an abbreviation of Comissão Interministerial de Restruturação das Empresas = Inter-Ministerial Commission for Enterprise Restructuring.

46 Management and workers can in principle acquire up to 20 per cent of the shares each.

47 The privatization unit in the Ministry of Finance, UTRE (see note 44), has an academic staff of seven. The unit for the restructuring of industrial enterprises in the Ministry of Industry, GREI, an abbreviation of Gabinete de Restruturação de Empresas Industriais, is staffed by two economists, one lawyer, two accountants and a secretary.

48 In 1993 a final agreement was reached to swap Mozambican debt of US$ 500 million for US$ 150 million worth of shares in Mozambican enterprises.

49 The quote is from the inspiring article Mandaza, 1994. Mandaza proposes the establishment of a kind of corporate 'social contract' between the emergent national bourgeoisie, a progressive state and wage-earners and peasants.

50 In Mozambique they are normally referred to as 'Industrial Free Zones'. See for example the periodical *Southern African Economist*, August 1992 and December 1992/January 1993 issues.

51 The missing strategic approach to industry is for example lamented in an informative, thoughtful and constructive article in the Mozambican business periodical *Economia* in June 1991. Re. Tibana, 1991.

52 Thus, the structural adjustment programme is evaluated on internal grounds, that is according to its own defined objectives. A full analysis of the programme should naturally also include variables outside the ones chosen by the programme.

53 Reference can be made to Abrahamsson and Nilsson, 1994; Bowen, 1992;
    Hanlon, 1991; Hermele, 1992; SIDA, 1988; Torp, 1989.
54 See for example Government of Mozambique, 1992, table 1.
55 The 4–5 per cent growth target is for example discussed in World Bank,
    1989, chapter 2.
56 Tarp, 1993 writes in his book *Stabilization and Structural Adjustment*
    (p.152): '... inflation has often been brought under control through real
    output increases, rather than credit ceilings'.
57 However, if the category is maintained, it is likely to increase somewhat
    in the coming years as it contains China, which has a powerful trading
    potential and practice with exports to Africa.
58 During the period of sanctions against South Africa many donors, and
    donor supported Mozambican institutions, made purchases in Swaziland
    in order to avoid direct imports from South Africa. However, only a
    minor part of the equipment, spares, building materials etc. originated
    from Swaziland.
59 See Direcção Nacional de Estatística (DNE), 1987.
60 Due to the transport link to Beira, coal mining in Tete province can only
    be developed under peace conditions. South African (Gencor) and
    Brazilian interests are lined up for investment and rehabilitation of the
    mines. South Africa's 'Anglo-American' company is the prime force
    behind a project to develop the immense Pande natural gas field in
    Inhambane province. Gold production is undertaken by 'Lonrho', and
    constituted US$ 7.1 of the 7.6 million earned on minerals exports in
    1992. In addition, Mozambique has an abundance of semi-precious stones
    and valuable minerals, such as titanium. Bauxite is also found, and with
    the cheap energy from Cahora Bassa some see aluminium smelting as a
    future export potential, although this perspective under current conditions
    appears highly unlikely.
61 The calculations are based on 83 per cent of all exports in 1992.
62 Exports to Africa totalled US$ 43 million out of overall exports of US$
    281 million in 1981. Re. SADCC, 1986c.
63 Reference is made to Interview, 1993d and Ministério do Comércio,
    1993b, table indicating the products and quota allocations in the
    Mozambique – South African Trade Agreement as per 1993.
64 The investment code is embodied in Law No. 4/84 of 18 August 1984.
    The main critique of the code is that some of the preferences are left too
    much open to negotiations in the individual investment case. MIGA stands
    for the Multilateral Investment Guarantee Agency and forms part of the
    World Bank Group.
65 The distribution on sectors of approved private foreign direct investment
    in the period 1985–91 is the following:

Sector	Million US$	Per cent of total
Agriculture	173.9	42.8
Tourism and hotels	106.0	26.1
Mineral resources and oil prospecting	59.2	14.6
Manufacturing	23.0	5.7
Transport and communication	22.0	5.4
Construction	9.5	2.3
Fishing	7.8	1.9
Others	4.8	1.2
Total	406.2	100.0

Source: Economist Intelligence Unit, 1992c

66 See for example SADCC, 1985e.

67 An interesting recent study of the Mozambican textile and clothing industry and its international competitiveness is Weinmann, 1991, which the author as mentioned above (note 27) incorporated in the book Weinmann, 1993.

68 See especially chapter 3.

69 In the first half of the 1980s second-hand clothes were imported to cover part of the market that the national clothing industry was not able to supply. They were especially used as incentive goods in the countryside, often in barter deals purchasing crops from the peasants. For a short, informative description and evaluation of the Swedish financing of transport of used clothes to Mozambique, see Abrahamsson, 1988. However, his recommendations of continued support to sending second-hand clothes to Mozambique, may be disputed, because he does not take into account the reduced effective demand of the population, and the harm done to local industry by continued second-hand imports, even though the theoretical/ideal demands for clothes have not been met. If the minimum needs for clothing are met by second-hand imports then the poor people will tend to use the little money available for other pressing needs such as food and housing and not for additional clothes.

70 Both Non-Governmental Organizations (NGOs) and government institutions, such as the agricultural produce commercialization company, Agricom, took part in this unfortunate practice. It is expected to be reduced following the peace accord, which makes access to rural Mozambique less difficult.

71 In an Italian consultancy report on the textiles and clothing sector in Mozambique sources are quoted that estimate 80 per cent of the garments sold in Maputo to have been imported illegally in the beginning of the 1990s. This is probably to the high side, but it underlines the seriousness of the problem. Re. Morest Services SRL, 1992.

72 Increasing from US$ 11 to 22 million. The majority of imported cloth is competing with locally produced cloth in the retail sector, and only a minor part is for further processing in the clothing factories. Re. Direcção Nacional Estatistica, 1992, table 6.9, which gives an overview of main import products. Cloth is a translation of the Portuguese category 'tecidos'.

73 This is naturally a relative statement, as the available foreign exchange in the years just before PRE were substantially lower – in 1986 US$ 4.7 million. The point is that funds under PRE are low in relation to internal demand in the textile and clothing industry for raw materials, spare-parts and machinery.

74 As mentioned earlier this is counteracted through an eight per cent rebate on purchases of tied aid funds under the new system of allocation of foreign exchange from 1992.

75 From 1980 to 1985 the only exports were sisal rope to the Soviet Union to the tune of US$ 1–2.5 million annually, according to CONTEX, 1993.

76 The company has for example established a bounded warehouse from where raw materials and finished products can move freely to and from the factory (without paying customs tariffs etc.) when producing for exports. Re. Interview, 1993f.

77 The two are 'Edgars' and 'Trueworth'.

78 Clothing exports are generally characterized by small quantities that change according to season and fashion, and that strictly must adhere to timetable and quality.

79 Calculated on the basis of data from CONTEX, 1993. Unfortunately, it is not possible to establish the production value in US$ after 1990.

80 The simultaneous implementation of structural adjustment programmes in many SADCC countries has reduced effective consumer demand considerably. However, the second largest textile mill won in 1992 an international tender on the delivery of cangas/capulanas to Angola. Unfortunately, the order was never effectuated, because of renewed hostilities in Angola.

81 China is said to be willing to finance and implement the rehabilitation of the third largest cotton mill, but to be effective a rehabilitation should be combined with technical assistance, training, export promotion and some kind of responsibility for the economic results of the factory. This is not likely to happen and therefore the future seems bleak for this company.

82 See for example World Bank, 1992b.

83 Reference is made to the discussion of trade in Southern Africa in chapter 3.

6   Summary and perspectives

6.1   An overview

With the analysis of the contents and implication of the structural adjustment programme in Mozambique the book has concluded its tour of the selected four main areas within the ambit of regional cooperation and integration in Southern Africa in the 1980s and the beginning of the 1990s: (1) general approaches; (2) industry, trade and SADCC's initiatives; (3) regional policies of the World Bank; and (4) the effects of a national structural adjustment programme.

It is an essential and normative point of departure for the book that regional cooperation and integration in one form or other is among the key prerequisites for sustained growth in Southern Africa. Another important assumption is that a regional market given the right conditions can be a beneficial stepping-stone for establishing a manufacturing sector, which at least in some sectors will develop world market competitiveness. The main questions which the book seeks to answer are: what did SADCC attempt in terms of regional cooperation within industry and trade and why did it fail? Which policies for regional cooperation and integration are directly and indirectly promoted by the key proponent for the new macroeconomic framework in the region, the World Bank? In order to have the necessary background and tools to deal with these issues the book discusses various general approaches to regional cooperation and integration and gives an overview over the industrial structure and trade flows in the region.

The first field of analysis general approaches, provides useful clues to the rest of the investigation. It ventures definitions of the two concepts cooperation and integration. The former places the emphasis on the flexible, joint solving of tasks while maintaining the nation state and its benefits on the centre stage. The latter includes market sharing and the creation of common mechanisms to minimize conflict and maximize benefits. The immense potential advantages of cooperation as an approach to regional economic interaction are recognized. But focus is likewise on the approach's limitations and apparent tendency to superficiality although the cooperation might cover many spheres. The five rung ladder of market integration is appreciated, as well as the dangers of polarization or bambazonke, as it is known in Southern Africa. Development integration has the obvious advantages of minimizing polarization and stressing the development angle. At the same time the problems of practical implementation are substantial. An approach in the making is identified: the adjustment adapted market integration approach. It represents a search for compatibility between structural adjustment and regional initiatives. The pragmatic and political motivations behind the approach are noted, as well as the flexibility of the approach in relation to speed and geographical coverage of reciprocal tariff reductions. Finally, among the general approaches focus has centred on the neo-functionalists. They gave useful insights and formulated hypotheses that furthered an understanding of the political processes surrounding regional cooperation and integration. SADCC in the period 1980–92 is seen as being based on a cooperation approach canalizing donor finance mainly for infrastructure projects in a regional context. It has advanced a common regional outlook and joint positions in relation to third parties, as well as having promoted a feeling of identity among the elites. It extends the scope of cooperation to other areas, but does not dig deeply into any of them. Agreements among leaders have not been sufficient to commit the countries as such and secure implementation. Donor finance for joint projects reduces the countries' reluctance to join SADCC and facilitates its work in certain sectors.

In the second area of focus it is argued that development of manufacturing industry is a must for escaping the trap of underdevelopment in Southern Africa. The precarious state of industry in Southern Africa is pinpointed. The figures clearly spell out the danger of polarization around South Africa and Zimbabwe. Trade between the SADCC countries is appallingly low: 4–5 per cent. An interesting aspect is that manufactured products constitute more than half of intra-regional SADCC trade. Moreover, regional trade has in reality already reached significant levels, also in international comparisons between South Africa, the SACU countries and a group of four SADCC members: Malawi, Mozambique, Zambia, and Zimbabwe. The book investigates the rise and fall of SADCC's plans for industry and trade development. Their failure is seen in the context of a shifting macroeconomic setting in the individual SADCC countries, unwillingness of donors to engage in the industrial sector, diverging interests among the SADCC countries themselves, and poor quality of projects as well the limitation embedded in the minimum common denominator negotiating style.

Thirdly, the principal advocate of the changed economic environment, the World Bank, has been put under scrutiny for the purpose of identifying its

214

possible policies on regional cooperation and integration in Southern Africa. On the general level two conflicting views emerge. One proposing the unilateral opening up of national economies towards the world market as the only solution, and another arguing for the firm need in Africa to promote regional cooperation and integration with a reasoning running close to the adjustment adapted market integration model. On the operational level two strategies or rather patterns of action are observed. Firstly, a halfhearted support for SADCC's cooperation approach and projects in the 1980s and beginning of the 1990s. Secondly, a recent initiative rather close to the recommendations of the adjustment adapted approach is noticed. However, it's future appears problematic, as it is implemented without any direct involvement of the existing regional organizations. The World Bank and the EC Commission seem to be pulling the strings while the countries are involved only through technical working groups. Thus, the initiative may be doomed by the lack of regional and local political ownership of the process. Moreover, the polarization effect is not taken up in the initiative, which may also jeopardize its viability.

The lack of consistency in theory and practice and between the two on the part of the World Bank necessitates a country focus. Therefore, the inclusion of the fourth and final area in the book: structural adjustment in Mozambique as a country example. There is not detected any direct references to regional cooperation and integration in the key documents concerning the country's structural adjustment programme. However, indirectly conditions for regional inter-linkages within trade and industry are affected through the effects of the general measures of the programme. Devaluations, liberalizations of trade and greater management autonomy furthered regional trade in manufactured goods. There is a pull in the opposite direction by the combined effects of interest rates that were perceived as prohibitive for industrial investments, unstable availability of foreign exchange due to dependence on donors, a cumbersome and protracted privatization process as well as the absence of a coherent industrialization strategy. An example from one industrial branch illuminates the seriousness of the crisis in the manufacturing sector at the beginning of the 1990s. Analysis of regional trade demonstrates South Africa's strong position covering a third of Mozambican imports and taking 15 per cent of Mozambique's exports. The figures underline how regional integration and cooperation within trade has a quite firm material basis among certain countries in Southern Africa. They also urge to caution as the danger of polarization is obvious.

Key overall conclusions of the book are that a number of discrepancies of policy exist. SADCC does not appear to adjust sufficiently to the change in the macroeconomic policies of its member states. The World Bank has conflicting strategies on the regional level; its activities to further regional cooperation and integration are not pursued convincingly, and its cooperation with the individual countries appears to neglect a regional angle to the adjustment programmes. However, concerted action from the region to advance regional cooperation and integration may link up to an increased understanding by the World Bank of the political and economic usefulness of regional markets. New initiatives are facilitated by democratic South Africa entering the regional equation, and the relatively high level of economic interaction between South Africa and a number of SADCC countries.

6.2   Chapter conclusions

The first substantive chapter focuses on the general approaches to regional cooperation and integration. Definitions of the two concepts are also ventured. Regional cooperation is defined as 'a process whereby nation states in common solve tasks and create improved conditions in order to maximize internal and external economic, political, social and cultural benefits for each participating state.' Emphasis is on the nation states achieving better results by working together than they would have been able to on their own. Cooperation can be as narrow or as comprehensive as the participants wish, and no specific institutional set up is required. Regional integration is defined as 'a process through which a group of nation states voluntarily in various degrees share each other's markets, and establish mechanisms and techniques that minimize conflicts and maximize internal and external economic, political, social and cultural benefits of their interaction.' Here the opening up of markets is a key element as well as the establishment of some sort of institutional framework that can facilitate the process of integration. A distinction is introduced between negative integration which is the breaking down of barriers between markets, and positive integration which indicates the building up of mechanisms to smooth and correct the integration process.

Regional cooperation as an approach to greater economic interaction is typically moulded in the following forms:

1   execution of joint projects, technical sector cooperation, common running of services and policy harmonization;
2   joint development of common natural resources;
3   joint stand towards the rest of the world;
4   joint promotion of production.

Regional cooperation can limit itself to sub-elements on this list or be all embracing. National interests are in focus and supra-national institutions are out of the question. Key words are flexibility, decentralization, an incremental, step-by-step attitude and a concentration on functional areas where the benefits of interaction appear obvious, where costs are low, and every partner gets a reasonable share of the cake. However, significant problems are the lack of obligation to fulfil commitments, and that the areas in which the nations cooperate often are not mutually supportive. Thereby, the cooperation might be stuck with the original tasks and unable to lead to higher levels of cooperation and integration. Thus, the areas of cooperation might be wide but often not go very deep into the subject matter. A consensus or common minimum denominator style of negotiation is predominant. It secures cohesion and stability, but limits speed and initiatives. Experiences with industrial cooperation appear discouraging.

Market integration is the first among four different approaches to regional integration that are looked into. The approach's analysis of the appropriateness of a given regional integration arrangement is based on the notion of trade creation and trade diversion. The former being the additional trade created between regional partners by cheaper purchases within the regional arrangement of products that earlier were produced locally but at higher prices. Trade diversion indicates that products produced cheaper, and previously imported from outside the region are rendered uncompetitive by high customs tariffs. Only when trade creation exceeds trade diversion can regional integration be recommended, according to the market integration approach. This implies that typical third world countries with low regional trade and a high level of world market trade are poor candidates for regional integration. The ideal type market integration approach consists of a progression in five steps from a free trade area, over a customs union and a common market to an economic, and eventually a political union. It is characteristic of the approach that positive integration in the form of common institutions and other arrangements only intensifies in the later stages of integration. The market approach, and its relevance for third world regional integration, has been criticized from various angles. Firstly, it is claimed to be based on unrealistic assumptions, for example perfect markets. Secondly, the static character of the approach is put into question. It cannot reflect how conditions for production can change in the course of time, for example through conscious intervention by a government. Thirdly, it is asserted that counting and comparing the effects of trade diversion and trade creation is not sufficient to judge the adequateness of a regional arrangement for a given country. A certain amount of trade diversion could for example be necessary in order to protect a manufacturing industry in its early stages. Thus, the region could be a training ground before world market exposure. Fourthly, there is the polarization effect: the market integration approach is criticized by G. Myrdal and others for allowing the most developed areas in the region to prosper, while the already economically weak parts become even more marginalized. This process is a natural consequence of the market forces, and it reinforces itself over time. A counteracting spread effect is relatively weak, especially in a third world setting. In Eastern and Southern Africa the tendency towards polarization is known from the Central African Federation with Harare (then Salisbury) as the centre, and the East African Community with Nairobi as the magnet for investment and trade. In the time of the Central African Federation the polarization effect became known as the bambazonke, meaning everything goes to Harare.

The background for the formulation of development integration approach lies in the critique of the market integration approach, not least the polarization effect. The development integration approach changes the objective, the timing and level of interstate binding commitments, and the distribution of costs and benefits. The objective is broadened to cover the improvement of social conditions and enhancement of development potential, with special emphasis on industry. The creation of common institutions, possibly with supra-national powers, and binding commitments between the countries comes at a rather early stage of the integration process. An attempt to create an equal distribution of the benefits and costs of the integration process is essential to the approach. Four main methods are identified in order to counteract the polarization process: (1) purely fiscal compensation; (2) improved conditions for development; (3) incentives for a changed pattern of production; (4) planning of new industries and agreements on distribution of production. The level of state intervention increases from the first to the fourth method. The first implies cash payments from the states, which experience most trade creation, to the less favoured countries. In Africa the only well functioning compensation scheme is part of SACU. However, the calculation of a reasonable level of compensation is extremely complicated and can ultimately only be decided politically. The use of customs receipts for redistribution in favour of the lesser developed countries will in the coming years suffer from the foreseen general reduction in the level of customs duties. The second method of improving general conditions of development is well known in the EC, where especially infrastructure investments are targeted. Improvements of education, not least technical disciplines, are also part of this way of attracting investments and creating jobs. The investments in the less privileged countries have in the EC often been part of package deals; for example, to make the poorer countries accept further trade liberalization. The third method of changing incentives for production has its own sub-categories. They can be brought about through development banks, special investment incentives, a slower rhythm of customs reduction, and the maintenance of certain tariffs. A common obstacle to this method has been that incentives only function with difficulty and are not transparent when markets are distorted, as they generally were in the third world in the 1970s and 1980s. Development banks often lacked clear objectives and funds. A slower customs rate reduction is technically feasible, but politically difficult among countries in the third world, which all have huge development needs. Maintenance of certain tariffs to protect lesser developed countries gives a complex tariff structure and there

218

is a danger that the industry in the region cannot benefit from the larger market. The fourth method on planned industrial development has proved immensely difficult. There is much national prestige attached to industrial development and countries at different levels of development – and with different industrial structures – simply often have contradictory material interests. The concept of a core state is important for the distribution of costs benefits in a regional arrangement. As the economically strongest state the core state might perceive a self-interest in overcompensating the lesser developed states in order to gain market access, and to be able to rally the whole region behind it on the international scene. However, when even the core states, such as South Africa in Southern Africa, have great development problems, then the area for manoeuvre is restricted.

The key characteristics of the adjustment adapted market integration approach are its supportive and complementary nature in relation to the structural adjustment programmes. Both have the ultimate aim of reaching the highest degree of opening towards the world market as possible. However, unilateral openings have experienced much political opposition and a slow rhythm of implementation in Africa. Therefore, the adjustment adapted market integration approach finds a detour worthwhile around a regional bend of the road. It argues that the end result will be lower tariffs than unilateral reforms would allow. Why? There are several reasons for that. Firstly, the positive connotations of regional integration in Africa. Secondly, the visible benefits that negotiations with neighbouring countries may bring. Thirdly, a regional agreement will be more difficult to topple than unilateral reforms for groups opposed to any opening of the economy. Fourthly, the social hardship may be reduced and the industrial sector may be able to avoid the potentially very drastic consequences of unilateral reform. The integration model of the adjustment adapted approach contains free flow of capital and labour, which should counteract the polarization process. The immense political obstacles to especially the free flow of labour is apparently not accounted for. A flexibility in relation to geographical coverage and rhythm of reform is also displayed. The decisive factor is which countries are willing to reduce barriers on a reciprocal basis. Existing regional organizations shall be vehicles for implementing the approach. The approach is reluctant to give special favours to lesser developed areas. At the same time it admits that political reasons can motivate some kind of fiscal compensation. A basic question that the approach appears to avoid, is whether it wants to advance its regional approach, even if a given government is willing to implement unilateral openings towards the world market?

The neo-functionalist approach is a refinement of older functionalist theory. The latter studies how international bodies may unite stubborn nationalism, and promote the view that it would be more rational to solve or administer together an increasing number of material functions of the nation states. The neo-functionalists adds to this a scientific study of the political processes surrounding cooperation and integration inspired mainly by the EC. Interest groups, political parties and technocrats are perceived as the prime movers of the integration process which is originally seen as rather linear. This is later modified and broadened somewhat. It is acknowledged that the integration process might end up in backlashes (spill-back), spill-around where interaction covers many areas but none profoundly, or self-encapsulation where the outside world is kept out and satisfaction with existing results prevails. Moreover, third world countries with little pluralistic tradition are not excluded from any prospect of progress in cooperation and integration. The process is just more difficult there. Central concepts are functional linkages, spill-over, and negotiating styles. The integration process is, according to the neo-functionalist approach, nurtured through small, relatively uncontroversial, incremental steps, which, however, have a functional linkage to the next steps on the integration ladder. Therefore, they are likely to be carried on, when the full potential of the first move is exhausted and has created its own momentum for further action. This is a spill-over process. The ideal negotiating style around such a process are package deals, where a compromise is reached on a higher level of integration and everybody can foresee potential benefits – often in different areas. Negotiating styles which may delay and block cooperation are according to the neo-functionalists, the zero-sum game where a loss to one is a gain to the other (splitting the difference style), or the lowest common denominator style where the most reluctant country sets the pace. Premature politization is also negative to cooperation and integration. This happens when a certain step towards greater integration moves into the centre of the political debate, before sufficient political backing has developed around the specific issue. The need for a regional group to act as a block towards other countries and international actors, externalization, often runs faster than the cooperation and integration itself. However, this may involve sensitive issues and thus hamper the integration process. When discussing how an integration process is started the neo-functionalist approach points to the importance of a dramatic act and persuasive ideological drive towards closer regional interaction. The committed 'Europeans' after the Second World War and the 'anti-dependencia school' in Latin America are cases in point. Finally, the neo-functionalists offer a framework for analyzing regional cooperation and integration using the three headings: integrative potential, process forces and consequences of integration.

Chapter 2 ends up with an attempt to define SADCC in the period 1980–92 in relation to the approaches presented. This is firmly done within the cooperation approach. The main reason is that SADCC does not implicate any sharing of markets. SADCC concentrates on: (i) execution of joint projects; (ii) the coordination of technical sectors; (iii) joint stand towards the outside world. SADCC has no supra-national institutions, no elaborate treaty and the cooperation does not impinge on national interest. Identity in outlook among Heads of State and government is an integrative potential, but the leaders have great difficulties in committing their countries to implementing regional decisions, beyond what common infrastructure projects entailed. An integrative potential for especially the Front-line states is the existence of a common enemy in the form of apartheid South Africa, but the South African destabilization is a negative process force. The expressed willingness of donors to fund SADCC projects is a positive integrative potential, as it makes the perceived costs of entering the regional group very low or nonexistent. The continued donor financing of projects is likewise an important process force. SADCC has undoubtedly led to greater regional elite identity and socialization than before, but it is not based on popular groups or driven by parties or interest groups. The inclusion of a democratic South Africa in SADCC raises interesting questions of a possible stronger interest group position in the region due to the synergetic influences from the relatively strong South African employers' organizations and trade unions.

The third chapter argues that Southern Africa must give priority to manufacturing industry development in order to raise living standards for its growing population. Prospects for increased world market prices for traditional exports from the region are bleak; also, they are threatened by technological developments and new aggressive exporters. It is established how manufacturing industry in Southern Africa both in terms of production and exports is diminutive and diminishing in the 1980s. Its geographic distribution is distorted. Among the ten SADCC countries Zimbabwe represents around 40 per cent of industrial production. However, even Zimbabwe is dwarfed when compared to South Africa, which has a manufacturing value added five time larger than that of all the SADCC countries combined. In South Africa and Zimbabwe manufacturing industry constitutes around a quarter of GDP; its sectoral composition is broad, and import-substitution has been rather successful within the existing and increasing constraints. In most of the remaining countries industry is weak and fragmented. Swaziland is a notable exception, due to special circumstances. The import-substitution industrialization strategy needs foreign exchange transfers from other sources in the economy. But the 1970s and 1980s experience a decline in earnings from traditional export products plus a decrease in export credits and investments as well as increased debt repayments. A vicious circle starts of diminishing and unstable foreign exchange availability for industry, low capacity utilization, lack of incentives to increase productivity and exports, falling production and increased centralized control over the economy. Deindustrialization is an apt description of the situation from the mid 1970s to the beginning of the 1990s. Concessional donor finance and debt relief seem the only solution. This in turn requires changes in macroeconomic policies mostly in the form of structural adjustment programmes. It also leads to dangerously high levels of donor dependence for some countries. The overview of trade in the region indicates the existence of three groups of countries among the SADCC member states in the 1980s: (1) Tanzania and Angola with very low or nonexistent trade with the rest of SADCC and with South Africa; (2) the SACU members receiving more than three quarters of their imports from South Africa; (3) Malawi, Mozambique, Zambia and Zimbabwe with levels of intra-SADCC imports and exports between 4–12 per cent of total trade and relatively high levels of trade with South Africa. This last group is potentially very important for SADCC's initiatives to increase intra-regional trade, and for future arrangements including a democratic South Africa. The data confirms Zimbabwe's dominant position among the SADCC countries, representing half of intra-regional exports and a third of imports. Trade between South Africa and SADCC is biased towards the former, which runs a huge trade surplus. However, it is argued that South Africa must also be seen as a giant market place and a source for easy purchases of imports, if prices and conditions are competitive. Another interesting observation is that over half of intra-SADCC trade consists of manufactured products and manufactured products constitute nearly half of Zimbabwe's exports to South Africa. Trade between South Africa and the African continent expanded rapidly around 1990. But within Africa, Southern Africa is totally dominant. It takes 19 per cent of South Africa's exports and accounts for five per cent of imports. The rest of Africa provides South Africa with less than one per cent of its imports and receives three per cent of South Africa's exports. Available information indicates that Africa absorbs more than half of manufactured exports from South Africa. Comparing the level of intra-regional trade in Southern Africa with levels in other regions of the world suggests that the intra-SADCC trade of 4–5 per cent is at the very low end, whilst the region including South Africa is in the forefront among African and Latin American nations.

SADCC's industry and trade programmes are introduced in 1981 and 1986 respectively. In the period 1981–89 the industry programme has a main focus on promoting industries which produced goods that fulfil basic human and development needs. Simultaneously, industrial services and the rehabilitation of industry are part of the programme. The analysis of the list of projects presented for financing reveals particularities that tend to distort the picture: two capital intensive sectors are, probably unintentionally, over-represented, and the bulk of the project value is concentrated in Tanzania, Mozambique and to some extent Malawi. Other countries do not take part in the programme. Apparently centralized economies have been able to shift national projects to a regional framework, while other countries have been hesitant to include any projects. Also, Tanzania and neighbouring countries may have been in a vantage position, because Tanzania coordinated the SADCC sector-secretariat. The response from donors was feeble. In the areas of industrial services and rehabilitation no progress could be observed and the strategy is revised in 1988/89. Most importantly, the priority basic needs industry projects are scrapped altogether. From 1989 to 1992 there is a triple focus on industrial services, improvement of the investment climate and creating a framework for the establishment of regional industrial projects. There is an increased emphasis on the market and business community. The regional industrial projects are of the utmost interest, but very problematic. They are promoted as part of a cooperation approach, but discussed by SADCC both within a market approach and a development integration approach. Up until the adaptation of the SADC Treaty the result is zero progress for the regional industrial projects, negligible advances for industrial services, and the outlook is bleak for both areas. The promotion of conducive macroeconomic structures in the region never becomes a main activity of SADCC. SADCC does promote regional business cooperation, but the venture seems to become too donor dependent, and to lack firm rooting in the national business associations as well as an independent and clear function in relation to SADCC. Initiatives which may have promoted investment also failed. They are designed to alleviate the stranglehold which the inward looking macroeconomic model had ended up in, but without changing the basic model. The Norsad fund and SADCC's cross border investment initiative are cases in point.

SADCC's trade programme is delayed in relation to initial expectations because the countries fear a possible damaging overlap with the PTA. Only in 1986 is a programme adopted which avoids direct conflict with the obligations towards the PTA. Focus is on direct trade measures and bilateral trade agreements; preferences; trade financing, and trade promotion. Again, it is an attempt within the existing macroeconomic framework to use the region for advancing the industrial development of the individual countries. Emphasis is on prearranged and balanced deals. Some of the trade proposals are linked up with the industrial programme, and as the latter comes to a halt the trade proposals also become redundant. However, in general, no progress of any significance can be observed in the period under scrutiny. The same applies to SADCC's seemingly uncontroversial trade financing schemes.

The discussion of the reasons behind the failure of SADCC's industry and trade programmes emphasizes the following points: (i) the different interests between the SADCC countries based on the diverging levels of industrial development and the differences in industry and trade policies; (ii) the miscalculation by SADCC of expecting donors to engage themselves with substantial amounts of public funding in industry and trade development; (iii) the non-optimal negotiating style, presentation and packaging of the projects as well as the lack of mutual obligations embedded in the programmes; (iv) the inability of leaders to commit administration and industry to the programmes; (v) pressure from interest groups and political parties to promote cooperation and integration has been weak; (vi) the most important reason is that while SADCC is busy formulating industry and trade programmes linked to the inward looking and centralized economic model with the state in a key role, the macroeconomy of the individual states is changing through agreements with the World Bank on structural adjustment programmes. They include internal and external liberalizations and has the private sector playing a dominant role. These characteristics contradict some of the proposals within SADCC's industry and trade programmes and make others irrelevant.

Therefore, focus switches towards the World Bank (chapter 4). Which general recommendations on regional cooperation and integration do the Bank encourage? How has the Bank actually performed in relation to regional cooperation and integration in the region? On the general level two conflicting analyses and recommendations are identified. In *World Development Report 1991* regional integration is discouraged on the basis of theoretical arguments, asserting that unilateral trade reform is a superior development path. While most can agree on this in principle, the discussion stops short of including real life market distortions or political processes, thereby reducing its relevance. This line of argument is contrasted with the analysis found in the World Bank's major publication from 1989 on Africa *From Crisis to Sustainable Growth*. There, increased regional cooperation and integration in Africa is one of the major recommendations presented to African decision-makers and donors. Functional cooperation is fully supported and integration is envisaged in a form very close to the adjustment adapted market integration approach. The regional path is economically a preparatory step on the way to world market competition. However, the key motivation to go regional is political. It is assumed that regional solutions will find easier acceptance than across the board unilateral liberalizations. There are also political motives behind recommendations to establish some kind of compensation mechanism to counteract polarization.

How the World Bank has transformed the diverging recommendation into policies and practice towards Southern Africa is explored through analyses of the Bank's interventions at SADCC's Annual Consultative Conferences. They express an initially strong verbal support for SADCC's cooperation approach with emphasis on common ground for national interests, such as for example infrastructure and communications. At the end of the 1980s emphasis is placed on promoting recommendations parallel to the ones contained in the adjustment adopted market integration approach and in *From Crisis to Sustainable Growth*. But essential questions such as compensation and phased tariff liberalizations are left out. Only a modest participation in SADCC's infrastructure programme is identified, and no direct support for SADCC's industry and trade programme can be found. Technical assistance for SADCC's Secretariat is discontinued after a short period and various studies do not seem to be well coordinated with SADCC. Neither the SADCC

224

nor the PTA Secretariat are confident that the World Bank really intends to put its considerable weight behind regional cooperation and integration. The World Bank's Cross Border Trade and Investment Initiative may have contributed to this. It is advanced outside the scope of the two organizations, and thus designed against the recommendations of the adjustment adapted market integration approach. Moreover, it does not contain any references to compensation in order to counteract polarization. The institutional turning point of the initiative is technical working groups in the participating countries. However, as the issues they deal with are politically controversial, there is a clear danger of premature politization. When this happens a backlash can occur, because the initiative is not anchored in the regional and national political leadership or, has the backing of strong socioeconomic forces in the region. In sum, the policies the World Bank pursues in practice are closest to *From Crisis to Sustainable Growth*, when compared to the recommendations in *World Development Report 1991*. At the same time they are far from having the important position they are intended to have in the proposed package of policies towards Africa, and key elements are left out. Therefore, the conclusion is that the policies are more ambiguous than they are coherent and effective; and consequently, an analysis of the World Bank's policies towards the individual countries becomes necessary.

Since it is impossible to go into the experiences of each country, chapter 5 argues for a focus on one of the non-SACU countries, as it is within that group of SADCC member states that we witness the move from closed to open economies. Mozambique is chosen as a case in point, because of its stable and broad structural adjustment programme with the World Bank from 1987 onwards, and because of the country's traditional support of regional cooperation and integration. The purpose is not to make sweeping generalizations or to advance any independent judgements of structural adjustment as such. The intention is to improve the level of discussion of regional cooperation and integration by pinpointing actual policies pursued, which in turn illuminate key issues of the book. The analysis of the basic documents guiding the structural adjustment programme in Mozambique does not reveal any direct references to regional cooperation and integration. Also, there is no mention of the obligations or perspectives that Mozambique's membership of SADCC and the PTA entails for the structural adjustment programme. The adjustment adapted market integration approach and recommendations found in *From Crisis to Sustainable Growth* are absent. This leads to the second strand of the analysis: the framework that is indirectly created for regional economic interaction through the various measures of the structural adjustment programme. It is established that all the measures are general in nature. No specific regional angle is given to tariff reform, allocation of foreign exchange or export promotion. However, exports to the region are also promoted by measures such as devaluation, liberalization of

225

trade and prices and greater management autonomy; but these positive elements seem to be counteracted by a depressed internal demand, high interest rates and credit ceilings that discourage industrial production and investment. Moreover, an industrial strategy is missing and industrial rehabilitation and privatization do not appear to receive sufficient priority from the involved parties.

Mozambican trade with the region is scrutinized. It constitutes a third of imports and 15 per cent of exports, with South Africa representing 80–85 per cent of each category. Trade with the region is highly unbalanced in Mozambique's disfavour. Exports of manufactured goods have experienced a noteworthy growth in the period under structural adjustment. A 1989 trade agreement with South Africa entails possibilities for Mozambican exports with low tariffs on manufactured products up to certain levels that are still not attained in 1992. Foreign investments have not reached the country in any significant amount. The Mozambican government lacks a clearly defined strategy on the question of foreign investment. The analysis of one specific industrial branch, textile and clothing, reveals rather sombre perspectives. The industry has greatly increased production in the initial years of structural adjustment, as imports of raw materials and spares enable the use of under-utilized capacity to satisfy the then high local demand. Exports also increase dramatically. However, production drops significantly in 1991 and 1992. This is a result of the combined effects of competition from imported second-hand clothes, clandestine imports, competition from high-tech East Asian producers, unstable availability of donor funds for imports, a depressed internal market, high interest rates and exports that in spite of an increase are too low to alleviate the other negative tendencies. In this way general structural adjustment measures whose internal logic are impeccable appear to become insufficient, when combined with specific country circumstances. There seems to be a need to adjust the adjustment in response to the specific conditions and take additional initiatives targeted at the uplifting of the manufacturing sector. One of those may be regional arrangements which facilitate trade in manufactured goods.

The Mozambican case seems to indicate that on a country level the World Bank in fact follows the recommendations on the primacy of unilateral trade reform advocated in *World Development Report 1991*, as opposed to what *From Crisis to Sustainable Growth* and the adjustment adapted market integration approach advocate. Mozambique is not included in the World Bank sponsored Cross Border Trade and Investment Initiative in the period under scrutiny. Regarding the industrial strategy the four categories defined by R.C. Riddell (and introduced in chapter 3) as responses to the emerging crisis in the 1980s may structure an analysis. The first is the continuation of a state driven industrial development policy simply modified to suit reduced means. In the second, the state keeps the overall closed and centralized model but abstains from intervention in industry. The third category represents the application of general structural adjustment measures without taking any specific initiatives regarding industry. Basically, industry adapts on its own according to market conditions. The fourth category reflects the possibility of combining a gradual transformation of closed economies towards market based systems with initiatives from the state in support of a restructuring of manufacturing industry. The emphasis is on productivity increases and international competitiveness. In the case of Mozambique the structural adjustment programme must be placed in the third category. In chapter 3 it is argued that SADCC's policies on regional industry and trade development could be compared to the policies of the first category.

The combined effect of conflicting strategies and practices on a regional and on a national level as well as between the two is an impasse in regional cooperation and integration within industry and trade in Southern Africa in the 1980s and the beginning of the 1990s.

6.3   Conceptual implications and perspectives

Let me start out this section by highlighting and reviewing some of the conceptual implications from the overall analysis of the book with special relevance to the future of regional cooperation and integration in Southern Africa. First and foremost a certain homogeneity seems to be necessary between the industrial and trade policies pursued by the various actors on the different levels in the appropriate fora. Neither SADCC nor the World Bank appears to pursue internally persistent and effective regional policies and there has been no synergetic force between the activities of the two organizations. Likewise the national states pursue or allow contradicting policies on the national and the regional level. Another lesson seems to be that the discussion of outward versus inward industrialization is increasingly irrelevant. Southern Africa appears well advised to seek increased industrial competitiveness and growth on all fronts: through production for the world market, the region, the rural sector, the informal market etc. The regional market can be an important training ground for gaining export experience, and increasing productivity and competitiveness before full world market exposure. Further conceptual implications concern low levels of civil society involvement in state and in regional endeavours and low levels of regional trade. Such conditions do, indeed, make cooperation and integration more cumbersome, but they shall not be seen as absolute hindrances to any initiatives, which in turn can stimulate popular involvement and raise levels of trade. Moreover, in the beginning of the 1990s the democratization process in South Africa and in the region in general, combined with the relatively high level of trade between South Africa and a number of SADCC members,

227

herald a new situation with more conducive conditions for cooperation and integration in the region. It shall also be borne in mind that in spite of obvious advantages, the pure cooperation approach with no market sharing or binding obligations, and a minimum common denominator negotiating style, has severe limitations in relation to increased levels of cooperation and integration. Conversely, carefully worked out package deals appear to facilitate more intense cooperation and integration. They resolve problems at a higher level of integration with benefits in one area or another for all involved. The core states may lubricate the negotiation process, but they are restricted by their own high development needs. Especial attention must be paid to the polarization effect, because the weakest states may opt out of a regional arrangement, if their situation is not sufficiently enhanced. Counteracting polarization is positive integration through adjustments to the pure market signals. A variety of measures can be applied, but one – the planned regional industrial development – seems to have encountered unsupportable hindrances. However, it may still be worthwhile exploring more narrow arrangements based on market signals. A cooperation and integration arrangement may be furthered by a certain flexibility regarding timing, depth and geographical coverage of its component parts. However, if too sophisticated systems are agreed upon the ability to function in practice is likely to suffer. A dramatic act and ideological conviction may be important to initiate the process. A general conceptual point is the importance of the political level in the different nation states. Political reluctance to implement sufficiently rapid openings towards the world market is a main motivating factor behind the adjustment adapted market integration approach. An ever present and relevant factor for analyzing the cooperation and integration process is the possibility of politization of integration issues, before enough political support has been built up behind the integration initiatives (premature politization in the neo-functionalist terminology). One must also be aware that the democratization process in Southern Africa not only opens up for political parties and interest group participation in regional initiatives. There will in all probability also be a sounding ground for and political actors who will pursue opportunistic nationalism: risks which have hitherto been reasonably avoided. There is an open and important field of research into the democratic wave in Africa and its influence on the crisis of the nation state, for example in relation to the state's legitimacy, its capacity to act decisively to improve the given country's conditions, and its ability to interact constructively and cede real power to both the local and the regional level.[1]

In the search for suitable general approaches to regional integration and cooperation in Southern Africa one must be aware of the interrelationship between three 'P's: paradigms, peace and power. The paradigm is the dominant model or ideal type of regional cooperation and integration in a given period. The quest for peace has been a strong motivating and normative force behind regional cooperation and integration, both in theory and in practice. Peace between nations, especially France and Germany, was in the forefront when the EC in the 1950s became the centre of inspiration for political theories of regional integration. The increased role of the UN in worldwide peace keeping efforts might give an impetus to regional cooperation. It is likely that the UN, both for practical and political reasons, will delegate responsibility to regional organizations.[2] In the mid 1990s in Southern Africa the maintenance of a hard won but fragile peace, and stabilizing democratic governments threatened by the military or other authoritarian forces, may develop into an important activity on a regional level. In its treaty from 1992 SADC opens up for the inclusion of peace and security in its ambit of activities,[3] but the issue may also be catered for by a separate forum. Turning to the third 'P' – the element of power – a united Europe was supported in the 1950s by the dominant world power, the United States. Further, in the 1950s and 1960s, the direct and indirect pervasive influence of the Western countries in the Third World naturally led to dominance of the market integration. In the 1970s with the upswing in Third World self-assertion, nationalizations, oil-price hikes and pressures for a New International Economic Order (NIEO), emphasis was shifted to the planning and control of internal and external economic actors within Third World regional integration models. Development integration was the order of the day. Then, in the 1980s with the failure of producer cartels and debt crisis in the Third World, and the shift of power back to the Western countries under the Reagan/Thatcher ideological umbrella of monetarism and universal free trade, regionalism as a development concept for the Third World was about to go under. In my view SADCC as a regional venture became a lone African success story within certain sectors in the 1980s, precisely because it was not based on market or development integration. However, as we have witnessed above, with the emergence of the adjustment adapted market integration approach there is a possibility of combining regional integration with the structural adjustment programmes, or similar policies under implementation in most developing nations in the 1990s. Whether this will become the dominant paradigm up to the turn of the century still remains to be seen, but chances are high that its key components will be found in the majority of integration attempts.

With the severe difficulties of international trade negotiations in the beginning of the 1990s some analysts foresee both the possibility of global bilateralism and/or a scenario of a division of the world into a relatively few large regional trading blocks with both developed, and developing countries participating in each.[4] With the absence of the common enemy of Communism rivalries between the blocks are likely to increase.[5] The establishment of NAFTA between Canada, Mexico and the US and the ever more frequent trade conflicts between the US, EC/EU and Japan may be an indication of this tendency. South American countries such as Chile may join NAFTA within a not too distant future. However, the East Asiatic region, including Japan, the ASEAN countries and not least the fast expanding China, is still the dark horse. It may develop into a block of its own, but in the foreseeable future it is likely to keep its door at least half open, because of dependence on exports to the rest of the world. In a long term view Asia might develop into a new centre for the defence of universal free trade, because Asia will then possibly host the world's most effective producers.[6] Already, East Asian goods are pouring into Africa, but less attention is paid to the effects of Asian growth on the demand for African products. The substantial and steady growth of India, with a population greater than that of the whole of the African continent, is likely to be of great importance, especially to Eastern and Southern Africa. To gain an even fuller picture the overall trends should ideally be compared to the consequences of the increased economic importance of the trans-national enterprises, the TNEs.[7] This is an area which calls for increased research, not least because foreign direct investment becomes increasingly crucial for the developing countries.

The implications to Africa of these trends are indeed uncertain. Europe seems too preoccupied with the former Soviet, Central and Eastern Europe to initiate a possible closer North-South partnership with Africa. The growth in Asia might also urge Africa to look for partnership there. However, symptomatic of how regional integration theory seems to develop, two leading World Bank economists are already in 1992 keen to dismiss any potential in South-South regional integration, and find that the optimal future model lies in blocks that contain countries from both the North and the South. On the basis of the discouraging experiences with regional integration in Latin America and Africa, they call it 'a mistake not worth repeating' and urge that 'any temptation to promote such schemes in the future should be resisted' (Melo and Panagariya, 1992a, pp.14 and 24).[8] It is their opinion that:

> [L]ooking at the future, North-South integration holds much promise for developing countries. Regional arrangements of this type can solidify past reforms, guarantee future access to a large market, and stimulate growth via increased direct foreign investment, more intense competition and faster technological diffusion (ibid., p.25).

Against this background they do not hesitate to recommend that: 'Clearly, it would be best for Sub-Saharan African countries to integrate with the EC and reap all the possible benefits. This, however, is a distant goal. The EC is simply not ready to grant entry ...' (ibid., p.20).

As indicated above I tend to agree with the last conclusion. Moreover, to count upon EC/EU farsightedness and benevolence does not appear to be the best strategy. This would tend to be a too idealistic understanding of how politics work. Even if it is accepted that closer a North-South cooperation and integration is desirable at some stage I disagree that South-South cooperation and integration should be avoided in Africa. On the contrary. A sequence of first defining, designing and operating a home-grown African regional scheme before approaching other continents seems to the present author to give better assurances of long term viability, than the sketched North-South model.[9] In a 1994 IMF study it is stated, without reference to specific country groups, that 'notwithstanding the conclusion of the Uruguay Round, interest in regionalism is expected to remain strong' (IMF Survey, 1994, p.354). The IMF study can accept the regionalism of the 1990s, because it is 'associated with outward-oriented strategies' and 'broadly compatible with the goal of multilateral liberalization' (ibid., pp.354–5). The study gives the following reasons for seeking regional solutions, which seem to match well to the situation in Southern Africa: (1) 'Exploit economies of scale, regional specialization and learning-by-doing, as well as to attract investment ...'; (2) 'enhancing regional political cohesion, managing immigration flows, and promoting regional security'; (3) 'the slow progress under the Uruguay Round and the desire to strengthen negotiation positions'; (4) '... to pre-empt future restrictions on market access and create a more stable and predictable trading environment ("safe haven"); (5) 'the ability to "lock in" domestic policy reform; and (6) 'the opportunity costs of remaining outside regional trading arrangements' (ibid., p.354).

On the basis of this, and judging from the dominant trends and distribution of power in the global system, it is in line with the three P's above that fundamental structures of a new regional dispensation in Southern Africa reflect the basic macroeconomic elements included in the adjustment adapted market integration approach. This may remedy the unfortunate disaccord and lack of consistency in the strategies and action that directly and indirectly affected regional cooperation and integration negatively in the 1980s and the beginning of the 1990s. In Central Africa the regional organization UDEAC initiated a reform process on the basis of an 'awareness ... that the policy instruments of UDEAC ... have not evolved to keep pace with changes in the economic environment' (World Bank, 1992d, p.i). However, let me stress that what I am referring to is not a fully fledged regional arrangement; my reference is to the key characteristics of the adjustment adapted market integration approach such as relatively low external tariffs, the dynamic and decisive role of the private sector and the market in economic activities, creating conducive conditions for local and foreign investment, development of financial markets, a flexible pragmatic, step by step approach, the granting of some kind of compensation to the weakest states and a meaningful role for existing regional organizations. This would secure a consistency between the national level and the regional level, and between the regional organizations and the international community represented by the World Bank and the IMF. However, on a common platform such as this, the countries of

Southern Africa must, indeed, introduce their own specific modifications and adjustments if the model is to fit the specific conditions and policy preferences of the area. If such a path is pursued it will be interesting to follow how Southern Africa in the context of a possible new regional cooperation and integration scheme handle areas such as:

– monetary policies;
– investment incentives, including export processing zones;
– migration;
– the environment/pollution;
– social aspects, including social standards and workers rights;
– common institutions and/or secretariat and the question of a supra-national authority;
– common positions towards the rest of Africa and the international community;
– participation in the regional endeavour by political parties and interest groups;
– the uphold of democratic and human rights in the member countries;
– promotion of peace and security.

An area of special interest to this book is the finding of a right mix of general and specific policies (re. Riddell's option four) which both on a national and possibly a regional level can stimulate and facilitate manufacturing industry development. This will enable Southern Africa's positions of strength to be identified and nurtured. One focus for such a policy may potentially be within the area of minerals benefication, where the region seems to have an advantageous point of departure.[10]

These areas come on top of the very delicate issue of how to find a rational solution to the duplication of activities and overlapping competence, at least potentially, between SACU, SADC and PTA: SACU being the functioning customs union, SADC an economic union in the making and PTA preparing to establish its common market, COMESA. There will be no easy or painless solution out of this unfortunate situation which the countries have brought upon themselves. In the 1990s in South Africa there have been voices that wanted the country to stand on the sidelines until the countries in the region had got their act together, while others advocated that South Africa joined both the SADC and the PTA in order to assist from within the organizations towards finding a solution.[11] In practice it seems as if a third path has been followed: South Africa joined SADC in August 1994 and in December the same year it appears that the majority of SADC member states refuse to advance COMESA, alleging that PTA must be split into a northern and a southern group of countries.[12] These developments may lead to a scenario with the coexistence of two regional groups: one for Eastern and the Horn of

Africa, including Tanzania, and the other for Southern Africa, possibly including Zaire and some Indian Ocean states. The Southern Africa group will probably as a subgroup contain a reformed SACU.[13] I agree with key analysts in Southern Africa that it would be a retroactive step if SACU is to be dissolved, unless something on an even higher level of integration is to replace it.[14] The three groups can then enter into flexible market sharing arrangements with each other. Apart from the possible market integration there will be a host of cooperation initiatives that can continue and be intensified. Their geographical coverage must match the requirements of the issue in focus and does not depend on the boundaries of possible market sharing arrangements. A 1993 study by the African Development Bank on regional integration in Southern Africa mentions the following areas for possible immediate intensification of regional cooperation (1993b, p.52):

> [P]roject investment and policy harmonisation in power, transport, telecommunications, river basin management, environmental management, sharing of agricultural technology and research, the regional rationalisation of food production, development of the region's key mineral resources and benefication, tourism development on a regional scale and the establishment of a regional network of commercial banking, development finance and capital market institutions.

In the majority of these sectors SADC already has a tradition for cooperation; as discussed earlier this may be as loose or as close as the countries wish it to be, and it can, for example, imply joint operational companies. It seems only natural that the market integration part and the sector coordination activities are joined in a common Southern African regional arrangement, probably with its own treaty, including binding obligations.

However, three observations are relevant to recap. First, that an overambitious treaty is worse than none. Non-fulfilment or failure can generate adverse effects which makes the situation even more desperate than before the regional arrangement was ventured. Second, and related to it, is Mitrany's point that only a country's interest in a certain function being solved or administered regionally can make countries give up their sovereignty. Formulas and treaties cannot do the trick. Third, to get a realistic picture of the prospects for regional corporation and integration it is necessary to get to the bone of what the national interests of the participating countries are. Let me quote from the frank statement by the then Deputy President of the ANC, W. Sisulu at the SADCC, Annual Consultative Conference in 1992 (African National Congress, 1992, p.5):

> Let there be no mistake: our concern to promote closer regional cooperation and eventually economic integration on these terms derives, in the first

233

instance, from our conviction that this would be in the best interests of our own people and national economy ... Already, some have suggested that an increase in regional trade could provide a much needed 'kick-start' for growth and development in a post-apartheid South Africa.

Realistic ambitions and open assessments of national interests combined with the involvement and commitment of parties and interest groups can be the basis for package deals involving the whole spectre of integration and cooperation. R. Davies has given some initial and preliminary thought to this issue and sketched how a market opening can be accompanied by, for example, significant South African purchases of energy, water, raw materials and transport services in the region. Mitigating arrangements are foreseen to accompany a reduction of foreign migrant workers in South Africa. South Africa will open its market for exports from the region; it will possibly support some development projects in the region, but at the same time be in an advantageous position to win tenders on international contracts; for example on civil works in the region (Davies, 1992, p.15 and Interview, 1993m). It has been suggested that a 'think tank' or a Southern African OECD type organization be created to further the study and presentation of concrete proposals concerning a new regional dispensation.[15] It may have an independent status, but taking into account the scarce resources it may be more productive to attach it to the secretariat of a future regional organization in Southern Africa. It appears logical that such an institution, if sufficiently flexible, highly calibrated and operationally minded, could play a very positive role.

Approaching the turn of the century there is little doubt that Southern Africa is balancing on a knife's edge between sliding into global marginalization and internal dissolution on the one hand,[16] and on the other hand the possibility for a launching of a new beginning. I will argue that a key element of the latter alternative is regional cooperation and integration. The countries in the region will in the words of T. Jefferson have to hang together or find themselves hanged separately.[17] Peace is at hand; but needs underpinning at a regional level. The power structure appears reasonably settled and an outline of a paradigm is available. Valuable experience has been gained during the last 30 years and some of the political leaders in the region have the ability to promote and push the issue. The material interest in doing so seems fortified with South Africa as a partner, and the democratization in the region enables broader social forces to participate in the endeavour. The end to apartheid and the silent revolution of the market may be said to constitute sufficient dramatic acts to foster action. It remains to be seen if, how and when the region will respond to this challenge, and possibly decisively define its own priorities and agenda within the given framework, linking it up consistently with the remaining elements of a development agenda.

Notes

1 See for example the interesting discussion of democracy, development and the crisis of the nation state in Munslow and Zack-Williams, 1990; and Davidson and Munslow, 1990.

2 The roles played by ECOWAS in Liberia and EC and the North Atlantic Treaty Organisation (NATO) in the conflict over Bosnia could be a forewarning of this.

3 Reference is made to SADCC, 1992c, articles 5 and 21.

4 See for example Buelens, 1992; Melo and Panagariya, 1992a, and Melo and Panagariya, 1992b.

5 Defending the General Agreement on Trade and Tariffs (GATT) before the US Congress President Kennedy declared in 1962:

> Our efforts to promote the strength and unity of the West are thus directly related to the strength and unity of Atlantic trade policies ... If we can take this step, Marxist predictions of 'capitalist' empires warring over markets and stifling competition would be shattered for all time ... and Communist efforts to split the West would be doomed to failure (here quoted from Buelens, 1992, p.127).

6 A role that Britain had in the 19th century and upheld till the 1930s, and the US took over after the Second World War. See for example Buelens, 1992, p.125.

7 See for example United Nations, 1993.

8 J. de Melo is Chief of the Trade Policy Division of the World Bank's Country Economics Department. A. Panagariya is Senior Economist in the Trade Policy Division of the Bank's Country Economics Department, according to *Finance & Development*, December 1992.

9 The inclusion of South Africa in a new regional dispensation would incidentally provide some of the mentioned benefits of a North-South arrangement for the less developed participants.

10 See for example Jourdan, 1992.

11 See for example Davies, 1994; Leistner, 1992a; Leistner, 1992b.

12 See for example *Financial Times*, 1994 and *Southern African Economist*, 1994.

13 The reforms could consist in introducing development oriented objectives and common institutions, allowing the free flow of capital and labour, lowering gradually the external tariffs and probably reducing the level of compensation somewhat.

14 However, I do not find it politically advisable that SACU is made the formal nuclei of a new regional dispensation. Reference is made to the following interviews made during my field studies in 1993: Interview,

1993a; Interview, 1993j; Interview, 1993k; Interview, 1993l. See also Ncube, 1992; and Maasdorp and Whiteside, 1993, p.41ff. The interviewed also found that a constructive role could and should be found for the Southern African Development Bank, which was created in connection with the apartheid regime's aborted regional plan from 1979, CONSAS.

15   Reference is made to Interview, 1993j; Interview, 1993l and Leistner, 1992b.

16   Reference is also made to the above IMF quote of high opportunity costs for neglecting regional cooperation and to Interview, 1993m in which Davies describes the 'boomerang effect' which will hit South Africa, if mutually beneficial agreements are not struck between the country and its neighbours; for example regarding migrant labour: South Africa would be flooded with illegal migrants, if it unilaterally would stop labour recruitment in Lesotho and not offer any satisfactory phased package deal in return. Internal dissolution is already found in an increasing number of African countries; examples from the 1990s are Liberia, Somalia, Sudan and Zaire. In Southern Africa, Angola still has to prove that it has left this category of countries for good.

17   I owe the inspiration to this to Green, 1980, p.A.43.

Bibliography

Primary sources
(Government publications, multilateral agency publications, press sources, documents)

African Development Bank/African Development Fund (1993a), *African Development Report 1993*, Abidjan.

African Development Bank (1993b), *Economic Integration in Southern Africa, Executive Summary*, Oxford.

African National Congress (1992), *Statement*, W. Sisulu, SADCC Annual Consultative Conference, January, Maputo.

Blejer, M.I. (1984), 'Economic Integration: An Analytical Overview' in Inter-American Development Bank, *Economic and Social Progress in Latin America. Economic Integration. 1984 Report*, Washington D. C.

Boletim Official de Moçambique (1964), 'Governo-Geral: Diploma Legislativo No. 2484', 1 Série, Número 22, 1 de Junho.

Boletim da República (1988), 'Decreto No. 20/88', Série 1, No. 52, 28 Dezembro.

Camdessus, M. (1993), 'Concluding Remarks', Boards of Governors, 1993 Annual Meetings, World Bank Group and International Monetary Fund, Washington D.C., *Press Release*, No. 71.

Central Statistical Office (1984), *Statement of External Trade 1983*, Harare.

Central Statistical Office (1986), *Quarterly Digest of Statistics*, June 1986, Harare.

Commission of the European Communities (1992a), *Community Structural Policies: Assessment and Outlook*, COM(92) 84 final, Brussels.

Commission of the European Communities (1993a), *EF-initiativernes Fremtid under Strukturfondene*, (in Danish on the initiatives of the Commission under the Structural Funds) KOM(93) 282 endelig udg., Brussels.

Commission of the European Communities (1993c), 'Letter from the EC Directorate General for Development to the Minister of Finance, Malawi', dated 19 January, Brussels.

CONTEX (1993), *Primary source material*, (mostly tables of volume and value of production, imports and exports), collected by the author, March, Maputo.

Daily Gazette, 1 March 1993, 'Domestic Tension'.

Direcção Nacional de Estatistica (DNE) (1987), Informação *Estatística 1986*, Maputo.

Direcção Nacional de Estatística (DNE) (1989), *Informação Estatistica 1988*, Maputo.

Direcção Nacional de Estatística (DNE) (1990), *Informação Estatistica 1989*, Maputo.

Direcção Nacional de Estatística (DNE) (1991), *Anuário Estatístico 1990*, Maputo.

Direcção Nacional de Estatística (DNE) (1992), *Anuário Estatístico 1991*, Maputo.

Economist Intelligence Unit (1992a), *Namibia, Botswana, Lesotho and Swaziland; Country Report*, No. 1, 1992, London.

Economist Intelligence Unit (1992b), *Zimbabwe. Country Report*, No. 3, 1992, London.

Economist Intelligence Unit (1992c), *Mozambique. Country Profile. 1992–93*, London.

Economist Intelligence Unit (1993), *Mozambique, Malawi, Country Report*, No. 1, 1993, London.

Financial Gazette, 15 July 1993.

Financial Times, 12 September 1994, 'Rivalries stymie African Body.'

Finansies & Tagniek, 4 October 1991, 'Só dryf SA handel met Afrika', (Afrikaans language article on trade between South Africa and Africa).

Government of Mozambique (1985), *Gorongoza Documents,1984 Desk Diary* (extracts), Maputo, 1985.

Government of Mozambique (1987), *Economic Policy Framework, 1987–89*, 5 May, Maputo.

Government of Mozambique (1988), *Economic Policy Framework, 1988–90*, 2 March, Maputo.

Government of Mozambique (1989), *Policy Framework Paper, 1989–91*, 21 February, Maputo.

Government of Mozambique (1990a), *Economic Policy Framework, 1990–92*, May, Maputo.

Government of Mozambique (1990b), *Constitution of the Republic of Mozambique*, Supplement to *Mozambique file*, No. 174.

Government of Mozambique (1991a), *Policy Framework Paper, 1991–93*, August, Maputo.

Government of Mozambique (1991b), *Strategy and Program for Economic and Social Development 1992–94*, October, Maputo.

Government of Mozambique (1992), *Policy Framework Paper, 1992 –94*, October, Maputo.

High Density Mirror, May 1994, 'Social Costs of ESAP'.

Horizon, July 1993, 'How ESAP Hurts the Workers'.

IMF Survey, November 14, 1994, 'Uruguay Round Outcomes Strengthens Framework for Trade Relations'.

International Monetary Fund (IMF) (1992), *Statistical Appendix*, SM/92/108, 1 June.

Interview (1993a), *SADCC Secretariat*, Senior Economist: Maphanyane, E., March, Gaborone.

Interview (1993b), *PTA Secretariat*, Senior Economist, Osafo, K., April, Lusaka.

Interview (1993c), *CONTEX*, Coordinating Unit for Textile and Clothing Industry subordinated the Ministry of Industry, Consultant to CONTEX and former Head of Economic Department at CONTEX: Bhatt, L. do C.T. and Head of Department for Provisions at CONTEX: Chiau, M.C., March, Maputo.

Interview (1993d), *Ministry of Commerce*, Head of Department for Relations to Multilateral Organizations: Ferrão, F. and Deputy Head of Department for Economics and Planning: Anastácio, M., March, Maputo.

Interview (1993e), *Ministry of Industry*, Head of Department of Economics and Planning: Chiale, A.R. and Coordinator: Moyane, A., March, Maputo.

Interview (1993f), *Textile and Clothing Factories: Texlom and Soveste*, General Directors: Tomo, J.P. and Carrajola, F.S., March, Maputo.

Interview (1993g), *World Bank Country Office*, Economist: Castro, R., March, Maputo.

Interview (1993h), *SADCC Regional Business Council, SRBC*, Development Officer: Munyavi, R., April, Gaborone.

Interview (1993i), *NORSAD Agency*, Senior Economist: Sipilä, S., April, Lusaka.

Interview (1993j), Ncube, P., Professor, University of Cape Town, March, Cape Town.

Interview (1993k), Maasdorp, G., Professor and Director, University of Natal, March, Durban.

Interview (1993l), McCarthy, C.L., Professor, University of Stellenbosch, March, Stellenbosch.

Interview (1993m), Davies, R., Professor and Co-Director, University of Western Cape, March, Bellville.

Jourdan, P. (1992), *Provisional Implications for the SADCC Mining Sector of a Post Apartheid South Africa*, prepared for SADCC Mining Sector Coordination Unit, final draft, Lusaka.

Leipziger, D.M. and Thomas, V. (1993), *The Lessons of East Asia. An Overview of Country Experience*, World Bank, Washington D.C.

Melo, J. de and Panagariya, A. (1992a), *The new Regionalism in Trade Policy. An interpretive Summary of a Conference*, World Bank and Centre for Economic Policy Research, Washington D.C.

Melo, J. de and Panagariya, A. (1992b), 'The New Regionalism', *Finance & Development*, December 1992.

Melo, J. de and Panagariya, A. (1992c), 'Regionalism in trade is back – and here to stay', *World Bank Policy Research Bulletin*, Vol. 3, No. 3.

Merchant Bank of Central Africa, Limited (1992), *Report on Cross Border Investment Facility*, prepared for SADCC Secretariat, Harare.

Ministério do Comércio (1993a), *Primary source material* (reports and tables, covering Mozambican foreign trade mainly in the period 1988–92), collected by the author, March, Maputo.

Ministério do Comércio (1993b), *Table indicating the products and quota allocations in the Mozambican – South African Trade Agreement*, as per 1993, collected by the author, March, Maputo.

Morest Services SRL (1992), *Estudo sobre: Situação do Sector Textil e de Confecções em Moçambique e Oportunidades de Desenvolvimento*, Solicitado por Consorcio Promoprato, Maputo.

Norsad Fund and Norsad Agency (1993a), *Annual Report for the Year 1 April 1991 – 31 March 1992*, Lusaka, 1993.

Norsad Fund and Norsad Agency (1993b), *Policy Guidelines for Norsad Fund and Norsad Agency*, Lusaka, 24 November 1992, revised 11 January 1993.

OECD (1987), *Geographical Distribution of Financial Flows to Developing Countries*, Paris.

OECD (1992), *Development Co-operation*, Paris

Organization of African Unity (1982), *Lagos Plan of Action for the Economic Development of Africa*, Geneva.

Organization of African Unity (1991), *Treaty Establishing the African Economic Community*, 3 June, Abuja.

Overseas Development Institute (1986), 'Industrialisation in Southern Africa', *Briefing Paper*, January.

Petersson, L. (1992), *Lesotho. Adjustment and Liberalization in Lesotho*, Macroeconomic Studies 35/92, The Planning Secretariat, SIDA, Stockholm.

Petri, P.A. (1993), *The Lessons of East Asia*, World Bank, Washington D.C.

PTA (1982), *Treaty for the Establishment of the Preferential Trade Area for Eastern and Southern African States*, United Nations Economic Commission for Africa, Addis Ababa.

PTA (1990), *PTA – The Objectives, Structure and Development Programmes*, PTA Secretariat, Lusaka.

PTA (1991), *Proposed Framework for Co-operation between the Preferential Trade Area and the World Bank*, Lusaka.

PTA (1992a), *Report of the Seventeenth Meeting of the Council of Ministers*, January, Lusaka.

PTA (1992b), *PTA Trade and Development Strategy*, Print Holdings, Harare.

PTA (1993a), *Report of The Eighteenth Meeting of the Council of Ministers*, January, Lusaka.

PTA (1993b), *The PTA, its Origins, Structure and Operations*, PTA Secretariat, Lusaka.

PTA (1993c), *Proposed Framework of Co-operation between the Preferential Trade Area and the International Monetary Fund (IMF)*, Lusaka.

SADCC (1983a), *Toward Regional Trade Development*, SADCC Secretariat, Gaborone.

SADCC (1983b), *A Strategy for the Integration of the SADCC Markets*, final report by consultants, International Funding Services, Brussels, Gaborone.

SADCC (1983c), *Minutes of Meeting of SADCC Trade and Finance Ministers*, Arusha, October, Gaborone.

SADCC (1983d), *The Proceedings*, Industrial Development and Food & Agriculture Conference, Maseru, January, Gaborone.

SADCC (1984a), *Extract from Records of the Council of Ministers*, Gaborone July, Gaborone.

SADCC (1984b), *Study on Payments and Clearing between Member States*, study by consultants, International Funding Services, Brussels, Gaborone.

SADCC (1984c), *Current Status of Industrial Projects*, Gaborone.

SADCC (1984d), *Report of the Workshop on Implementation of SADCC Industrial Projects*, Harare, January, Gaborone.

SADCC (1984e), *Progress of the SADCC Regional Plan of Industrial Co-operation*, Gaborone.

SADCC (1984f), *SADCC. A Handbook*, Gaborone.

SADCC (1985a), *Workshop on Rehabilitation and Upgrading of Priority Industries in the SADCC Region, Objectives, Rationale and Approach, and Initial Set of Projects*, Arusha, August, Gaborone.

SADCC (1985b), *SADCC Industrial Development Activity, Progress and Proposals for Assistance*, Consultative Conference, January/February, Mbabane.

SADCC (1985c), *Minutes: SADCC Council of Ministers*, Maseru, May, Gaborone.

SADCC (1985d), *SADCC's First Five Years. Industrial Development*, Gaborone.

SADCC (1985e), *Macro-Economic Survey 1986*, Gaborone.

SADCC (1986a), *Annual Progress Report 1985–86*, Gaborone

SADCC (1986b), *Macro-Economic Survey. Report on the Lilongwe Workshop – August 1986*, Gaborone.

SADCC (1986c), *SADCC Intra-Regional Trade Study*, Bergen and Gaborone.

SADCC (1986d), *Industry, Strategies for the Next Five Years*, Consultative Conference, Harare, January, Gaborone.

SADCC (1986e), *Investment Policies and Mechanism of SADCC Countries*, compiled by SITCD, Dar es Salaam.

SADCC (1986f), *Minutes: Meeting of SADCC Ministers of Trade*, March, Gaborone.

SADCC (1986g), *Regional Investment Promotion Meeting for SADCC Countries*, Harare, November, Dar es Salaam.

SADCC (1986h), *The 10th Meeting of SADCC Industry Officials Sub-Committee*, September, Dar es Salaam

SADCC (1987a), *Industry and Trade*, Consultative Conference, February, Gaborone.

SADCC (1987b), *SADCC: Investment in Production*, February, Gaborone.

SADCC (1987c), *The Proceedings*, 1987 Consultative Conference, February, Gaborone.

SADCC (1988a), *Industry and Trade, Mining, Tourism*, Consultative Conference, Arusha, January, Gaborone.

SADCC (1988b), *Development of Infrastructure and Enterprise*, Consultative Conference, Arusha, January, Gaborone.

SADCC (1988c), *The Proceedings*, 1988 Consultative Conference, Arusha, January, Gaborone.

SADCC (1988d), *The Proceedings*, Conference of Businessmen, Southern Africa: Opportunities for Investment and Trade, Harare, February, Gaborone.

SADCC (1989a), *Industry and Trade, Mining, Tourism*, Consultative Conference, Luanda, February, Gaborone.

SADCC (1989b), *SADCC: The Productive Sectors – Engine of Growth and Development*, Consultative Conference, Luanda, February, Gaborone.

SADCC (1989c), *The Proceedings*, 1989 Consultative Conference, Luanda, February, Gaborone.

SADCC (1990a), *Industry and Trade*, Consultative Conference, Lusaka, January/February, Gaborone.

SADCC (1990b), *The Second Decade – Enterprise, Skills and Productivity*, Consultative Conference, Lusaka, January/February, Gaborone.

SADCC (1990c), *The Proceedings*, 1990 Consultative Conference, Lusaka, January/February, Gaborone.

SADCC (1991a), *Industry and Trade*, Consultative Conference, Windhoek January/ February, Gaborone.

SADCC (1991b), *Annual Report, July 1990 – June 1991*, Gaborone.

SADCC (1991c), *The Proceedings*, 1991 Consultative Conference, Windhoek, January/February, Gaborone.

SADCC (1992a), *Industry*, Consultative Conference, Maputo, January, Gaborone.

SADCC (1992b), *SADCC: Towards Economic Integration*, Consultative Conference, Maputo, January, Gaborone.

SADCC (1992c), *Treaty of the Southern African Development Community*, August, Gaborone.

SADCC (1992d), *Towards the Southern African Development Community. A Declaration by the Heads of State or Governments of Southern African States*, August, Gaborone.

SADCC (1992e), *Protocol to the Treaty Establishing the Southern African Development Community on Immunities and Privileges*, August, Gaborone.

SADCC (1993a), *Industry and Trade*, Consultative Conference, Harare, January, Gaborone.

SADCC (1993b), *Southern African, A Framework and Strategy for Building the Community*, Consultative Conference, Harare, January, Gaborone.

SADCC (1994), *Industry and Trade*, Consultative Conference, January, Gaborone.

SADCC Regional Business Council, SRBC (1992), *Business Monitor*, Vol. 2, No. 1, Gaborone.

SAPEM, March 1994, 'Structural Adjustment without a Human Face'.

SIDA (1988), *Country Report: Mozambique*, Stockholm.

SIDA (1989), *Study of Possible Swedish Support to the Central American Bank for Economic Integration (CABEI)*, Stockholm.

South Scan, 12 November 1993.

Southern African Economist, August 1992 and December 1992/January 1993 issues (various articles on Export Processing Zones).

Southern African Economist, Vol. 6, No. 10, 1993, 'Step by Step'.

Southern African Economist, Vol. 7, No. 4, 1994, 'ESAP's Winners and Losers'.

Southern African Economist, Vol. 7, No. 10, 1994, 'A house divided'.

Tarp, F. (1992), *Angola*, Danida, Ministry of Foreign Affairs, Copenhagen.

Tarp, F. (1993a), *South Africa, Background and Possibilities for Danish Transitional Assistance*, Danida, Ministry of Foreign Affairs, Copenhagen.

UNDP/World Bank (1992), *African Development Indicators*, New York, Washington D.C.

UNIDO (1985a), *Industrial Cooperation through SADCC*, UNIDO/IS.570, 15 October 1985, V.85–32131, Vienna. As source for Haarlov, J. (1988) a 'revised draft' of the UNIDO document of 25 March 1985 was used.

UNIDO (1986a), *African Industry in Figures 1986*, Vienna.

United Nations (1993), *World Investment Report. Transnational Corporations and Integrated International Production*, UNCTAD, New York.

World Bank (1988), *Report to the Consultative Group for Mozambique on the Government's Economic Rehabilitation Program*, October, Washington D.C.

World Bank (1989), *Sub-Saharan Africa. From Crisis to Sustainable Growth. A Long Term Perspective Study*, World Bank, Washington D.C.

World Bank (1991a), *World Development Report 1991*, Oxford University Press, New York.

World Bank (1991b), *Intra-Regional Trade in Sub-Saharan Africa*, Report No.7685–AFR, Washington D.C.

World Bank (1991c), Background Paper on Privatization, 25 October, Washington D.C.

World Bank (1992a), *World Development Report 1992*, Oxford University Press, New York.

World Bank (1992b), *Mauritius. Expanding Horizons*, A World Bank Country Study, Washington D.C.

World Bank (1992c), 'Regionalism in trade is back – and here to stay' in *World Bank Policy Research Bulletin*, Vol. 3, No. 3.

World Bank (1992d), *Regional Cooperation for Adjustment: A Program of Trade and Indirect Tax Policy. Reforms for Member Countries of the Customs Union of Central African States (UDEAC)*, Report No. 9747–AFR, Washington D.C.

World Bank (1992e), *Conference Papers*, Document 1 and 2, Interventions at SADCC's 1992 Consultative Conference, Maputo.

World Bank (1992f), *Annual Report 1992*, Washington D.C.

World Bank (1993a), *World Development Report 1993*, Oxford University Press, New York

World Bank (1993b), *Global Economic Prospects and the Developing Countries*, World Bank, Washington D.C.

World Bank (1993c), *The East Asian Miracle Economic Growth and Public Policy*, Oxford University Press, New York.

World Bank (1993d), *Conference Paper*, Intervention at SADCC's 1993 Consultative Conference, Harare.

World Bank (1994), *World Development Report 1994*, Oxford University Press, New York.

Secondary Sources
(Books, journals, working papers/occasional papers)

Aalborg, H. (1986), *Regional Økonomisk Integration i Mellemamerika*, (in Danish on regional industrial development in Central America), Masters Thesis, Faculty of History, University of Copenhagen, Copenhagen.

Abrahamsson, H. (1988), *Den Nakna Sanningen* (in Swedish on the issue of NGO's sending second hand clothes to Mozambique), Area Forecasting Institute, Gothenburg.

Abrahamsson, H. and Nilsson, A. (1994), *Mozambique: Macro-Economic Developments and Political Challenges in the Nineties*, background paper for Danida Workshop, Gothenburg.

Abreu, A.P. de and Baltazar, R.A. (1992), 'Monetary Policy in Mozambique', *Conference Paper* from the Regional Economic Integration Conference, 3 and 4 December, SAFER, Harare.

Anglin, D.G. (1983), 'Economic Liberalization and Regional Cooperation in Southern Africa: SADCC and PTA', *International Organization*, Vol. 37, No. 4.

Axline, W.A. (1977), 'Underdevelopment, Dependence, and Integration: The Politics of Regionalism in the Third World', *International Organization*, Vol. 31, No. 1.

Balassa, B. (1961), 'Towards a Theory of Economic Integration', *Kyklos*, Vol. 14, No. 1.

Balassa, B. (1962), *The Theory of Economic Integration*, George Allen & Unwin, London.

Balassa, B. (1965), *Economic Development and Integration*, Centro De Estudios Monetarios Latinoamericanos, Mexico.

Barber, W.J. (1961), *The Economy of British Central Africa*, Oxford University Press, London.

Black, A. (1992), 'Industrial Strategy: lessons from the Newly Industrialized Countries' in Aberdian, I. and Standish, B. (eds.), *Economic Growth in South Africa. Selected Policy Issues*, Oxford University Press, Oxford.

Boidin, J.-C. (1988), 'Regional cooperation in the face of structural adjustment', *The Courier*, No. 112, November–December 1988.

Bowen, M.L. (1992), 'Beyond Reform: Adjustment and Political Power in Contemporary Mozambique', *Journal of Modern African Studies*, Vol. 30, No. 2.

Browne, R.S. and Cummings, R.J. (1985), *The Lagos Plan of Action vs. the Berg Report*, Howard University, Washington D.C.

Buelens, F. (1992), 'The Creation of Regional Blocs in the World Economy', *Intereconomics*, Vol. 27, No. 3.

Callaghy, T.M. (1990), 'Lost Between State and Market: The Politics of Economic Adjustment in Ghana, Zambia and Nigeria' in Nelson J.M. (ed.) (1990), *Economic Crisis and Policy Choice: The Politics of Adjustment in the Third World*, Princeton University Press, Princeton.

Campbell, and Stein, H. (eds.) (1991), *The IMF and Tanzania. The Dynamics of Liberalisation*, SAPES Trust, Harare.

Chenery, H. et al. (1986), *Industrialization and Growth: A Comparative Study*, Oxford University Press for the World Bank, New York.

Chitepa, C. (1993), 'Malawi' in Adepoju, A. (ed.) (1993), *The Impact of Structural Adjustment on the Population of Africa. The Implications for Education, Health and Employment*, UNFPA in association with Heinemann and James Currey, London.

Chitepa, C. and Davies, R. (1992), *Regional Relations and Cooperation Post-Apartheid: A Macro-Framework Study*. Study made for and on behalf of the SADC Secretariat, University of Malawi and University of the Western Cape, Bellville.

Christiansen, T.L. (1992), *SADCC 1980–90*, (in Danish on SADCC's first 10 years), Masters Thesis, Faculty of History, University of Copenhagen, Copenhagen.

Cooper, C.A. and Massell, B.F. (1965a), 'Toward a General Theory of Customs Unions for Developing Countries', *The Journal of Political Economy*, Vol. LXXIII.

Cooper, C.A. and Massell, B.F. (1965b), 'A New Look at Customs Unions Theory', *The Economic Journal*, Vol. 75.

Creighton, T. (1960), *The Anatomy of Partnership: Southern Rhodesia and the Central African Federation*, Faber & Faber, London.

Davidson, B. and Munslow, B. (1990), 'The Crisis of the Nation-state in Africa', *Review of African Political Economy*, No. 49.

Davies, R. (1990), 'Key Issues in Reconstructing South-southern African Economic Relations after Apartheid', *Working Paper Series*, No. 2, Centre for Southern African Studies, University of the Western Cape, Bellville.

Davies, R. (1991), 'Perspectives on Regional Co-operation from South Africa's Mass Democratic Movement', *Backgrounder*, Centre for Southern African Studies, University of the Western Cape, Bellville.

Davies, R. (1992), 'Integration or Co-operation in a Post-Apartheid Southern Africa: Some Reflections on an Emerging Debate', *Southern African Perspectives, A Working Paper Series*, No. 18, Centre for Southern African Studies, University of the Western Cape, Bellville.

Davies, R. (1994), 'Approaches to regional integration in the Southern African context', *Africa Insight*, Vol. 24, No. 1.

Foroutan, F. (1992), *Regional Integration in Sub-Saharan Africa: Past Experience and Future Prospects*, World Bank and CEPR Conference on New Dimensions in Regional Integration, April 2–3, Session 2, Paper No. 3, Washington D.C.

Geffray, C. and Petersen, M. (1986), 'Sobre a Guerra na Provincia de Nampula: Elementos de análise e hipóteses sobre as Determinações e Consequências Sócio-Económico', *Revista Internacional de Estudos Africanos*, Vol. 4–5, Decembro.

Gersony, R. (1988), 'Summary of Mozambican Refugee Accounts of Principally Conflict-Related Experience in Mozambique', *Report* submitted to the Director for Bureau for Refugee Programs and Assistant Secretary of African Affairs, April, Washington D.C.

Gibbon, P., Bangura, Y., and Ofstad, A. (eds.) (1992), *Authoritarianism, Democracy, and Adjustment. The Politics of Economic Reform in Africa*, The Scandinavian Institute of African Studies, Uppsala.

Green, R.H. (1980), 'Toward Southern African Regionalism: The Emergence of a Dialogue' in Legum, C. (ed.) (1980), *Africa Contemporary Record 1978/79*, Vol. 11, Africana Publishing Company, Holmes & Meier Publishers, London.

Green, R.H. (1981), 'Southern Africa: Constellation, Association, Liberation: Economic Coordination and the Struggle for Southern Africa' in C. Legum (ed.) (1981), *Africa Contemporary Record 1979–80*, Africana Publishing Company, Holmes & Meier Publishers, London.

Green, R.H. (1991), *The Struggle against Absolute Poverty in Mozambique*, SDA Project, National Directorate of Planning, Maputo.

Groes, N. et al. (1989), *The Nordic/SADCC Initiative: A Nordic Review*, Chr. Michelsen Institute, Bergen.

Haarlov, J. (1987), 'Konflikten i Mozambique', (in Danish on the conflict in Mozambique in yearbook of world conflicts) in Thune, C. (ed.) (1987), *Konflikternes Verden 1987*, Dansk Røde Kors, Nyt Nordisk Forlag, Copenhagen.

Haarlov, J. (1988), *Regional Cooperation in Southern Africa. Central Elements of the SADCC Venture*, CDR Research Report No. 14, Centre for Development Research, Copenhagen.

Haas, E.B. (1958), 'The Uniting of Europe: Political, Social and Economic Forces 1950 –57' in Keeton, G.W. and Schwarzenberger, G. (eds), *The Library of World Affairs*, No. 42, Steven & Sons, London.

Haas, E.B. (1963), 'International Integration: The European and the Universal Process', in Stichting Grotius Seminarium (1963), *Limits and Problems of European Integration*, The Conference of May 30–June 2, 1961, Martinus Nijhoff, The Hague.

Haas, E.B. (1964), *Beyond the Nation-State: Functionalism and International Organisation*, Stanford University Press, Stanford.

Haas, E.B. (1971), 'The Study of Regional Integration: Reflections on the Joy and Anguish of Pretheorizing' in Lindberg, L.N. and Scheingold, S.A. (eds.), *Regional Integration: Theory and Research*, Harvard University Press, Cambridge, Massachusetts.

Haas, E.B. (1975), *The Obsolescence of Regional Integration Theory*, Research Series No. 25, Institute of International Studies, University of California, Berkeley.

Haas, E.B. and Schmitter, P.C. (1965), *The Politics of Economics in Latin American Regionalism: The Latin American Free Trade Association after*

Four Years of Operation, Vol. 3, Monograph No. 2, University of Denver, Denver.

Hanlon, J. (1985), 'Conflict and Dependence in Southern Africa', *Third World Affairs*, Third World Foundation, London.

Hanlon, J. (1986), *Beggar your Neighbours*, CIIR in collaboration with James Currey and Indiana University Press, London and Bloomington.

Hanlon, J. (1991), *Mozambique: Who Calls the Shots?*, James Currey and Indiana University Press, London and Bloomington.

Hansen, E. (1987), 'The Economic Commission for Africa and African Development' in Hansen, E. (ed.) (1987), *Africa – Perspectives on Peace and Development*, United Nations University and Zed Books, New York and London.

Hawkins, A.M. (1992), 'Economic Development in SADCC Countries' in Maasdorp, G. and Whiteside, A (1992).

Hazlewood, A. (1985), 'The End of the East African Community: What are the Lessons for Regional Integration Schemes?' in Onwuka, R.I. and Sesay, A. (eds.) (1985), *The Future of Regionalism in Africa*, Macmillan, London.

Henderson, R.D.A. (1985), ' The Southern African Customs Union: Politics of Dependence' in Onwuka, R.I. and Sesay, A. (eds.) (1985), *The Future of Regionalism in Africa*, Macmillan, London.

Hermele, K. (1990), *Mozambican Crossroads. Economics and Politics in the Era of Structural Adjustment*, Report 1990, 3, Chr. Michelsen Institute, Bergen.

Hermele, K. (1992), 'Stick and Carrot: Political Alliances and Nascent Capitalism in Mozambique' in Gibbon P., Bangura, Y. and Ofstad, A. (eds.) (1992), *Authoritarianism, Democracy, and Adjustment*, The Scandinavian Institute of African Studies, Uppsala.

Hirschman, A.O. (1958), *The Strategy of Economic Development*, Yale University Press, New Haven, Conn.

Hoohlo, S.G. (1990), 'The Southern African Customs Union (SACU) and the Post-Apartheid South Africa: Prospects for Closer Integration in the Region' in Santho, S. and Sejanamane, M. (eds.), *Southern Africa After Apartheid. Prospects for the Inner Periphery in the 1990s*, SAPES Trust, Harare.

Hyden, G. (1983), *No Shortcuts to Progress: African Development Management in Perspective*, University of California Press, Berkeley.

Hyden, G. and Karlstrom, B. (1993), 'Structural Adjustment as a Policy Process: The Case of Tanzania', *World Development*, Vol. 29, No. 9.

Johnson, P. and Martin, D. (eds.) (1986), *Destructive Engagement. Southern Africa at War*, Zimbabwe Publishing House, Harare.

Jourdan, P. (1991), 'Mining and Southern African Regional Integration: The "Bambazonke" Problem', *Southern Africa*, SAPES, Vol. 5, No. 2.

Kiljunen, K. (ed.) (1990), *Region to Region Cooperation between Developed and Developing Countries. The Potentials for Mini-NIEO*, Avebury, Aldershot, Hants.

Kitamura, H. (1966), 'Economic Theory and the Economic Integration of Underdeveloped Regions' in Wionczek, M. (ed.), *Latin American Economic Integration. Experiences and Prospects*, New York.

Kumar, U. (1992), 'Southern African Customs Union: Lessons for the Southern African Region', *Southern African Perspectives, A Working Paper Series*, No. 16, Centre for Southern African Studies, University of the Western Cape, Bellville.

Leistner, E. (1992a), 'South Africa's Options for Future relations with Southern Africa and the European Community', *Discussion Document*, South African Chamber of Business.

Leistner, E. (1992b), Designing the framework for a Southern African Development Community', *Africa Insight*, Vol. 22, No. 1.

Lewis, S.R. (1987), 'Economic Realities in Southern Africa (or, One Hundred Million Futures)', *Discussion Paper 232*, Institute of Development Studies, University of Sussex, Brighton.

Leys, C. and Pratt, C. (1960), *A New Deal in Central Africa*, Heinemann, London.

Lipsey, R.G. (1960), 'The Theory of Customs Unions: A General Survey', *The Economic Journal*, Vol. 70, September.

List, F. (1885), *The National System of Political Economy*, Longman Green, London.

Maasdorp, G. (1982), 'The Southern African Customs Union – An Assessment', *Journal of Contemporary African Studies*, Vol. 2, No. 1.

Maasdorp, G. (1992a), 'Economic Co-operation in Southern Africa: Prospects for Regional Integration', *Conflict Studies 253*, Research Institute for the Study of Conflict and Terrorism, London.

Maasdorp, G. (1992b), 'Trade Relations in Southern Africa – Changes Ahead' in Maasdorp, G. and Whiteside, A. (eds.).

Maasdorp, G. (1992c), 'Overview: regional prospects and rapid technological change' in Whiteside, A.G. (1992), *Industrialization and Investment Incentives in Southern Africa*, James Curry Publishers, University of Natal, Pietermaritzburg.

Maasdorp, G. and Whiteside, A. (eds.) (1992), *Towards a Post-Apartheid Future. Political and Economic Relations in Southern Africa*, Macmillan, London.

Maasdorp G. and Whiteside, A. (1993), *Rethinking Economic Cooperation in Southern Africa: Trade and Investment*, Konrad Adenauer Stiftung, Johannesburg.

Mandaza, I. (1994), 'Where is the African National Bourgeoisie?', *SAPEM*, November.

249

Mansoor, A. (1992), 'Experiences of Economic Integration in Sub-Saharan Africa: Lessons for a Fresh Start' in H.H. Bass et al. (1992), *African Development Perspectives Yearbook 1990/91*, University of Bremen, LIT Verlag, Münster/Hamburg

Mansoor, A. and Inotai, A. (1990), 'Integration Efforts in Sub-Saharan Africa: Failures, Results and Prospects – A Suggested strategy for Achieving Efficient Integration', *Conference Paper*, Nairobi, June.

Maphanyane, E. (1990), 'Economic Development in southern Africa – A SADCC Perspective', *Conference Paper*, from the seminar: Rethinking Strategies for Mozambique and Southern Africa, Instituto Superior de Relações Internacionais, May, 21–24, Maputo

McCarthy, C. (1992), 'The Southern African Customs Union in a changing Economic and Political Environment', *Journal of World Trade*, Vol. 26, No. 4.

Mikesell, R.F. (1963), 'The Theory of Common Markets as Applied to Regional Arrangements among Developing Countries' in Harrod, R. and Hague, D. (eds.) (1963), *International Trade Theory in a Developing World*. Proceedings of a Conference held by the International Economic Association, Macmillan, London.

Minter, W. (1989), 'The Mozambican National Resistance (Renamo) as described by Ex-participants', *Report* submitted to Ford Foundation and SIDA, Washington D.C.

Mitrany, D. (1963), 'Delusion of Regional Unity', in Stichting Grotius Seminarium: *Limits and Problems of European Integration*, The Conference of May 30 –June 2, 1961, Martinus Nijhoff, The Hague.

Mitrany, D. (1966), *A Working Peace System*, Quadrangle Books, Chicago.

Mkandawire, T. (1985), 'Dependence and Economic Co-operation: The Case of SADCC', *Zimbabwe Journal of Economics*, Vol. 2, No. 1.

Morgan, G. (1990), 'Violence in Mozambique: Towards an Understanding of Renamo', *Journal of Modern African Studies*, Vol. 28, No. 4.

Munslow, B. (1984), 'State Intervention in Agriculture: the Mozambican Experience,' *Journal of Modern African Studies*, Vol. 22, No. 2.

Munslow, B. and Zack-Williams, A.B. (1990), 'Democracy and Development', *Review of African Political Economy*, No. 49.

Myrdal, G. (1957), *Economic Theory and Under-Developed Regions*, Gerald Duckworth & Co., London.

Mwase, N. (1985), 'The African Preferential Trade Area: Towards a Sub-Regional Economic Community in Eastern and Southern Africa', *Journal of World Trade Law*, Vol. 19, No. 6.

Ncube, P. (1992), 'Economic Co-operation and Integration in Eastern and Southern Africa – some future prospects', *Conference Paper*, S.A.F.E.R., Regional Economic Integration Conference, December, Harare.

Ndegwa, P. (1984), 'Economic Co-operation: The Engine of Growth in Sub-Saharan Africa', (mimeo) published in *Journal of Development Planning* (1985), Vol. 15.

Ndlela, D.B. (1987), 'The Manufacturing Sector in the East and Southern African Subregion with Emphasis on the SADCC' in Amin, S., Chitala D. and Mandaza I. (eds.) (1987), *SADCC. Prospects for disengagement and Development in southern Africa*, The United Nations University/Third World Forum, Studies in African Political Economy, London.

Nelson J.M. (ed.) (1990), *Economic Crisis and Policy Choice: The Politics of Adjustment in the Third World*, Princeton University Press, Princeton.

Nye, J.S. (1968), 'Comparative Regional Integration: Concept and Measurement', *International Organization*, Vol. 22, No. 3.

Nye, J.S. (1971), 'Comparing Common Markets: A Revised Neo-Functionalist Model' in Lindberg, L.N. and Scheingold, S.A. (eds.) (1971), *Regional Integration: Theory and Research*, Harvard University Press, Cambridge, Massachusetts.

Oestergaard, T. (1989a), 'Industrial development in southern Africa and the role of SADCC', *CDR Working Paper 89.4*, Centre for Development Research, Copenhagen.

Oestergaard, T. (1989b), 'Aiming beyond Conventional Development Assistance: An Analysis of Nordic Aid to the SADCC Region' in Odén, B. and Othman, II. (eds.) (1989), *Regional Cooperation in Southern Africa. A Post Apartheid Perspective*, The Scandinavian Institute of African Studies, Uppsala.

Oestergaard, T. (1993), 'Classical Models of Regional Integration: What Relevance for Southern Africa?' in Odén, B. (ed.) (1993), *Southern Africa After Apartheid*, The Scandinavian Institute of African Studies, Uppsala.

Ofstad, A. (1993), 'Will PTA be Relevant in the Post-Apartheid Era?' in Odén, B. (ed.), (1993), *Southern Africa After Apartheid*, The Scandanavian Institute of African Studies, Uppsala.

Ojo, O. (1985), 'Regional Co-operation and Integration' in Ojo, O., Orwa, D.K. and Utete, C. M.B. (eds.) (1985), *African International Relations*, Longman, New York.

Orantes, I.C. and Rosenthal, G. (1977), 'Reflections on the conceptual framework of Central American economic integration,' *CEPAL Review*, No. 3.

Palmer, R. and Parsons, N. (1977), *The Roots of Rural Poverty in Central and Southern Africa*, University of California Press, Berkeley.

Peet, R. (1984), *Manufacturing Industry and Economic Development in the SADCC Countries*, Energy, Environment and Development in Africa No. 5, The Beijer Institute, Stockholm and the Scandinavian Institute of African Studies, Uddevalla, Uppsala.

Ravenhill, J. (1985), 'The Future of Regionalism in Africa', in Onwuka, R.I. and Sesay, A. (eds.) (1985), *The Future of Regionalism in Africa*, Macmillan, London.

Riddell, R.C. et al. (1990), *Manufacturing Africa. Performance and Prospects of Seven Countries in Sub-Saharan Africa*, Overseas Development Institute, London in association with Heinemann, Portsmouth (N.H.) and James Curry, London.

Riddell, R.C. (1993), 'The Manufacturing Sector' in African Development Bank (1993), *Integration in Southern Africa*, Abidjan, Vol. 2, chapter 4 (final draft manuscript).

Robson, P. (1983), *Integration, Development and Equity. Economic Integration in West Africa*, George Allen & Unwin, London.

Robson, P. (1985), 'Regional Integration and the Crisis in Sub-Saharan Africa' *The Journal of Modern African Studies*, Vol. 23, No. 4.

Robson, P. (1990), *The Economics of International Integration*, Unwin Hyman, 3rd edition, London.

Rosenthal, G. (1989), 'Latin American and Caribbean development in the 1980s and the outlook for the future' *CEPAL Review*, No. 39, 1989.

Saigal, J.C. (1985), *Economic Cooperation and Integration in Latin America. (A review of historical experience)*, paper prepared for the Conference on South Asian Regional Co-operation organized by the Bangladesh Economic Association, Dhaka.

Schmitter, P.C. (1969), 'Three Neo-Functional Hypotheses about International Integration', *International Organization*, Vol. 23, No. 1.

Schmitter, P.C. (1970), 'Central American Integration: Spill-over, Spill-around or Encapsulation?', *Journal of Common Market Studies*, Vol. 9, No. 1.

Schmitter, P.C. (1972), *Autonomy or Dependence as Regional Integration Outcomes: Central America*, Research Series No. 17, Institute of International Studies, University of California, Berkeley.

Seidman, A. (1986), 'The need for an Appropriate Southern African Industrial Strategy', *ROAPE Conference Paper*, Liverpool.

Simba, I. and Wells, F. (1984), Development *Co-operation in Southern Africa: Structures and Procedures*, Development Centre of the OECD, Paris.

Stein, H. (1991), 'Economic Policy and the IMF in Tanzania: Conditionality, Conflict and Convergence' in Campbell and Stein, H. (eds.) (1991), *The IMF and Tanzania. The Dynamics of Liberalisation*, SAPES Trust, Harare.

Stoneman, C. (1989), 'Tips for SADCC Industry Planners', *The Southern African Economist*, Vol. 1, No. 6, December 1988/January 1989.

Takirambudde, P.N. (1993), 'Rethinking regional integration structures and strategies in Eastern and Southern Africa' *Africa Insight*, Vol. 23, No. 3.

Tarp, F. (1993), *Stabilization and Structural Adjustment. Macroeconomic frameworks for analysing the crisis in sub-Saharan Africa*, Routledge, London.

Thomas, C. (1974), *Dependence and Transformation. The Economics of the Transition to Socialism*, Monthly Review Press, New York.

Tibana, R.T. (1991), 'Indústria Moçambicana: Os Limites de uma Reabilitação sem Estratégia de Industrialização', *Economia*, No. 3, 2.a Série.

Tinbergen, J. (1965), *International Economic Integration*, Second Revised Edition, Elsevier Publishing Company, Amsterdam.

Torp, J.E. (1979), *Industrial Planning and Development in Mozambique. Some Preliminary Considerations*, Research Report No. 50, The Scandinavian Institute of African Studies, Uppsala.

Torp, J.E. (1983), 'SADCC Industrial Cooperation within Manufacturers: Country Case Study on Mozambique', *CDR Project Papers A.83.4.*, Centre for Development Research, Copenhagen.

Torp, J.E. (1989), 'Mozambique' in Szajkowski, B. (ed.) (1989), *Mozambique, São Tomé and Príncipe*, Marxist Regime Series, Pinter Publishers, London.

Traoré, A. (1993), 'Regional Integration', *The Courier*, No. 142, November–December.

Vaitsos, C.V. (1978), 'Crisis in Regional Economic Cooperation (Integration) among Developing Countries: A Survey', *World Development*, Vol. 6.

Viner, J. (1950), *The Customs Union Issue*, Carnegie Endowment for International Peace, New York.

Vletter, F. de (1992), 'Microenterprise Credit Strategies. Lessons from Mozambique's Adjustment Process', *Seminar Paper*, International Council for Small Business, 'Prosperity for Africa – the Small Business Way', May, Johannesburg.

Weinmann, C.D. (1991), *Indústria Textil em Moçambique*, Final Report from Field Study as part of Masters Thesis, Faculty of Economics, Berlin Free University, Berlin.

Weinmann, C.D. (1993), *Textilen in Mosambik: Industrialisierung 'von unten'*, Bremer Afrika-Studien, Bd. 7, LIT Verlag, Münster and Hamburg.

Weiss, J. (1988), *Industry in Developing Countries. Theory, Policy and Evidence*, Routledge, London.

Whiteside, A.G. (1992), *Industrialization and Investment Incentives in Southern Africa*, James Curry Publishers, University of Natal, Pietermaritzburg.

Winters, A. (1992), *The European Community: A Case of Successful Integration?*, World Bank and CEPR Conference on New Dimensions in Regional Integration, April 2–3, Paper No. 11, Washington D.C.

Wionczek, M. (ed.) (1966), *Latin American Economic Integration. Experiences and Prospects*, New York.

Wionczek, M. S. (1978), 'Can the Broken Humpty-Dumpty Be Put Together Again and By Whom? Comments on the Vaitsos Survey', *World Development*, Vol. 6.

Wong, J. (1985), 'ASEAN's Experience in Regional Economic Cooperation', *Asian Development Review*, Vol. 3, No. 1.

Zehender, W. (1983), 'Cooperation versus Integration: The Prospects of the Southern African Development Coordination Conference (SADCC)', *Occasional Papers* of the German Development Institute (GDI), No. 77, Berlin.